The Challenge of Pluralism

The Challenge of Pluralism

Church and State in Five Democracies

Second Edition

Stephen V. Monsma and J. Christopher Soper

ROWMAN & LITTLEFIELD PUBLISHERS, INC.
Lanham • Boulder • New York • Toronto • Plymouth, UK

ROWMAN & LITTLEFIELD PUBLISHERS, INC.

Published in the United States of America
by Rowman & Littlefield Publishers, Inc.
A wholly owned subsidary of The Rowman & Littlefield Publishing Group, Inc.
4501 Forbes Boulevard, Suite 200, Lanham, Maryland 20706
www.rowmanlittlefield.com

Estover Road, Plymouth PL6 7PY, United Kingdom

British Library Cataloguing in Publication Information Available

Library of Congress Cataloging-in-Publication Data
Monsma, Stephen V., 1936-
   The challenge of pluralism : church and state in five democracies / Stephen V.
Monsma and J. Christopher Soper. — 2nd ed.
      p. cm.
   Includes bibliographical references and index.
   ISBN-13: 978-0-7425-5416-0 (cloth : alk. paper)
   ISBN-10: 0-7425-5416-3 (cloth : alk. paper)
   ISBN-13: 978-0-7425-5417-7 (pbk. : alk. paper)
   ISBN-10: 0-7425-5417-1 (pbk. : alk. paper)
   eISBN-13: 978-0-7425-5740-6
   eISBN-10: 0-7425-5740-5
   1. Church and state—History—20th century. 2. Democracy—Religious aspects—
Christianity—History—20th century. 3. Religious pluralism—Christianity—History—
20th century. I. Soper, J. Christopher. II. Title.
   BV630.3.M66 2009
   322'.1090511—dc22

                                                                    2008015685

Printed in the United States of America

⊗™ The paper used in this publication meets the minimum requirements of
American National Standard for Information Sciences—Permanence of Paper
for Printed Library Materials, ANSI/NISO Z39.48-1992.

~

Contents

~

Preface to the Second Edition

In the ten years since this book was published, we are tempted to say that everything is the same and everything is different when it comes to church-state issues in the United States, the Netherlands, Australia, England, and Germany. One of our purposes in writing the first edition of this book was to stress that the manner in which the United States resolves religious freedom and religious establishment issues is distinctive when compared to the practices of other political democracies. Like its predecessor, this edition reaches that same conclusion: the United States is exceptional among political democracies in how it approaches such issues as the reach and meaning of religious free exercise rights, the place of religion in public schools, state support for religious schools, and government money going to religious nonprofit social service agencies. What also remains the same ten years later is the importance of inherited church-state institutions and practices in resolving contemporary issues. The names of some of the religious groups have changed over time, as have the specific religious freedom and establishment issues in question, but the church-state practices of the past continue to create a powerful stream that shapes the contours of the current debate.

On the other hand, the world of religion and politics in these five countries is radically different from what it was ten years ago. Most notably, the European states and Australia have become more religiously pluralistic than at any time in these countries' histories. This is largely a consequence of immigration, particularly the immigration and settlement of large numbers of Muslims and other religious minorities into the Netherlands, Australia, England,

and Germany. Ten years ago, political conflict around religion in Europe seemed to some a thing of the past, a relic of a bygone era when religion had cultural sway and political power, but a factor that would continue to recede as secular forces took over. Secularism remains a powerful force in western Europe and Australia, but the repoliticization of religious disputes in each of the countries in our study negates the naive assumptions that religion would somehow disappear as a political variable. Issues that were barely on the horizon ten years ago, such as state aid to Islamic schools, the teaching of religions other than Christianity and Judaism in public schools, and the meaning of freedom for non-Christian religious minorities are now at the forefront of politics in the Netherlands, Australia, England, and Germany. In this way, Australia and Europe have come to look more like the United States, where religion was and remains an important political variable.

In revising the first edition, we benefited greatly from the advice of various people who read drafts of our chapters and made very helpful comments. In particular, we would like to thank Michael Hogan, Gerhard Robbers, Chris Janse, and Sophie C. van Bijsterveld. We would also like to acknowledge the support of our colleagues at Pepperdine University and the Henry Institute of Calvin College who assumed more than their fair share of administrative tasks while we shut ourselves in our offices working on our manuscript. The book would not have been possible without the numerous interviews we conducted with activists and scholars in each country for this project. In every case, those interviewees were generous with their time, helpful with their insights, and gracious in more ways than we can possibly recount. Finally, we wish to thank the staff at Rowman & Littlefield for encouraging us in this second edition and for being patient when we were running up against, and even past, deadlines. In particular, we owe Susan McEachern a debt of gratitude for her patience and support.

At home, we continue to receive loving support for our efforts, but we also get the necessary encouragement to leave the world of church and state behind in order to involve ourselves in the daily lives of our respective families. Our families richly deserved the dedication to the first edition of the book, and we are happy to rededicate this volume to them as well.

Preface to the First Edition

American society continues to be deeply divided on the question of the proper relationship between the institutions of church and state. Almost every year the Supreme Court is marked by sharp divisions in the church-state cases that come before it, divisions that mirror the disagreements and controversies of the broader American society. It was while we were discussing church-state practice in the United States that it occurred to us that a comparative analysis of how other western pluralistic democracies resolve church-state tensions might shed new light on this enduring issue in American politics. This book, then, is a comparative study of church-state policy in the United States, the Netherlands, Australia, England, and Germany. We do not pretend that this book will resolve a political debate in the United States that is as abiding as it is frustrating to the groups and individuals involved in it, but it is our hope that it will provide a different perspective on it.

As we delved further into the study of these five countries, we were struck at how contemporary church-state practice had much to do with each nation's unique history and cultural assumptions about the proper place of religion in public life. This book is not an apology for the church-state practice in any one of these countries, but we have attempted to be sensitive to each nation's particular history in the story we have told. At the same time, our study has convinced us that sufficient similarities in the church-state experiences of the five countries exist that allow us to make some general conclusions that would apply to each. Democracies, we believe, can and should learn from each other.

The lessons these countries offer are particularly important now. Increasing levels of religious pluralism in the modern world raise tensions among religious groups and challenge the inherited church-state models of the nations in our study. In addition, the growth of the welfare state has led to an expansion of government involvement in almost all aspects of society, including religious life, and threatens to undermine past relations between religious and political institutions.

We are convinced that the answer to these growing conflicts is to be found in a church-state policy that is genuinely neutral among all religious groups and between religious and secular perspectives generally, and that accommodates and promotes the religious pluralism that is a natural feature of each nation. We do not believe that the state can attain genuine neutrality, or even-handedness among religious and secular groups in society, with a church-state policy that supports only some religious groups and practices but not others, nor through a no-aid-to-religion standard that ends up favoring secular over religious perspectives. Either of these policies would violate the standard of government neutrality that we believe should lie at the heart of a country's church-state policy. It is to the extent that the five nations in our study fall short of this goal that we are critical of their practices, while it is to the degree to which each attains this evenhandedness that they serve as a model from which we hope to draw some lessons.

We have received assistance and cooperation from many people in our research for this book. We would like to thank the dozens of people whom we interviewed in each country for our study. They gave freely of their time and expertise, provided us with invaluable insight about the church-state practices of their countries, and were a constant source of support with the hospitality they extended to us. We also owe a considerable debt to the following people who read portions of the manuscript and gave numerous suggestions that helped us avoid errors and generally strengthened the book: J. P. Balkenende, Sophie van Bijsterveld, Gary Bouma, Stanley Carlson-Thies, Lothar Cönen, Michael Hogan, Cees Klop, Frans Koopmans, George Moyser, Jørgen Rasmussen, Gerhard Robbers, and Jerry Waltman. We also would like to thank Lothar Cönen for his help in arranging for many of the interviews in Germany. The blame for any remaining errors of fact or interpretation is, however, ours alone. Stephen Wrinn, our editor at Rowman & Littlefield, provided just the right combination of encouragement and suggestions to strengthen our manuscript, and he wisely selected an outside reviewer for the book who read the entire manuscript carefully and made very helpful comments. We would also like to thank the American Political Science Association and Pepperdine University for providing us with grant money for travel to each of these countries.

Finally, we would like to thank our families for their constant love, moral support, patience, and interest in our work: our wives, Jane and Mary, and our children, Katharine and David, and Martin and Kristin. They all richly deserve the dedication of this book.

CHAPTER ONE

~

Introduction

From Plato's discussion of religion in the *Laws*, to the conflict between Pope Gregory VII and King Henry IV in the Middle Ages, to present-day debates about the proper role of religious groups in the making of public policy, the world has seen no lack of debate and discussion about how two of the most powerful and longest lasting of human institutions—the church and the state—are to relate to each other.[1] Religion is such a pervasive, deeply ingrained aspect of human existence that few, if any, examples can be found of human societies in which religion does not play a prominent role. Similarly, government is such an omnipresent feature of human societies that again few, if any, examples can be found of human societies with no political or governmental frameworks. As a result of the enduring presence and power of both the church and the state in all human societies, one of the perpetual issues with which all societies must struggle is how these two vital spheres of human endeavor should relate to each other.

This book explores how five western liberal democracies—the United States, the Netherlands, Australia, England, and Germany—have sought to deal with this issue. All five are successful, stable, democratic nations, yet they have approached the question of church-state relations in different ways. In the United States church-state issues have remained on the front burner of discussion and debate. There are interest groups committed to one side or the other of church-state questions, Congress struggles each year with constitutional amendments that seek to change the ground rules of church-state relations, issues such as prayer in public schools regularly enter into

1

presidential campaigns, and almost every year the Supreme Court decides church-state cases marked by closely divided decisions and at times embarrassingly vitriolic opinions. In the other democracies considered here, new, challenging church-state issues are being raised by changing immigration patterns that have brought sizable numbers of Muslim and other non-Christian immigrants into them, creating significantly greater religious pluralism. How well are preexisting church-state practices able to recognize and accommodate these religious newcomers? The rise of a small, but real, violence-prone Islamist movement within Islam has also posed new challenges to old church-state arrangements. This book compares the approaches these five western democracies are pursuing in church-state relations. Our goal is to give new guidance to all democracies and to the United States in particular in their attempts to relate church and state to each other in a manner that is supportive of their citizens' religious freedoms and the role of religion in them.

Exploring the issue of church-state relations in these countries has taken on a new importance because there is increasing talk of devolving certain activities and programs previously run by government agencies to private, usually nonprofit organizations, many of which have a religious history or orientation. In the United States this trend can be clearly seen in President George W. Bush's faith-based initiative.[2] As western governments look to private, often religiously based organizations to play larger roles in society, questions of church and state are bound to be magnified. If programs and activities that were previously run by government agencies are to devolve to private, religiously based agencies, usually with accompanying governmental funds, are their religious orientations likely to be toned down or eclipsed? Should they be? If religiously based agencies are excluded from governmental funding programs—as is largely done in the United States in the case of elementary and secondary schools—is that a form of discrimination against religious entities? These questions are not new. What is new is that if governments are to move in the direction of public policies that depend more and more heavily on private agencies for education, welfare, health, and other services, these questions will come to be written much larger than they have been in even the recent past.

In this introductory chapter we set the context for our study by first considering three basic church-state questions that repeatedly arise in democratic polities. In subsequent chapters we explore how each of the five countries has responded to these questions. The next section sets out a basic religious liberty goal that we use as a standard against which to evaluate the strengths and weaknesses of the five countries' approaches to church-state issues. The third section describes three models of church-state relationships, and the final section explains why we selected these five democracies for this study.

Three Questions

Questions of church and state have often proven contentious even in stable, successful democracies. More specifically, there are three very basic questions that, at various points in history and today as well, have confronted democratic societies. One question is: *How far can a democratic polity go in permitting religiously motivated behavior that is contrary to societal welfare or norms?* There is general agreement that when the exercise of religious freedom by one group has the effect of endangering the health or safety of others or of significantly disrupting the smooth functioning of life lived in society, the claims of religious freedom must yield to the welfare of the broader society. On this basis, most western democracies require, for example, religious burial practices to meet normal health standards and those organizing religious processions on public streets to obtain the normal permits regulating the timing and size of such processions. But this leaves many questions. How serious must the threat to public health and safety be before the government insists that even religiously motivated practices must be curtailed? How significant must the disruption to the normal functioning of society be before government has a right to limit or forbid a religiously motivated practice?

There is also the matter of religious groups violating deeply held societal norms. Modern democracies—no matter how committed to religious pluralism—would not allow human sacrifice, even if it were part of a group's sincere religious beliefs. Allowing human sacrifice would so violate such deeply held norms as respect for human life that society would be torn apart if it were allowed in the name of religious freedom. Democratic societies that are fully committed to freedom of religion have decided there are certain norms or values so fundamental to human existence and so deeply held that religion cannot be used as a basis for their violation. In such cases religion must yield to the claims of the broader society and its values. When religious groups violate those principles the force of law can be brought to bear on them. The political order sometimes outlaws and punishes certain religiously motivated practices.

Here also questions arise over where to draw the line between practices that are legally permissible and impermissible in the name of religion. Human sacrifice may be out, but what about polygamy—a burning issue in nineteenth-century America. Or today what about female circumcision—or female genital mutilation, as its opponents term it? It is practiced by certain

African cultures as a religious rite, but should it be allowed when their members are living in western societies? Or what is to happen when Muslim schools in western societies teach attitudes and values—such as those relating to the role of women in society—that are today rejected by those societies? These are not trivial questions. Religious freedom is a fundamental freedom. Many Americans, when referring to religious freedom as the "first freedom," have more than its location in their Bill of Rights in mind. The horrors of religious wars and of western societies burning religious heretics at the stake not that many years ago stand as vivid testimonies to the importance of religious freedom. Let no one take it for granted or look lightly on attempts even to nibble away at its fringes.

But societal unity and welfare are also of crucial importance. What makes a society into a society is much more than a conglomeration of persons occupying the same territory. Instead, a society is marked both by cooperative efforts promoting societal welfare that make possible life lived in a complex, interdependent society and by shared values, myths, and memories that lead persons to identify themselves as a people. It is as persons identify themselves as members of a common society that cooperative tasks, sacrifices for the larger good, and other basics of human civilization are made possible. When common values and beliefs of a fundamental nature are shattered, or when some persons' practices endanger and disrupt the lives of others, society is threatened with disintegration: at best, cooperation is made difficult and, at worst, barbarism and civil war result. Post–Saddam Hussein Iraq stands as an early-twenty-first-century symbol of the horror that can result when bonds of respect and civility are absent.

In addition, something more than societal unity may be at stake. Many theorists have contended that free, democratic government is finally dependent upon a populace with certain internalized values and habits of the mind. Clinton Rossiter once wrote, "It takes more than a perfect plan of government to pursue ordered liberty. Something else is needed, some moral principle diffused among the people to strengthen the urge to peaceful obedience and hold the community on an even keel. . . . [Democratic] government rests on a definite moral basis: a virtuous people."[3] If, in fact, a "virtuous people" is essential for a successfully functioning democracy, any movements—including religious ones—that work to build up a sense of virtue or morality among the public and that teach respect for the welfare of others become crucial for a healthy democracy, and any movements that undercut or subvert a sense of virtue, morality, and consideration for others pose a significant threat to democratic government. Does democratic self-preservation thereby mean religious movements that undercut a sense of public virtue and morality, or that subvert respect for the welfare of others, should not receive religious freedom protection? Germany, Australia, the Netherlands, and England are all struggling with this question as they work to balance the religious freedom of their Muslim citizens—a small number of whom seem to be resisting assimilation into the majority culture—with the need for national unity resting on liberal democratic values.

In short, religious freedom, on the one hand, and shared values and beliefs and public health and safety, on the other hand, are enormously important. Political theorist Will Kymlicka highlights this need for balance when he writes that "any plausible or attractive political theory must attend to both the claims of ethnocultural minorities and the promotion of responsible democratic citizenship."[4] The stakes in resolving the question of how far a polity can go in permitting behavior contrary to societal welfare and norms that is justified on the basis of religious beliefs are indeed high.

This leads to the second basic question related to religion and society that confronts democratic polities today: *Should the state encourage and promote consensual religious beliefs and traditions in an attempt to support the common values and beliefs that bind a society together and make possible limited, democratic government?* This is the positive version of the first question just raised.

If certain shared values are crucial for societal unity and democratic governance, should government perhaps not only oppose those religious practices and movements that would undercut those values, but also encourage these values in a positive manner through the promotion of certain consensual religious values and symbols? As we will see more fully later, in nineteenth-century America the common schools were seen as being extremely important precisely because they taught not only knowledge and skills but also values and beliefs. Horace Mann and his fellow New England school reformers saw the common school as the key device by which democracy would be safeguarded in the face of a rising tide of uneducated frontier farmers and millions of immigrants from foreign lands. Thus Bible reading, prayers, and moral lessons were an integral part of the common school. It was a consensual, civil religion that marked the common schools, but it was thought crucial that the state play an active role in supporting and propagating religion of this sort. In England today the established Church of England is often seen as important in inculcating a sense of national unity, honor, and morality that is crucial for free, democratic government. But when the state supports religion of this sort, does it perhaps violate the norm of religious freedom for all? After all, there are many people holding to distinctive, minority religious beliefs or to clearly secular worldviews who are left out of a consensual civil religion. They may very well see a state-supported consensual religion as undermining their own faith or secular worldview.

A third basic question emerges from a fundamental fact of life in all industrialized, urbanized western democracies: the expansion of the modern administrative state into almost all areas of life. Whether it is economic regulation and stimulation, health care, education (from preschool preparatory programs to postdoctoral fellowships), care for the elderly, land-use planning and zoning, radio and television licensing and regulation, preservation of historical sites, or regulation of abortion and other health services, the modern administrative state is active in regulating, supporting, and providing services. But almost all the areas just cited as examples of state activity are also areas in which religious communities have been and continue to be active. This leads to the question: *When religious groups and the state are both active in the same fields of endeavor, how can one ensure that the state does not advantage or disadvantage any one religious group or either religious or secular belief systems over others?* If the state, for example, collects taxes from the entire population in order to fund its own schools and to help fund the programs of the schools of the traditional, well-established religions, but does not fund the schools of newer, nonmainstream religions, is it not advantaging some religions and disadvantaging others? Or if the state funds its own secular social service programs and those of secularly based nonprofit agencies, but leaves religiously based groups involved in the same social service programs to struggle on without state help, is not religion clearly being disadvantaged? But if the state inserts religion into its own activities or funds the activities of religious groups, does it not run the risk of favoring one religious group over another or of favoring religion over secular belief structures? As the modern state has entered more and more areas to regulate, fund, or provide services, questions of evenhandedness among all religious groups and between secular and religious groups arise.

In the following chapters we consider how the five countries whose church-state principles and practices we have chosen for analysis have responded to these three questions.

A Basic Goal

In discussing and at some points suggesting answers to the three questions raised in the prior section, we hold to the basic ideal or goal of governmental neutrality on matters of religion. We define neutrality as government neither favoring nor burdening any particular religion, nor favoring or burdening religion as a whole or secular systems of belief as a whole. Governmental religious neutrality is attained when government does not influence its citizens' choices for or against certain religious or secular systems of belief, either by imposing burdens on them or by granting advantages to them. Instead, government is neutral when it is evenhanded toward people of all faiths and of none. This concept of state neutrality on matters of religion is what the American legal scholar Douglas Laycock has termed *substantive neutrality* and what Stephen Monsma calls *positive neutrality*.[5] Laycock describes substantive neutrality as being achieved when the government minimizes "the extent to which it either encourages or discourages religious belief or disbelief, practice or nonpractice, observance or nonobservance."[6]

We believe this goal takes precedence over any specific theory or means that at one time or another and in one polity or another has been put forward to structure church-state relations, such as an established church, a multiple establishment, no aid at all for religion, a wall of separation between church and state, and financial support for a wide range of religious expressions. All these and more have been tried and implemented at one time or another in the democracies considered here. But we believe none of them should be taken as ends or goals in themselves. The appropriate goal should be governmental neutrality toward all religious groups and toward religion as a whole and secular worldviews as a whole. That is the standard against which specific church-state principles and theories, or specific means to implement those principles and theories, should be judged. It is when this goal of neutrality is fully realized that the moving words of U.S. Supreme Court Justice Potter Stewart take on life and meaning: "What our Constitution indispensably protects is the freedom of each of us, be he Jew or Agnostic, Christian or Atheist, Buddhist or Freethinker, to believe or disbelieve, to worship or not worship, to pray or keep silent, according to his own conscience, uncoerced and unrestrained by government."[7]

This basic goal or ideal of governmental neutrality on matters of belief—whether religiously or secularly based—is largely in keeping with the liberal tradition within western society, yet differs in some important ways from that tradition. That tradition emerged on the western scene in the eighteenth-century Enlightenment, received a concrete manifestation in the French Revolution, was a strong social and political movement in the nineteenth century, and is a very active force down to today in all five democracies considered here.[8] In fact, in a generalized way one can say that virtually all of western society today is liberal. Individual rights are universally respected (in theory and usually in practice), inherited class distinctions are not seen as giving special political prerogatives, the principle of "one person, one vote" is the norm, and selecting political leaders by free, competitive elections is fully accepted. In the sense of holding to principles such as these, all five of the countries included in this book are liberal democracies.

Liberalism can, however, also be seen as a more specific, philosophical theory or movement. Liberalism in this sense is often referred to as Enlightenment liberalism. It reacted with horror to the religious wars of the seventeenth century and to the often conservative nature of religious bodies that supported hereditary privileges and authoritarian government and opposed democratic reforms. Liberals placed great faith in human reason, believing that if people were freed from existing economic, political, and religious constraints they could, through the exercise of their reason, reach a consensus on the virtues and institutions needed for a free and prosperous society. Religion in its particular manifestations was seen as rooted in authority and superstitions and—when brought into the political arena—as a dangerous force, since it would work to divide society and become a basis for one group to use the political order to force its will onto others. On the other hand, basic, consensual religious beliefs were both discoverable by human reason and adequate to construct a free, prosperous society. Enlightenment liberalism believed religion in its particular manifestations should be banned from the public realm as a dangerous, divisive force; it saw religion in its rational, consensual manifestation as potentially having a positive, unifying role to play in the public realm.

Enlightenment liberals, therefore, typically called for a strict separation of church and state. They believed such a separation would spare the state from the dangerous divisions particularistic religion posed, yet would not harm particularistic religion, since it would continue to flourish in the purely private realm. Religious belief was something that people would be free to express in their private lives, but was of no concern to the state. The state would thereby be neutral on matters of religion. It would neither help nor hinder any particular religion. The state would only support and identify with rational, consensual religious themes, such as duty, honesty, responsibility, and respect, on which all religions and even all reasonable nonreligious people agreed. It thereby equated government neutrality on matters of religion and strict church-state separation. This meant Enlightenment liberals also saw religious freedom as being wholly a negative freedom, that is, as consisting of the right to be free from government restrictions or restraints on one's exercise of religion. They, for the most part, did not see it as also containing an element of positive freedom, that is, as requiring certain positive governmental actions that would make it possible for people to live out their religious faiths. All that was necessary for people to be fully free was for government to stay out of religious affairs.[9]

Enlightenment liberalism was often at odds with the existing church authorities, since they resisted both the liberals' theoretical assumptions and the practical political consequences of those assumptions. This meant Enlightenment liberalism often had an anticlerical nature. Today it is sometimes forgotten that the French Revolution was as much a revolution against the organized church and social class privileges as it was a revolution against an authoritarian monarchy.

All five countries considered in this book had strong Enlightenment liberal movements, and the story of church-state relations in each of them is to a significant degree the story of the varied ways in which the conflict between the Enlightenment liberals and opposing movements played out. We return to this issue in subsequent chapters.

The concept of governmental neutrality on matters of religion as defined earlier in this section is clearly in the tradition of liberalism as a generalized force in western societies, but differs in some important respects from the assumptions and beliefs of Enlightenment liberalism. Enlightenment liberalism rested on three interrelated assumptions: that particularistic religion could be safely assigned to the purely private sphere without infringing on the religious beliefs and practices of its adherents, that a public realm stripped of all religious elements would be a neutral zone among the various religious faiths and between religious and secular belief systems, and that religious freedom would flourish in the absence of governmental restraints and with no need for positive governmental actions to equalize the advantages enjoyed by religious and secular groups. On the basis of these assumptions the Enlightenment liberal perspective equates strict church-state separation and government religious neutrality.

These liberal assumptions, however, are coming under increasing attack in today's world. As Robert Bellah and his associates have written: "Yet religion, and certainly biblical religion, is concerned with the whole of life—with social, economic, and political matters as well as with private and personal ones. Not only has biblical language continued to be part of American public and political discourse, the churches have continuously exerted influence on public life right up to the present time."[10] As will become clear as this book progresses, the religious communities of all five countries considered in it are concerned with a wide range of public policy questions and are active in providing education, health care, and other social services. If indeed religion has a strong public facet to it and if religious groups, as well as government, are involved in providing educational, health, and social services, the Enlightenment liberal belief that limiting religion to the purely private realm leads to state neutrality on matters of religion is simply not accurate. If this is the case, removing all religious elements from the public sphere and seeing religious freedom as requiring no positive steps to recognize or support religion are, at the least, drawn into question. That is why earlier in this section we defined government neutrality not in terms of strict church-state separation or any other specific church-state arrangement, but in terms of an evenhandedness among people of all faiths and of none. We view neutrality in terms of government not influencing by its actions its citizens' choices for or against any particular religious or secular system of belief. It should neither advantage nor burden religion. We do not assume that withdrawing all government support for particularistic religion, extending government support for generalized, consensual religion, or merely removing all government restraints on the exercise of religion necessarily equates to neutrality.

Three Models

Even a cursory look at church-state relations in the five democracies to be considered reveals that they all have followed different church-state policies. In thinking more systematically about church-state relations in these countries and in organizing the mass of observations we will be making, it is helpful to think in terms of three basic models of church-state relations that modern, western democracies have followed. None of the five countries under review here follow any one of these models in a pure form, but starting out with these three models in mind helps to organize and focus the many observations we make.

One model is the strict church-state separation model. Under this model—which traces its roots to the Enlightenment liberal view of society and politics—religion and politics are seen as clearly distinct areas of human endeavor that should be kept separate from each other. Religion is seen as a personal, private matter, best left to the realm of personal choice and action. When religion and politics are mixed—with either the state dictating religious beliefs or practice or religion using the state to advance its cause—both religion and politics suffer. The state should be neutral on matters of religion and this neutrality is assumed to be achieved best by keeping religion and politics separate. Those who support this model point to the religious wars of the seventeenth century and present-day religious strife in the Middle East and elsewhere as examples of what happens when religion and politics mix. Of the five countries under consideration here the United States comes the closest to following the strict separation model, although as we will see it has recently been moving away from this model.

A second model—at the opposite end of the continuum from the church-state separation model—is the established church model. Under this model the state and the church form a partnership in advancing the cause of religion and the state. Church and state are seen as two pillars on which a stable, prosperous society rests. The state provides the church with recognition, accommodation, and often financial support; the church provides the state with an aura of legitimacy and tradition, recognition, and a sense of national unity and purpose. In present-day modern democracies it is usually seen more as a traditional, innocuous, but also helpful holdover from earlier times, than as a living, vibrant church-state model essential in today's world.

Religious establishment can take several different forms. It can, first, be either formal or informal. In formal church establishments the government recognizes and supports one particular church or denomination, and while other religions are tolerated, they clearly do not occupy the favored position the established church does. Religious establishment may also be more informal in nature. Here one particular church is favored by the state, and that church supports the existing political order, but both occur not because of formal, legal provisions, but because of certain informal forces such as those of tradition or the overwhelming numerical or cultural strength of one religion. Church establishment can also be marked either by only one particular established church or by a system of multiple church establishment. Under the latter system, the state seeks to favor and work with two or more favored religious bodies. Here the state may promote a generic "religion-in-general"[11] that is more of a civil religion, supportive of the state and its traditions, than a particularistic faith. Of the five countries considered in this study, England is the only one with a formally established church, although some observers would make the case that in Germany there is an informal multiple establishment.

The third church-state model is the pluralist or structural pluralist model.[12] Under this model "society is understood as made up of competing or perhaps complementary spheres."[13] Included among these spheres or realms of societal activities are education, business, the arts, and the family—and religion and government. These spheres have distinct activities or responsibilities, and they are to enjoy autonomy or freedom in their efforts to fulfill them. But it is crucial to note that the pluralist model sees religion not as a separate sphere with only limited relevance to the other spheres as the liberal strict separationists do, but as having a bearing on all of life. Pluralists also stress the existence of secular perspectives or worldviews that play a similar role to religion in society. "Pluralism is a matter of political respect by the state for the many world views held by the different kinds of institutions that fulfill the differentiated needs of a free society."[14] Government is not to take sides among the plurality of religious and secular worldviews swirling about in society. It is to seek equal justice for all of them, with justice essentially defined as giving them all their freedom and neither advantaging or disadvantaging any of them. The Netherlands is probably the clearest example of a country that has self-consciously sought to follow this model. Germany—in addition to possessing some aspects of the multiple, informal establishment model— and Australia also possess some features of this model.

In the following chapters we describe church-state relations in the five countries and seek to classify the five countries in terms of these three models, even while recognizing that none of them are pure examples of any of them.

Five Stable Democracies

As explained earlier in the chapter this book explores how five stable, western, liberal democratic countries have sought to respond to key questions posed by the intersection of those two great human institutions: the church and the state. We believe the five countries chosen for our study to be particularly well suited for our purposes for three basic reasons. First, they are all stable democracies whose successful commitment to religious freedom is generally recognized. Germany has the Nazi regime in its past and the eastern part of the country emerged from an oppressive communist past only recently, but for fifty years West Germany—into which East Germany was absorbed—has been recognized as part of the family of liberal western democracies. Thus the five countries selected fit our purpose of wishing to explore how polities recognized as mature, successful democracies have dealt with the issue of church-state relations.

Second, all five countries are religiously pluralistic, with predominantly Christian traditions, both Protestant and Catholic, but also with many smaller religious minorities. In the case of Germany and the Netherlands Protestants and Catholics are today about numerically equal, but in those countries Protestants have been dominant in a social and political sense through most of the modern era, and thus it was the Protestants that set the tone or played the dominant role in working through church-state issues. In all five there is a religious pluralism, characterized by large numbers of both Catholics and Protestants, and the Protestants in turn are divided into a variety of groups. Also, each of these countries has come to be marked in recent years by sharply increasing numbers of adherents of non-Christian faiths—and especially the Muslim faith—and people of no religious faith. Religiously, all five nations are indeed facing the challenge of pluralism.

A third characteristic of the five countries is that, despite their similar cultural, Christian heritages, they have chosen distinctly different approaches to church-state issues. England has an officially established church; the United States has followed a route emphasizing strict church-state separation; Australia has constitutional provisions very similar to those found in the American Constitution but has interpreted and implemented them in a quite different manner; the Netherlands is known for following a self-conscious policy of religious pluralism; and Germany, although not having an officially established church, has a long history of close cooperation between the state and the church. Thus the five countries are not carbon copies of each other. They offer a rich texture of differences that make them excellent subjects for comparative study.

Each of the following five chapters deals with one of the five countries and follows the same basic outline. Each chapter first gives a brief description of some salient characteristics of the nation and next gives an historical summary of church-state relations in that country. Church-state relations have clearly been shaped by the unique history of each country, and this section seeks to explain these unique sets of circumstances and how they have led to certain theories, assumptions, and mind-sets that have guided church-state relations in that nation. Each chapter then considers how—in light of its history and its church-state theories and assumptions—the country has handled the issue of the free exercise of religion, especially for minority religious groups. Then the chapter considers how the country has dealt with the issue of state accommodation of and support for religion, with special attention being paid to public policies as they relate to issues of education and religiously based social service organizations. The final section of each chapter offers some concluding observations and evaluations of the country's church-state policies.

Notes

1. Throughout this book we will follow conventional American usage and use the term "church" to refer generically to religion in its various manifestations.

2. On this initiative, see John DiIulio Jr., *Godly Republic: A Centrist Blueprint for America's Faith-Based Future* (Berkeley: University of California Press, 2007); and Amy E. Black, Douglas L. Koopman, and David K. Ryden, *Of Little Faith: The Politics of George W. Bush's Faith-Based Initiative* (Washington, D.C.: Georgetown University Press, 2004).

3. Clinton Rossiter, *Seedbed of the Republic* (New York: Harcourt, Brace & World, 1953), 447. Also see James Q. Wilson, *The Moral Sense* (New York: Free Press, 1993).

4. Will Kymlicka and Wayne Norman, "Citizenship in Culturally Diverse Societies: Issues, Contexts, Concepts," in Will Kymlicka and Wayne Norman, eds, *Citizenship in Diverse Societies* (Oxford: Oxford University Press, 2000), 1.

5. See Douglas Laycock, "Formal, Substantive, and Disaggregated Neutrality Toward Religion," *DePaul Law Review* 39 (1990), 1001–6; Stephen V. Monsma, *Positive Neutrality* (Westport, Conn.: Greenwood, 1993), chap. 5; and Stephen V. Monsma, *When Sacred and Secular Mix: Religious Nonprofit Organizations and Public Money* (Lanham, Md.: Rowman & Littlefield, 1996), chap. 6. It should be noted that this goal of governmental religious neutrality is itself not neutral. It makes a choice in favor of a certain type of governmental religious neutrality and thereby reflects certain assumptions and values that differ from those, for example, of Erastian or Enlightenment liberal thinking.

6. Laycock, "Formal, Substantive, and Disaggregated Neutrality Toward Religion," 1001.

7. From Stewart's dissent in *Abington School District v. Schempp*, 374 US at 319–320 (1963).

8. On Enlightenment liberalism and its impact in western society, see Peter Gay, *The Enlightenment: An Interpretation* (New York: Knopf, 1966); and Henry A. May, *The Enlightenment in America* (New York: Oxford University Press, 1976).

9. In addition to the sources cited in note 8, see Monsma, *Positive Neutrality*, 173–75.

10. Robert Bellah, Richard Madsen, William M. Sullivan, Ann Swindler, and Steven M. Tipton, *Habits of the Heart* (New York: Harper & Row, Perennial Library, 1986), 220.

11. The term is Martin Marty's. See Martin Marty, *The New Shape of American Religion* (New York: Harper & Row, 1958), 2, 31–44.

12. On this model, see Carl H. Esbeck, "A Typology of Church-State Relations in Current American Thought," in Luis Lugo, ed., *Religion, Public Life, and the American Polity* (Knoxville: University of Tennessee Press, 1994), 15–18; and Monsma, *Positive Neutrality*, 137–71.

13. John G. Francis, "The Evolving Regulatory Structure of European Church-State Relationships," *Journal of Church and State* 34 (1992), 782.

14. Esbeck, "A Typology of Church-State Relations," 15.

CHAPTER TWO

~

The United States:
Strict Separation under Fire

In 1947 the U.S. Supreme Court declared in ringing words:

> No tax in any amount, large or small, can be levied to support any religious activities or institutions, whatever they may be called, or whatever form they may adopt to teach or practice religion. Neither a state nor the Federal government can, openly or secretly, participate in the affairs of any religious organizations or groups and *vice versa*. In the words of Jefferson, the clause against establishment of religion by law was intended to erect "a wall of separation between church and state."[1]

Later the Court went on to insist that the wall between church and state "must be kept high and impregnable."[2] There is, however, more than a little irony in the fact that the Court decided—after articulating these ringing words of strict, even absolute, church-state separation—that the First Amendment allows government to aid religious schools in the form of subsidies to transport children to them. As one of the dissenting justices complained, the Court's decision reminded him "of Julia who, according to Byron's reports, 'whispering "I will ne'er consent,"—consented.'"[3]

There is much in this early decision that typifies the Supreme Court's approach to church-state issues. It made "no aid to religion" the key principle guiding its interpretations of the First Amendment's religious freedom language, but time and again it finds itself unable to hold strictly to that principle in actual practice. Yet it cannot agree on legal principles that clearly articulate when no aid to religion ought to be followed and when and under what conditions other principles should take precedence. In fact, in recent years that principle has begun to crumble even while it continues to exert influence. This has resulted in a series of church-state decisions in which the Court has been closely divided and, as one Court observer expressed it, by "contradictory principles, vaguely defined tests, and eccentric distinctions."[4]

This chapter explores the American approach to issues of church and state, noting the strong commitment to strict church-state separation, efforts in practice sometimes to hold firm to it and sometimes to modify it, and the resulting state of affairs. We do so in six sections. First, we give relevant information on the American society and political system, next we give some necessary historical background. The next three sections consider free exercise theories and practices, establishment theories and practices as they relate to education, and establishment theories and practices as they relate to other issue areas. Finally, we make some concluding observations.

The Nation

With a population of three hundred million drawn from most of the other nations of the world, the United States is by far the most populous and most diverse of the five countries considered in this book. It is also a stable democracy. The United States has the oldest written constitution in the world, and its religious freedom protections are thereby the oldest written constitutional protections of religion.

Two characteristics of the American people are especially relevant to this study and worth noting. The first of these is the great religious diversity of the American people, a diversity that is clearly greater than that of the other countries considered in this book. From the founding of the nation through the nineteenth century the United States was an overwhelmingly Protestant country. There was diversity within this Protestantism, but by the mid-nineteenth century the large mainline denominations—Methodists, Presbyterians, Congregationalists, Episcopalians, Baptists, and Lutherans—dominated the religious life of the nation. Since then much has changed. The mainline denominations are aging and rapidly declining in numbers, and both conservative, evangelical Protestants and Roman Catholics now surpass mainline Protestants in numbers and perhaps in cultural and political influence. Numerically, approximately 18 percent of the population can be considered white mainline Protestants, 26 percent white evangelical Protestants, 7 percent black Protestants, and 24 percent Roman Catholics.[5] Equally important, the social and educational gap that once existed between Catholics and

Protestants has closed and evangelical Protestants, constituting about one-fourth of the American electorate, are clearly a potent political force.

Adding to American religious diversity is the 2 percent of the population that is Jewish, the 2 percent that is Mormon, and the 0.6 percent that is Muslim.[6] Muslims are a smaller percentage of the population in the United States than in the other four countries considered in the book. More importantly, they are "largely assimilated, happy with their lives, and moderate with respect to many of the issues that have divided Muslims and Westerners around the world."[7] A 2007 survey showed that only 2 percent of American Muslims fell into the low-income category, and 71 percent agreed that most people who want to get ahead in the United States can do so if they are willing to work hard.[8]

Secularists—those without any religious affiliation—now constitute 16 percent of the population.[9] In addition, one finds many small faith groups in the United States, including Hinduism, Buddhism, Native American religion, New Age spirituality, and a variety of sects. It is no exaggeration to say that any religious group present in the world has its adherents in the United States.

The end result of this religious diversity, and especially the combination of declining numbers among mainline Protestants and the rise of both Catholics and evangelical Protestants, is that no one religious tradition is socially or politically dominant in the United States today. Christianity is, of course, the dominant religion, but it is fractured into literally thousands of separate groups.

A second important characteristic is Americans' high rate of religious membership and activity, when compared to the people of other modern, industrialized countries. In a series of polls conducted by the Pew Forum between 1996 and 2005, the percentage of Americans reporting they attend religious services at least weekly varied from a low of 38 percent to a high of 43 percent (in the latest poll [2005] it was at 41 percent).[10] This compares to 15 percent in Germany and 14 percent in Britain.[11] Seventy-eight percent of Americans report prayer is an important part of their daily lives, and 83 percent report that they never doubt the existence of God.[12]

Politically, it is important to keep in mind the crucial role played by the U.S. Supreme Court in constitutional interpretation. The nine life-appointed justices of the Supreme Court have the final word in interpreting the religious freedom language of the First Amendment. They can hold any act by any branch of the national, state, or local governments to be in violation of the First Amendment and therefore null and void. Thus the story of church-state relations in the United States is to a large degree a story of the Supreme Court's interpretations of the basic, simple—yet devilishly elusive—words of the First Amendment: "Congress shall make no law respecting an establishment of religion, or prohibiting the free exercise thereof." Before we turn directly to these struggles, it is important to consider some key elements in the history of the development of church-state attitudes, practices, and principles.

Historical Background

American church-state theory and practice has gone through five distinct stages during the past three hundred years. The first stage was the establishment of religion during the colonial era of the seventeenth and eighteenth centuries. When the American colonies were first settled, most followed the prevailing European pattern of creating established churches. The English Puritans in New England, the Dutch Reformed in New Amsterdam, the Anglicans in Virginia, and other colonists elsewhere assumed that "the pattern of religious uniformity would of necessity be transplanted and perpetuated in the colonies."[13] The assumption was that religious unity was essential for political unity. Thus the favored churches were granted tax supports of different types, dissenters were subjected to penalties of varying severity, and civil authorities exercised control over certain ecclesiastical affairs.

The second stage in American church-state theory and practice emerged in the second half of the eighteenth century, when a movement to disestablish the churches materialized at about the same time as the movement for independence from Britain. This disestablishment was the result of two dissimilar movements that came together in a "strange coalition."[14] The first of these movements was the Great Awakening, a religious revival that swept through the colonies, starting in the 1740s. It is hard to exaggerate the breadth and depth of this revival. It featured itinerant preachers, mass exhibitions of religious fervor, and renewed religious commitments by the masses. It also had a strong anti–established church emphasis, since it was reacting against the perceived formalism and dead orthodoxy of the existing, usually established churches.

The second partner in the "strange coalition" consisted of the Enlightenment liberal rationalists. Led by figures such as Thomas Jefferson and James Madison these people were religious, even Christian, in a broad, generic sense, but largely rejected or saw as irrelevant to government the traditional doctrines of historic Christianity. They were well read, cosmopolitan, and revolted by the religious persecutions that had marked Europe in the recent past and that were also present in the colonies. They were rationalists who felt that human reason could discern the basic precepts of religion that were necessary for a stable, moral society and political order. Doctrines peculiar to the various religious traditions were unnecessary and even dangerous for the public order, and thus they could and should be separated from the public realm and relegated to the private sphere.

These two movements came together in the last quarter of the eighteenth century to provide the impetus for the disestablishment of the churches. The Enlightenment liberals, as an intellectual and political elite, provided most of the rationale in support of disestablishment; the popular Great Awakening provided mass support for disestablishment. The events surrounding the disestablishment of the Anglican church in Virginia proved to be especially crucial for the subsequent development of church-state concepts. Events began to unfold in 1776 when the Virginia legislature repealed most of the legal privileges that had been granted Anglicans and suspended the collection of taxes for the Anglican church.[15] Then, in 1784, Patrick Henry introduced a General Assessment Bill that made clear there was to be no established church, but also provided for a tax whose proceeds were to be distributed in support of all Christian churches. It appeared to have majority support in the legislature, but Madison won a year's postponement of the vote on it. In the meanwhile Madison wrote his soon-to-be-famous "Memorial and Remonstrance against Religious Assessments." In it he condemned all public tax support for churches, arguing "that the same authority which can force a citizen to contribute three pence only of his property for the support of any one establishment, may force him to conform to any other establishment in all cases whatsoever."[16]

With Madison supplying the intellectual firepower, the dissenting churches with roots in the Great Awakening—largely Baptist and Presbyterian—supplied the popular opposition to the Henry bill. In 1785 the Virginia legislature turned down Henry's General Assessment Bill and enacted instead Jefferson's "Bill for Establishing Religious Freedom" that provided, in part, "no man shall be compelled to frequent or support any religious worship, place or ministry whatsoever . . . but all men shall be free to profess, and by argument to maintain, their opinions in matters of religion, and that the same shall in no wise diminish, enlarge, or affect their civil capacities."[17] Subsequently other states that had had laws creating various forms of religious establishment repealed them. In 1833, Massachusetts, the last of the states to abandon church establishment, did so.

Soon after these events and the writing of the First Amendment, church-state relations entered a third stage, from roughly 1800 to 1950, marked by an informal reestablishment of Protestant Christianity. At the beginning of the nineteenth century Christianity seemed to be losing its presence in society. The churches had lost their establishment status, and only about 10 percent of the population professed to be members of any church.[18] Yet in 1888 James Bryce, the respected English commentator on U.S. government and society, wrote: "The National Government and the State governments do give to Christianity a species of recognition inconsistent with the view that civil government should be absolutely neutral in religious matters. . . . The matter may be summed up by saying that Christianity is in fact understood to be, though not the legally established religion, yet the national religion."[19] One cause of this reestablishment of religion—Protestant Christianity to be exact—was the Second Great Awakening in the early years of the nineteenth century.[20] Church membership swelled, as revival again swept through the land, especially on the rapidly growing frontier. Another cause for the reestablishment of religion was the fact that the eighteenth-century disestablishment movement was clearly committed to the formal, legal disestablishment of churches, but never directly addressed the question of whether or not to allow a host of public supports for religion more generally. Clearly, the heirs of the Great Awakening assumed that government support for such measures as Sunday observance, suppression of gambling, and other such marks of a "Christian society" would continue. Even Enlightenment liberals such as Madison and Jefferson were ambiguous on this issue. Madison as president, for example, issued proclamations calling for days of national prayer and approved chaplains to be paid from public funds for the Congress, although he later wrote that on reflection he felt such actions unconstitutional.[21]

Thus, when Christianity experienced a surge in the early nineteenth century, a vigorous, populist Protestant Christianity overwhelmed any tendencies to maintain a more strict separation of church and state. Prayers and Bible readings were a regular part of state-supported common schools, Christian missions to Native Americans were subsidized by government, and laws enforced Sunday observance. In 1890 most state colleges and universities had chapel services and some even required Sunday church attendance.[22]

It is especially important in understanding what happened later in church-state relations to understand the origins and rationale underlying the creation of a vast system of common schools—today's public schools—in the nineteenth century. From the founding of the nation in 1789 Americans have worried about how to maintain national unity in the face of wide geographic distances, sharp class differences, and disparate, recurring waves of immigration. The answer Americans developed in the nineteenth century and have largely clung to since is the common school. In the early nineteenth century, European efforts at universal, state-run education caught the attention of Horace Mann and other New England elites. These reformers viewed the common school as the basic means by which the children of all classes—but especially the children of the lower, uneducated classes—would be taught social and political virtues. The common school advocates consistently saw the common school primarily in terms not of teaching skills in such areas as reading and mathematics, but in teaching the virtues thought necessary for national unity and free, democratic society.

When immigration surged in the middle decades of the nineteenth century, the concept of the common school was already well launched among the elites of the young American nation and readily available for application to this new turn of events. Surging immigration from Ireland, Italy, and other predominantly Catholic countries from which the United States had previously had relatively few immigrants raised fears of American society being overwhelmed and undermined by millions of hard-to-assimilate immigrants unschooled in democratic values. These fears turned the common school ideal from an elite theory into a popular ideal broadly held in American society. Charles Glenn reports, "What in the 1830s was a cause appealing to a relatively limited elite, concerned to shape the American people in their own image, came in the next two decades to be perceived as an urgent necessity by virtually all Americans of social and political influence."[23] The common school came to be seen as an increasingly crucial means for achieving national unity, assimilation, and the inculcation of habits of good citizenship.

Religion of a particular type played an important role in the vision of the common school as the crucial inculcator of civic virtue and as the key instrument of cultural and national assimilation. Mann was a Unitarian—as were many of his fellow New England education reformers—and as such rejected both particularistic religion and nonreligious secularism. The schools were to be rational, Christian, and consensual.[24] Mann once wrote:

> Although it may not be easy theoretically, to draw the line between those views of religious truth and of christian faith which are common to all, and may, therefore, with propriety be inculcated in school, and those which, being peculiar to individual sects, are therefore by law excluded; still it is believed that no practical difficulty occurs in the conduct of our schools in this respect.[25]

Carl Kaestle has described the resulting common school ideology as being "centered on republicanism, Protestantism, and capitalism, three sources of social belief that were intertwined and mutually supporting."[26] The common school ideal thereby was definitely within the tradition of Jefferson, Madison, and other Enlightenment liberals.

There were some protests to this form of liberal religion both from a few evangelical Protestants and from Roman Catholics, but Catholics in the nineteenth century were largely marginalized politically and socially, and evangelical Protestants surprisingly came largely to accept the vision of the common school religion espoused by Mann and others. Especially in light of the perceived threat arising from large numbers of Catholic immigrants flooding into the United States, many conservative Protestants—by far the numerically dominant group within nineteenth-century Protestantism—felt common schools that included Bible readings and moral lessons represented a bulwark against the Catholic threat, even if it was not exactly biblical, orthodox Christianity that was being taught. Os Guinness has expressed it well: "In the nineteenth century, therefore, Protestant evangelicals were public-spirited in supporting state-run public schools. But it was also their way of 'establishing' a vague, nonsectarian, and moralistic Protestantism as the de facto civil religion."[27] There was virtual unanimity among the culturally dominant Protestant elites that in the common school the ideals of democracy, America, and Christianity were joined together in a powerful device for uniting the nation. The elements of Christianity in the common schools meant that the then-dominant conservative evangelical Protestants saw no need for their own separate schools, and enabled them to join fully in the common school enterprise. The common school movement was supported by the same "strange coalition" that had led the disestablishment movement of the late eighteenth century. It was a crucial part of the informal, de facto establishment of a genial, vague Protestantism in the 1800 to 1950 period.

After World War II, at mid-twentieth century, the United States entered a fourth stage of church-state relations, one that lasted until the 1980s and continues to exert great influence. It can be termed the second disestablishment of religion. Enlightenment liberal thinking reemerged and came to dominate Supreme Court decisions and the thinking of society's leadership echelon, even if not of the broader public. The 1947 words of the Supreme Court decision quoted at the beginning of this chapter signaled this decisive turn of events. It established no aid to religion as a bedrock principle for interpreting the First Amendment and embraced Jefferson's wall of separation metaphor. As will be seen in more detail later, the Supreme Court banned religious elements from the public schools, declared almost all aid to religiously based schools unconstitutional, and found other forms of church-state cooperation or recognition unconstitutional. The liberal view of society clearly triumphed in the United States. Enlightenment liberalism in the other democracies considered in this book was forced into compromises with more conservative religious forces. But this did not happen in the United States. The paradox is that in what is clearly the most religious of the five countries considered in this book, religion, at least for a time, had the least impact in protecting a legitimate role for itself in the public life of the nation.

Then, from the early 1980s to the present day, the United States entered a fifth stage of church-state relations, one marked by a still-emerging principle of neutrality or equal treatment. As one observer wrote in 2000, "The Supreme Court is on the verge of replacing the principle of strict separation with a very different constitutional principle that demands equal treatment for religion."[28] In this new era the strict separation, no-aid-to-religion strand of thinking is clashing with the new equal-treatment, equal-access strand of thinking. A closely divided Supreme Court leans first one way and then the other. Heated battles are being fought among clashing advocacy groups, and in the news media and Congress—and among Supreme Court justices. The exact contours of those clashes will becomes clear as the chapter proceeds.

The Free Exercise of Religion

All five democracies included in this study support religious freedom for all. No person will be fined or imprisoned for whether, where, and how he or she worships God (or gods). Nevertheless, the United States—along with its fellow democracies—faces some contentious issues over the exact meaning and application of religious freedom. Most difficult is the question of whether religiously motivated behavior that is thought to be contrary to societal welfare or norms should be protected. No democracy would allow child sacrifice as part of a religious ritual, no matter how sincere the adherents of that religion. But much more difficult, borderline cases remain.

The First Amendment states: "Congress shall make no law . . . prohibiting the free exercise [of religion]." Historically and down to today, the Supreme Court has tended to interpret this clause very narrowly. It has not proven to be a robust basis for protecting minorities' freedom to practice their religions as they see fit. This tendency can be seen in the first case to come before the Court that called on it to interpret these words. It was an 1879 case that dealt with a federal law that prohibited polygamy, which was being challenged by Mormons who at that time practiced polygamy as a part of their religious beliefs. The Supreme Court ruled that the federal law did not violate the constitutional rights of Mormons since it was beliefs, and not actions, that the First Amendment protected: "Laws are made for the government of actions, and while they cannot interfere with mere religious beliefs and opinions, they may with practices."[29] The decision then went on to argue that to hold otherwise "would be to make the professed doctrines of religious belief superior to the law of the land, and in effect to permit every citizen to become a law unto himself."[30]

This belief-action distinction led to what has been termed the secular regulation rule: as long as the government has a valid secular purpose in mind and otherwise has the legal authority to engage in a certain form of regulation, the fact that it interferes with or hampers people's free exercise of their religion is not a basis for them to escape the regulation.[31] The secular regulation rule and the belief-action dichotomy on which it rests raise the question of what is left of free exercise protections. If the free exercise clause protects only beliefs and not religious practices, and if any law with legitimate secular purposes can be enforced on religious groups irrespective of sincerely and deeply held religious beliefs underlying their practices, is there any protection given by the free exercise clause? There are two responses to this question. One is that the Supreme Court continues to hold that any law that intentionally singles out a religious group for disadvantages or limitations violates its free exercise rights. In 1993, for example, the Supreme Court struck down several ordinances of the city of Hialeah, Florida, on the basis they were specifically aimed at outlawing animal sacrifices of the Santeria religion. "The ordinances had as their object the suppression of religion."[32] It reached this conclusion on the fact that the ordinances had been narrowly drawn to outlaw the religious sacrifice of animals, but not to outlaw such practices as hunting, the slaughter of animals for food, and the kosher slaughter of animals. Since they were specifically aimed at the ritual sacrifice of animals as practiced by the Santeria religion, they were held to be in violation of the free exercise clause.

A second answer to the question of what is left of free exercise protections in light of the secular regulation rule is what is termed the compelling state interest test. This is an area of legal uncertainty. The Supreme Court has wavered in its application of this test. The compelling state interest test holds that if an apparently neutral, secular law has the effect of significantly burdening or disadvantaging people's exercise of their sincerely held religious beliefs, that law can only be enforced on those persons if the state has a compelling reason for doing so. It thereby modifies the secular regulation rule. On this basis the Supreme Court held that the Amish did not have to send their children to school beyond the eighth grade, a Seventh-day Adventist could not be excluded from receiving unemployment benefits because she refused Saturday work, and a pacifist could not be refused unemployment compensation when he lost his job because of refusing to work on manufacturing armaments.[33] In all three of these cases the Court ruled that the government had not demonstrated a compelling societal interest that would be endangered if exceptions to existing law were made in order to accommodate religious convictions.

The Supreme Court, however, has never consistently or fully followed the compelling state interest standard. In 1961 the Court failed to extend free exercise protections to Orthodox Jewish businesspeople who had been disadvantaged by Sunday closing regulations. In 1982 it did the same in the case of an Amish employer and his Amish employees who felt their religious scruples were violated by having to pay Social Security taxes, and in 1986 it did not rule in favor of an Orthodox Jewish air force officer who had insisted on wearing a yarmulke as required by his faith.[34] In all three cases, the Supreme Court essentially followed the compelling state interest standard, but set a low threshold for meeting it, holding each time that the government had successfully demonstrated a compelling interest that overruled the claimed free exercise right.

Then, in 1990, the Supreme Court considered a case dealing with adherents of a Native American religion who had used peyote as part of a traditional religious ceremony. As a result they had tested positive for drug use, were fired from their jobs, and were denied unemployment compensation since they were held to have been fired "for cause." The Court held that "an individual's religious beliefs [do not] excuse him from compliance with an otherwise valid law prohibiting conduct that the State is free to regulate."[35] The compelling state interest test was left in shreds: "To make an individual's obligation to obey . . . a law contingent upon the law's coincidence with his religious beliefs, except where the State's interest is 'compelling[,]' . . . contradicts both constitutional traditions and common sense."[36]

Widespread criticism greeted this decision of the Supreme Court. People and groups that traditionally had been divided on questions of religious establishment united in condemning it. A coalition of these groups came together and persuaded Congress to pass the Religious Freedom Restoration Act (RFRA) in 1993. This act reads in part: "Government may substantially burden a person's exercise of religion only if it demonstrates that application of the burden to the person is in furtherance of a compelling governmental interest; and is the least restrictive means of furthering that compelling governmental interest."[37] The act sought to write into law the compelling state interest standard the Supreme Court had first articulated, never fully applied, and then largely abandoned. In 1996, however, the Supreme Court again demonstrated its limited understanding of the free exercise clause when it declared this law unconstitutional.[38] Congress reacted by passing in 2000 the more limited Religious Land Use and Institutionalized Persons Act (RLUIP).[39] It seeks to protect the rights of churches to build or expand in areas where zoning laws are a barrier and the freedom of prisoners to exercise their religious beliefs while incarcerated.

RFRA, and now RLUIP; the wide coalition of groups that came together in support of them; and the wide margins by which they passed Congress stand as testimonies to the normal commitment of the broader society and its political institutions to protecting religious freedoms. When that normal commitment breaks down, however, unpopular religious minorities are vulnerable, and the free exercise clause, as interpreted by the Supreme Court, is at best an uncertain protection.

Nevertheless, the United States has not faced the same level of controversy over the free exercise rights of Muslims as have some other of the countries considered in this book. The question of Muslim women being allowed to wear head scarves or other distinctive Muslim clothing at school or work has been an issue in some of the other democracies considered in this book, but outside of a few scattered cases that were quickly resolved, it has not been an issue in the United States.[40] No such cases have come before the Supreme Court. Most free exercise issues involving Muslims have come from prisoners who have asserted they have not been able to exercise their Muslim faith and its required practices freely while incarcerated. Even here accommodations have gradually been made.[41] The comparatively small number of Muslims in the United States, their success at assimilating into American society, and the largely tolerant attitudes of Americans toward Muslims[42] help to explain why free exercise issues for Muslims have not been as large an issue in the United States as in some other countries.

One final point: The comparative weakness of the free exercise clause, as interpreted by the Supreme Court, can also be seen in the fact that on several occasions the Supreme Court has rejected arguments that sought to use the free exercise clause to assert certain positive religious rights, as has sometimes been done in other democracies considered in this book—especially in Germany. The concept here is that if people are to enjoy full religious freedom, not only must they be free from direct legal restrictions on their right to act on their religious beliefs, they may sometimes need to be aided by government in doing so, especially if nonreligious people are being assisted by government to act on their secular beliefs. Two examples of the Supreme Court's rejection of such reasoning are instructive. The first comes from two basic decisions in which the Court ruled eight to one that neither a state-composed prayer nor the Lord's Prayer and a Bible reading could be a part of public school programming.[43] The lone dissenting justice in both these cases was Potter Stewart and in both cases he made a free exercise argument. He wrote, "There is involved in these cases a substantial free exercise claim on the part of those who affirmatively desire to have their children's school day open with the reading of passages from the Bible."[44] He then went on to explain more fully that

> a compulsory state educational system so structures a child's life that if religious exercises are held to be an impermissible activity in schools, religion is placed at an artificial and state-created disadvantage. Viewed in this light, permission of such exercises for those who want them is necessary if the schools are truly to be neutral in the matter of religion. And a refusal to permit religious exercises thus is seen, not as the realization of state neutrality, but rather as the establishment of a religion of secularism, or at the least, as government support of the beliefs of those who think that religious exercises should be conducted only in private.[45]

Stewart went on to argue that if public school religious exercises could be made voluntary in nature, the free exercise rights of those who desired them would be protected without violating the rights of those who did not desire them. As we will see later, this is the precise position the German Constitutional Court has taken. But the U.S. Supreme Court decisively rejected it.

Similarly, some justices have made a free exercise argument in cases dealing with public aid to religiously based schools. Justice Byron White, for example, in one such case dissented on free exercise grounds from the conclusion of the Court majority that public aid to religious schools violates the First Amendment:

> The Establishment Clause, however, coexists in the First Amendment with the Free Exercise Clause and the latter is surely relevant in cases such as these. Where a state program seeks to ensure the proper education of its young, in private as well as public schools, free exercise considerations at least counsel against refusing support for students attending parochial schools simply because in that setting they are also being instructed in the tenets of the faith they are constitutionally free to practice.[46]

In another case that also dealt with public aid to religious schools he again made a free exercise argument when he argued that denying parents who send their children to such schools any financial relief "also make[s] it more difficult, if not impossible, for parents to follow the dictates of their conscience and seek a religious as well as a secular education for their children."[47]

But Justices Stewart and White have been lonely voices on the Supreme Court. The Court has consistently held that First Amendment restrictions on the establishment of religion trump a positive right to government support in freely exercising one's religion. It has not seen the free exercise clause as requiring government to take positive actions to assure room or space for religious people to practice their faith. In fact, it has, at best, been ambiguous in protecting religious people from laws that would hamper and disadvantage them in practicing what their religious consciences demand. As interpreted by the Supreme Court, the free exercise clause has remained limited, truncated in nature. It thereby has not been effective in affording wide protections to religious minorities when popular sentiment and the elected branches of government fail to do so.

The Establishment of Religion and Education

The place of religion in schools has been *the* key battleground where the American system has largely hammered out the meaning of the First Amendment's establishment clause. Here, more than in any other area, one can see the continuing influence of the common school ideal; the triumph of the strict separation, no-aid-to-religion principle in the post–World War II era; the challenges to strict separation since the1980s by the equal treatment principle; and the continuing influence of strict separation as a key to understanding the American approach to no-establishment of religion. In this section we first consider the issue of religion in the public schools and then the issue of governmental funding of private, religiously based schools.

The strict separationist era can be clearly seen in positions adopted by the Supreme Court on *the question of the permissible place of religion in the public schools.* The thinking of the Supreme Court was clearly signaled in the early 1960s when the Supreme Court decided that prayer and Bible readings in the public schools violated the Constitution. In the first of these decisions the Court held that a brief, nondenominational prayer the New York authorities had composed for recitation at the start of the school day ("Almighty God, we acknowledge our dependence upon Thee, and we beg Thy blessings upon us, our parents, our teachers and our Country") violated the establishment clause of the First Amendment ("Congress shall make no law respecting an establishment of religion . . ."). The Court argued that "in this country it is no part of the business of government to compose official prayers for any group of the American people to recite as a part of a religious program carried on by government."[48] A year later the Court ruled that programs of Bible reading and recitation of the Lord's Prayer at the start of the school day were also unconstitutional. Here the Court argued that what was at issue were "religious exercises, required by the States in violation of the command of the First Amendment that the Government maintain strict neutrality, neither aiding nor opposing religion."[49] The Court further ruled that to pass establishment clause scrutiny "there must be a secular legislative purpose and a primary effect that neither advances nor inhibits religion."[50] Prayers and Bible readings passed neither of these tests. The fact that the religious exercises were voluntary (children who objected could be excused) made no difference, since a violation of the establishment clause does not require coercion to be present.

The Supreme Court also took a strict separationist position in its rulings on integrating religion into the public school curriculum. It ruled unconstitutional a released time program in which the schools and religious groups would cooperate by the schools releasing the students for an hour or so a week with various religious groups coming into the school to offer instruction to the adherents of their faiths. Students not desiring any religious instruction were given alternative activities. Justice Hugo Black spoke for the Court majority when he reasoned that such programs utilized "the tax-established and tax-supported public school system to aid religious groups to spread their faith."[51] The mind-set of the Court at that time can be seen in that merely allowing parents to have their own children instructed in their family's own faith was mischaracterized as enabling "religious groups to spread their faith." A few years later the Court pulled back from this strict separationist ruling when it allowed a similar program, but one where the classes of religious instruction were held on sites away from the public schools.[52]

As we will shortly see the Supreme Court has since the 1980s moved away from strict separation in some church-state areas, but the Court has continued to take a strict separation position in regard to religion having an officially sanctioned place in the public schools. It ruled against prayers at ceremonial occasions such as graduations, moments of silence at the start of the school day for prayer or meditation, and a Louisiana law requiring that whenever evolution is taught as a theory of human origins, equal time must also be given to a literal version of creationism.[53] In all these decisions the Court has primarily relied on the principle that government may not favor, encourage, or promote religion. Strict no aid to religion is still the guiding norm.

It is important to recognize that the Supreme Court has always insisted it is not hostile to religion. It has stated that public schools are permitted to teach about religion, to teach about the role religion has played in history, and to teach the Bible as literature. In one decision, for example, the Court stated that the "study of religions and of the bible from a literary and historic viewpoint, presented objectively and as part of a secular program of education, need not collide with the First Amendment's prohibition [against supporting religion] . . . ."[54]

These decisions of the Supreme Court can be seen both as being rooted in the common school ideal and as going against that ideal. They are rooted in the common school tradition in the Court's attempts to assure that the public schools are welcoming and evenhanded toward children of all faiths and of none. To do so, the Court has worked to remove all religious observances from the schools. But they can also be seen as going against the common school tradition in that that tradition had accepted—indeed even seen as vital—the incorporation of broadly consensual religious beliefs and observances into the educational process.

As a result of this latter factor, there have been continuing efforts to overturn some of these decisions of the Supreme Court by way of a constitutional amendment, legislation, or finding loopholes in the Court's decisions, spurred no doubt by the public's continuing support for certain religious elements in the public schools.[55] George Gallup reported in 1989: "Since the U.S. Supreme Court's 1962 and 1963 rulings that religious exercises and devotional Bible reading in the public schools were unconstitutional, the courts have consistently struck down efforts to restore those practices. Surveys show that Americans have just as consistently favored some form of school prayer."[56] A 2006 survey showed that not much has changed in the intervening seventeen years: almost 70 percent of the American public agreed that "liberals have gone too far in trying to keep religion out of the schools and the government."[57]

As noted earlier, however, the Supreme Court has since the 1980s been moving—uncertainly, in starts and stops—into a new era of church-state interpretations. This movement toward an equal treatment approach began in 1981 when the Supreme Court ruled that a state university could not bar a religious, student-initiated club from using university facilities for its meetings, as long as it allowed a host of other student clubs to use its facilities.[58] Then, in 1984, Congress applied the same principle to public high schools when it passed the Equal Access Act, which provided that if a school allowed extracurricular clubs to use school facilities outside normal instructional hours, it could not refuse a religiously based club to form and also use school facilities. The Supreme Court upheld this law when it ruled that clubs formed under it do not violate the establishment clause, as long as "a religious club is merely one of many different student-initiated voluntary clubs. . . ."[59] Then, in 2001, the Supreme Court held that an elementary school could not exclude a parent-sponsored religious club for children held in the school after normal class hours.[60] The Court relied on equal treatment reasoning: since the school had allowed a variety of nonreligious groups to use its facilities for after-school activities, it could not exclude a religious group. The Court stated that the religious student club "seeks nothing more than to be treated neutrally and given access to speak about the same topics as are other groups."[61]

Nevertheless, strict separation doctrines forged thirty to forty years ago continue to exert an influence. Recently, for example, in Michigan a school chorus wished to sing the "Lord's Prayer" as a part of the school's graduation ceremonies in order to honor a classmate who had been killed in an automobile accident, but was told by the school superintendent it could not do so under current law.[62] At times individual schools or school districts, sometimes with the support of the lower courts, have gone beyond what even the Supreme Court would seem to require. A fifth-grade teacher was told she could not keep a Bible on her desk or silently read it during her class's silent reading period. A federal Court of Appeals upheld the school.[63] A ninth-grade teacher assigned her class a research paper and when one of her pupils wrote on the life of Jesus Christ she gave her an "F" on the paper, explaining that "the law says we are not to deal with religious issues in the classroom." The lower federal courts upheld the teacher.[64] In another instance a student was told she could not sing a Christian song at a school talent show.[65] Instances such as these may be due to overly zealous teachers, principals, or local school boards, but help demonstrate that strict separation, no-aid-to-religion thinking still exerts a significant influence in the United States.

Also, even under equal treatment interpretations, the role of religion in public schools has been limited to extracurricular clubs and activities. The line that has time and again been drawn excludes any official recognition or support for religion. At the same time, the public schools have been called increasingly to deal with morally sensitive issues such as teenage pregnancies, AIDS awareness, racial and ethnic respect, school violence, juvenile crime, and good citizenship. The very issues that religion has sought to address and that a majority of Americans turn to their communities of faith for answers must now be addressed in a thoroughly secular fashion by the schools. This results in a dilemma that the Supreme Court and most American societal elites have failed to recognize. On the one hand, for the public schools to integrate certain religious perspectives into the curriculum or to conduct certain religious exercises would violate the norm of governmental neutrality on matters of religion. Even generalized, consensual religion that has the support of a majority of the community—maybe even the overwhelming majority—is rejected by some parents in the community. Those parents and their children would be disadvantaged by such practices. And allowance for individual students to be excused from religious exercises or from lessons with religious dimensions may stigmatize those students in the eyes of their peers as "different." Thus teacher-led prayers, the teaching of religiously based accounts of creation, and the incorporation of consensual religious exercises into the public schools would be a violation of religious neutrality. Under the influence of Enlightenment liberalism this has been rightly recognized and given weight by the Supreme Court and societal elites.

On the other hand—and this is what the Supreme Court and American elites have failed to recognize—once religion is removed from the schools what is left is not a zone of neutrality between religion and secularism. What is left is secularism. As A. James Reichley has written, "Banishment of religion does not represent neutrality between religion and secularism; conduct of public institutions without any acknowledgment of religion *is* secularism."[66] The result is not the explicit promotion of secularism as an antireligious movement, but its implicit promotion as a latent ethos or force. If issues such as environmental ethics, AIDS, hate speech, and racism must all be discussed without reference to religion as an active moral force—not even in in-school released time programs—the implicit message is that religion is either irrelevant or unimportant. Thus removing religion from the public schools also violates the norm of governmental neutrality, since government is then indirectly and implicitly favoring secularism. Religious parents and their children are thereby disadvantaged.

There may not be a completely satisfactory answer to this dilemma, but in-school released time programs for religious instruction and moments for silent private prayer or reflection represent efforts to recognize or honor the faith communities of the students in a manner that makes allowances for the rich religious diversity of most public schools. Some of the other democracies considered in the book have gone this route and this has led to a greater measure of neutrality than would either incorporating certain consensual religious elements or banning all religion. Yet even in-school released time programs and moments of silence for prayer or reflection continue to be banned by the Supreme Court's interpretations of the First Amendment. Those decisions, as well as the reasoning the Court has used in reaching them and other decisions in regard to religion in the public schools, reveal that the Court does not recognize the dilemma outlined above. It sees only the first horn of the dilemma. As we will see in the following chapters, most of the other democracies studied here have taken a different approach to this issue.

This brings us to the second key church-state question in regard to education, namely, *governmental funding of private, religiously based schools*. Here also the Supreme Court took a strict separation, no-aid-to-religion approach in the 1960s and 1970s, but here one can clearly see the shift of the Supreme Court's thinking toward equal treatment or neutrality beginning in the 1980s. The initial decision in this area from which we quoted at the start of this chapter laid down the terms clearly: there was to be a "high and impregnable" wall between church and state and no taxes could go to support "any religious activities or institutions." It was twenty-four years later, in *Lemon v. Kurtzman* (1971), that the Court clearly and decisively ruled against public funds going to support private religious schools. In doing so it articulated a three-part test that has remained highly controversial today, even among many Supreme Court justices. Nevertheless, it has been used in many subsequent establishment clause decisions. To pass muster under the so-called *Lemon* test, a government program must meet all three of the following standards: "First, the statute must have a secular legislative purpose; second, its principal or primary effect must be one that neither advances nor inhibits religion; finally, the statute must not foster 'an excessive entanglement with religion.'"[67]

The Court ruled in the 1970s and early 1980s that in most cases involving state aid to nonpublic schools that there was a valid secular purpose: to help provide a general education for the children attending the nonpublic schools. But a number of state attempts to aid religious schools were held to fail the second part of the *Lemon* test: that they must not have the principal or primary effect of advancing or inhibiting religion. The third aspect of the *Lemon* test is that there must be no excessive government entanglement with religion. The Supreme Court used this test to invalidate a New York City program that supported remedial assistance for children from low-income families in nonpublic schools.[68] It ruled that the system New York had established to make certain that religious elements were not being introduced into the remedial program resulted in an excessive entanglement of church and state.

But, especially in the 1990s, the Supreme Court's decisions began to shift, using equal treatment or neutrality reasoning. This can clearly be seen in a 1997 decision that overruled two of its earlier decisions just mentioned that outlawed public school teachers coming into religiously based schools to teach remedial or enrichment courses. The Court declared an incentive in favor of religion is not present when the aid is allocated by evenhanded, neutral criteria that do not favor either religious or secular schools.[69] In 2000 the Supreme Court upheld the constitutionality of a federal program that made money available to schools—public and private alike—for computers, library books, and other teaching materials. The opinion of the Court, quoting from the earlier decision just described, concluded that the challenged program "is allocated on the basis of neutral, secular criteria that neither favor nor disfavor religion, and is made available to both religious and secular beneficiaries on a nondiscriminatory basis."[70] Then in 2003, the Court upheld the constitutionality of a program in Cleveland, Ohio, that provided vouchers to students from failing central city schools that could be used by the parents at other public and private schools, both secular and religious in nature. The vast majority of the parents opted to send their children to religious schools. The Court used two standards in reaching its decision. One is that the public funds went to religious schools only by an indirect process, since the money, in effect, went to the parents and they decided to which schools to direct the money by deciding to which schools to send their children. The second principle the Court used was the neutrality, or equal treatment, principle: "In sum, the Ohio program is entirely neutral with respect to religion. . . . It permits . . . individuals to exercise genuine choice among options public and private, secular and religious."[71] It is important to note that government funds were clearly flowing to religiously based schools, but the indirect nature of the funding and the fact there was no attempt to favor religion resulted in the Supreme Court holding there was no establishment clause violation. Here, as in some other areas to be considered later, the Supreme Court has clearly moved away from its strict separation, no-aid-to-religion position of the 1960s and 1970s.

The Supreme Court has been more willing to uphold the constitutionality of some forms of governmental funding of religiously based schools than to permit religious elements into the public schools. Paradoxically, however, there is less popular support for governmental funding of religiously based schools and more popular support for including religious elements in the public schools. The common school ideal, as noted earlier, has deep roots in the American culture, apparently resulting in societal leaders and a majority of the public seeing religious schools as divisive and running contrary to the ideal of all children learning together. A 1988 nationwide public opinion survey, for example, found societal leaders in academia, the media, government, and business opposing financial aid to religiously based schools by margins of two to one to three to one. Among academicians, 74 percent opposed it, among leaders in the media, 67 percent did so, and among both high-ranking federal executive branch officials and business leaders, 62 percent did so.[72] The same survey found the general public sharply divided on the question of whether government should provide financial help to religiously based schools, with 41 percent favoring such aid and 50 percent opposing it.[73] In several states there have been ballot measures to institute statewide voucher programs. All have been rejected by voters, usually by wide margins. For example, in 2000 voucher proposals were defeated in both California and Michigan by margins of two to one in spite of well-financed campaigns in their favor.

The greater willingness of the Supreme Court to uphold government funding of religious schools than to uphold religious observances in the public schools can be seen in the history of funding for religiously based higher education. Even in the heyday of strict separation in the 1970s the Court ruled in favor of several government funding programs for religiously based colleges and universities. Three cases challenging programs sending government funds to religiously based colleges and universities came before the Supreme Court in the 1970s; in all three cases the Court held that the public funding programs did not violate the First Amendment establishment clause. The Supreme Court was able to maintain its strict separation, no-aid-to-religion line of reasoning while approving aid programs to religiously based colleges and universities, largely because of its application of two legal principles.

One of these legal principles is the sacred-secular distinction. The aid programs under challenge were approved, first, because the Supreme Court was willing to accept the separability of the secular and sacred aspects of education at religiously based colleges, and therefore it could accept the theory that public funds were supporting the secular mission, but not the religious mission of the colleges. By making a clear-cut distinction between the religious and the secular elements in a college education and then funding only the secular elements, one could have government financial aid to a religious college without giving aid to religion (at least in legal theory). In one of the cases, the Court observed that the challenged program of aid "was carefully drafted to ensure that the federally subsidized facilities would be devoted to the secular and not the religious function of the recipient institutions."[74] Another decision noted that "the secular and sectarian activities of the colleges were easily separated."[75]

But this approach in itself does not distinguish the cases dealing with higher education from those dealing with elementary and secondary education, since the Supreme Court at the same time as these decisions was largely rejecting federal funding to religiously based elementary and secondary schools. To do so the Supreme invoked a second legal principle, namely the pervasively sectarian standard. The Supreme Court held that religiously based colleges and universities are not "pervasively sectarian," while religiously based elementary and secondary schools are. If an institution is "pervasively sectarian" it would be impossible to separate out the secular and religious. Thus it is only possible financially to support the secular programs of an organization without supporting the religious aspects of those programs if an organization is not "pervasively sectarian." In a case dealing with a South Carolina program assisting in the construction of college and university buildings, the Court made the point concerning the importance of a pervasively religious nature: "Aid normally may be thought to have a primary effect of advancing religion when it flows to an institution in which religion is so pervasive that a substantial portion of its functions are subsumed in the religious mission. . . ."[76]

Less clear, however, are the exact characteristics that distinguish a pervasively sectarian from a nonpervasively sectarian institution. In recent years many justices have expressed dissatisfaction with the idea of pervasively sectarian as a legal standard, but it has never been expressly overturned. It remains "a vaguely defined work of art,"[77] as Justice Harry Blackmun once described it, and its exact legal standing is in doubt.

The Establishment of Religion: Other Issues

The clashing of the no-aid-to-religion, strict separation line of reasoning of the 1960s and 1970s and the neutrality, equal treatment line of reasoning of the present era can be seen clearly in three additional issue areas dealing with the establishment of religion: government funding of a religious student publication, symbolic recognition of religion by government, and government funding of faith-based nonprofit organizations. We will see how these various forms of aid or recognition have been expanded in recent years, but in such a way that no-aid-to-religion thinking is still exerting an influence.

The key decision that dealt with funding for a religious student publication was the 1995 decision in *Rosenberger v. Rector*. It illustrates more clearly than any other decision the distinct, clashing no-aid-to-religion and neutrality principles and how, in this instance, the neutrality principle won out by a razor-thin five to four division of the justices. The University of Virginia had refused to fund a Christian student publication, even though it was funding fifteen other student opinion publications, since it was convinced that doing so would violate church-state separation. The Court majority held that the university's refusal to fund the publication violated the students' free speech rights, and that funding it would not violate the establishment clause. The majority opinion is clearly rooted in the equal treatment, or neutrality, principle. It states:

A central lesson of our decisions is that a significant factor in upholding governmental programs in the face of Establishment Clause attack is their neutrality towards religion. . . . We have held that the guarantee of neutrality is respected, not offended, when the government, following neutral criteria and
evenhanded policies, extends benefits to recipients whose ideologies and viewpoints, including religious ones, are broad and diverse.[78]

A program funding a clearly—some would say pervasively—religious publication was saved from establishment clause violation because religion was
not singled out for favored treatment and the funding was extended to "the
whole spectrum of speech, whether it manifests a religious view, an antireligious view, or neither."[79]

The neutrality line of reasoning is clearly illustrated in this decision. It allows limited forms of governmental accommodation and assistance—even financial assistance—to religious groups and their activities as long as that assistance is offered equally to all religious groups and to religious and
nonreligious groups on the same basis. The four dissenting justices in the
Rosenberger case clearly saw that the decision undermined the no-aid-to-religion principle and the sacred-secular distinction under which religious
groups had earlier been permitted to receive public funds. They wrote: "Even
when the Court [in the past] has upheld aid to an institution performing both
secular and sectarian functions, it has always made a searching enquiry to ensure that the institution kept the secular activities separate from its sectarian
ones, with any direct aid flowing only to the former and never the latter."[80]
They went on to advocate the continued reliance on "the no-direct-funding
principle" over "the principle of evenhandedness."[81] As will be seen later, the
other democracies considered in this study have tended to use variations of
this equal treatment line of reasoning rather than the no-aid-to-religion approach the U.S. Supreme Court followed in the strict separation era.

Another issue that has periodically come up before the Supreme Court
has been the permissible limits of the government in giving recognition or
honor to religion and its role in American history and society. In 1984, for
example, the Court approved a municipal Christmas display that included a
scene of Mary, Joseph, and the baby Jesus, as well as secular symbols of the
Christmas season such as candy canes and a Santa.[82] But the influence of the
no-aid-to-religion principle can be seen in the Court's reasoning. It only approved the display as not violating the establishment clause because it argued
that the presence of secular holiday symbols, along with the religious ones,
sent the overall message that the display was secular, not religious in nature.
It argued that the depiction of the Holy Family was really no longer religious

and thus could approve the display and still uphold its no-aid-to-religion principle. The highly respected Justice William Brennan suggested in a dissenting opinion that such symbolic recognitions of religion by government as the "In God We Trust" motto on coins can be squared with the no-aid-to-religion principle because they are a form of "ceremonial deism" that has "lost through rote repetition any significant religious content."[83] The Court was willing to say that what most people would say is religious really is not.

But in more recent years, the Court has, under the equal treatment principle, been willing to approve symbolic recognitions of religion without denying their religious nature. In 1995 the Supreme Court upheld the Christmas display of a Christian cross on the grounds of the Ohio State Capitol Building on equal treatment grounds: "We find it peculiar to say that government 'promotes' or 'favors' a religious display by giving it the same access to a public forum that all other displays enjoy. . . . [I]t is no violation for government to enact neutral policies that happen to benefit religion."[84] Gone is any attempt to argue that the cross in this instance had lost its religious significance; it was the fact that a host of other displays were allowed on the capitol grounds that swayed the Court majority. Equal treatment of religious and secular displays was the underlying principle that saved the cross from establishment clause problems.

Both the nature of the equal treatment line of reasoning and its limitations were illustrated by two 2005 decisions, one upholding the constitutionality of a display of the Ten Commandments on the Texas State Capitol grounds and one holding unconstitutional a display of the Ten Commandments in a Kentucky courthouse.[85] The Texas display was upheld on clear equal treatment grounds, since there were many other, secular displays, honoring such historic or cultural figures as Texas pioneer women and the Texas cowboy. To exclude a religious symbol would be to discriminate against religion. But in the Kentucky case, the local authorities had first displayed the Ten Commandments by themselves, then with some other religious historic documents, and finally with both religious and secular documents. This, the Court ruled, indicated the authorities had an underlying motive to favor religion, and thus the display of a religious text violated the First Amendment.

A third area of growing controversy is the government's funding of private nonprofit service organizations, many of which are religiously based.[86] In a recent year, for example, 65 percent of the Catholic Charities' revenue came from government sources, as did 75 percent of the Jewish Board of Family and Children's Services' revenues and 55 percent of the Lutheran Social Ministries' revenues.[87] One study found that a majority of religiously based child and family service agencies received over 40 percent of their budgets from government sources.[88] A study of welfare-to-work programs in Los Angeles, Chicago, Dallas, and Philadelphia found that about one-half of the faith-based programs received government funding, including 58 percent of the most deeply religious ones. The amount of government funds they received was significant—about 30 percent of the budgets of the most deeply religious programs came from government sources.[89]

Despite large amounts of public tax dollars going to religiously based service organizations, only two cases have come before the Supreme Court challenging this practice, and in both instances the Court found the practice constitutional. One case, from the end of the nineteenth century, dealt with aid to a District of Columbia Catholic hospital. The Supreme Court based its approval of the program of aid on the sacred-secular distinction. The Court saw the hospital as "simply the case of a secular corporation being managed by people who hold to the doctrines of the Roman Catholic Church."[90] The secular nature of the hospital's function assured the constitutionality of the aid.

The constitutional issues at stake were raised more clearly in the 1988 case of *Bowen v. Kendrick*. The Adolescent Family Life Act (AFLA) had authorized federal grants for both public and private nonprofit organizations for the purpose of providing services relating to teenage sexuality and pregnancies. By a close five to four vote, the Supreme Court ruled that on its face the act did not violate the First Amendment establishment clause and remanded the case to the lower courts to determine whether it did so as actually administered. The key issue with which the Court struggled concerned the second part of the *Lemon* test, namely, whether the act advanced religion. The Supreme Court majority ruled that "the programs established under the authority of the AFLA can be monitored to determine whether the funds are, in effect, being used by the grantees in such a way as to advance religion."[91] The money could only go to support the secular aspects of the agencies' programs. Further, the Court majority ruled that the agencies receiving government funds were not pervasively sectarian, but seemed to be more like colleges and universities for whom public funds had previously been approved than like elementary and secondary schools for whom public funds had largely been rejected: "In this case, nothing on the face of the AFLA indicates that a significant proportion of the federal funds will be disbursed to 'pervasively sectarian' institutions."[92] One clearly sees that the Supreme Court's basis of approving this aid was the sacred-secular distinction and the pervasively sectarian standard, not primarily the newer equal treatment or neutrality standard. The Court approved this funding without abandoning its no-aid-to-religion standard. Some key implications of this will be shortly noted.

The no-aid-to-religion principle—in spite of the recent rise of the equal treatment principle—continues to exert a powerful force on the Supreme Court and among leaders in the media and the political arena. This can be seen in the controversy that has surrounded what has been termed "charitable choice" and President George W. Bush's faith-based initiative. It is helpful to look at these events closely. In 1996 a bill made its way through Congress that enacted major changes in the Aid to Families of Dependent Children (AFDC) program. Among other changes it was renamed Temporary Assistance to Needy Families (TANF) and made work or training a requirement for those receiving assistance. It also included section 105, which came to be termed "charitable choice." It provided that states could contract with private organizations or create voucher systems to deliver welfare services, and that any state that did so would have to allow funding of religious organizations on an equal basis with secular organizations. Most significantly, it then went on to protect the religious freedom rights of religious agencies that receive government funds, by providing that agencies receiving such funds shall maintain the right to develop and express their religious orientation, may keep religious pictures and symbols in their facilities, and may favor members of their own religious faith in hiring decisions.[93] This amendment was adopted by wide margins in Congress, President Clinton did not raise objections to it in signing the bill into law, and it was not widely criticized in the media.

But then early in his presidency President George W. Bush created a White House Office of Faith-Based and Community Initiatives, charged with the specific task of removing barriers for faith-based and small, community-based organizations from receiving governmental financial support for their charitable activities. This ignited a firestorm of criticism and controversy that continues today. Generally, Republican members of Congress lined up in support of these efforts and Democratic members of Congress and strict separationist advocacy groups lined up in opposition to it.[94] Controversy especially focused on the provision that religiously based organizations receiving public funding would not lose their right to make hiring decisions based on religion. Religiously based organizations had been explicitly given this right in the 1965 Civil Rights Law that had generally outlawed discrimination in hiring based on religion, and this provision had been unanimously upheld by the Supreme Court.[95] Nevertheless, strict separationist advocates and their congressional allies lined up to denounce this provision in President Bush's initiative. Congressman Bobby Scott of Virginia, for example, proclaimed, "Every legislative version of charitable choice up to this point included a specific provision that you may discriminate on the basis of religion in hiring. . . . The essence of charitable choice is the right to discriminate."[96] A similar perspective can often be seen in comments from leading newspapers and commentators. For example, a *New York Times* editorial referred to an attempt by the House of Representatives to allow faith-based agencies running Head Start programs and receiving government funds to hire persons of their own faith as a "smashing of constitutional and civil rights protection," and "discrimination based on religion."[97] The perspective that this might protect the religious autonomy of the agencies receiving government funds and thereby help maintain religious pluralism never entered in at all.

Meanwhile many court cases challenging various aspects of President Bush's initiative are making their way through the lower courts.[98] Some have been decided in favor of government funding on terms favorable to the faith-based groups; others have gone the other way. None has yet reached the Supreme Court, but it is likely that is where these issues will ultimately be decided.

The reason the issues surrounding President Bush's initiative have proven so controversial is the fact that the Supreme Court's sacred-secular distinction and the no-aid-to-religion doctrine have never been overturned by the Supreme Court and continue to shape the prevailing mind-set among much of the cultural and media elite in the United States. An equal treatment approach would argue that the basis for the constitutionality of government funding lies in the government funding religious and secular activities of a similar or parallel nature without favoring one or the other. In fact, it would say that to fund the secular activities and not the religious ones would be to discriminate against religion. This is what the Supreme Court held in the *Rosenberger* case dealing with a Christian student publication at the University of Virginia. But to date it has not applied this reasoning to funding faith-based social service organizations. As noted earlier, in the two cases where the Supreme Court approved programs of direct funding of religious organizations, it sought to maintain the principle of no aid to religion. It has done so on the theory that the government is only aiding the secular aspects of the program, which have been carefully split off from the religious or sacred aspects of the program. It is only in cases of indirect funding—as was the case in the Cleveland voucher case—that the Court has based its decision on equal treatment reasoning.

One crucial consequence of using the sacred-secular distinction as the basis for approving public funding of religiously based organizations is that questions arise over whether religious elements may be integrated into the presumably secular activities that are being subsidized. May religious pictures or symbols be displayed in a homeless shelter receiving public funds? May a religious college receiving public funds hire only faculty members of its own faith? May a home for abused children insist on standards of behavior for its staff in keeping with the religious beliefs of the sponsoring faith? The problem is that if in actual fact religious organizations such as these are truly providing purely secular services with no relevance to their religious beliefs, it is hard to think of logical reasons why they should have a right to insist that certain religious standards or elements be a part of them. In addition, ambiguity is present due to the pervasively sectarian standard that the Supreme Court has sometimes ignored and sometimes criticized, but has never officially overturned. It opens the way for officials administrating programs or the lower courts to pressure religious agencies to give up certain religiously motivated practices. It is not surprising that questions and controversy remain over what is and is not permitted in regard to government funding of faith-based, nonprofit delivery of health and social services. As will be seen in the following chapters, most other democracies have avoided such uncertainty by not embracing a strict no-aid-to-religion standard and by granting public funds to faith-based organizations on equal treatment or evenhandedness grounds rather than on a sharp sacred-secular distinction.

Concluding Observations

As seen in this chapter the United States is currently wavering between two different church-state models that remain in tension with each other: the liberal Enlightenment strict separation, no-aid-to-religion model and the neutrality or equal treatment model. The basic terms of the strict separation model are still in place, while the American public and the Supreme Court have been increasingly willing to make decisions based on the equal treatment model. When Congress or the Supreme Court approves government-sponsored religious displays, government funding of educational or social services, and other forms of government cooperation with religion, they seek to do so in such a way that their actions can be defended on strict separation grounds that are strained at best and disingenuous at worst. Pervasively sectarian versus nonpervasively sectarian, direct versus indirect funding, religious instruction versus secular instruction: all these have become standards that must be applied, but they are not clearly defined and therefore can be interpreted to match the desired conclusion.

Most of the other countries considered in this book—and most clearly the Netherlands, which we consider in the next chapter—avoid these conflicts and uncertainties by clearly basing their church-state thinking on equal treatment or neutrality grounds, not on a rigid no-aid-to-religion standard, a standard that in practice is sometimes and unpredictably modified or abandoned.

In this concluding section we return to the question of why the United States has taken this position and seek a tentative evaluation of it. The most persuasive explanation for the United States' continuing ideological commitment to a strict separation, no-aid-to-religion standard, even when it in practice is increasingly being abandoned, lies in nineteenth-century American history. At that time, as we saw earlier, Enlightenment liberals and the dominant Protestants came together to oppose Catholic influence in the United States and to impose their own generalized Protestant establishment on all of society. Throughout the nineteenth and into the twentieth century Protestants were the dominant force in this liberal-Protestant coalition. But by the mid-twentieth century, conservative Protestantism had been routed in internal church battles and replaced by a liberal Protestantism that accepted many of the basic tenets of Enlightenment liberalism. Neither evangelical Protestantism nor Catholicism was numerically or socially powerful enough to command the political and media influence to make their positions felt in the courts and among the influential elites. As a result the Enlightenment liberal view of church and state was left in a commanding position in the post–World War II world, and came largely to be incorporated into Supreme Court interpretations of the First Amendment, especially in relation to the public schools that traditionally had been seen as playing a crucial leveling, assimilating role in an otherwise divided society. It continues to assert a major influence on the American mind-set—to some degree among the American people and certainly among American social and cultural elites. Thus the American mind-set still largely thinks in terms of strict separation, no-aid-to-religion, and only grudgingly makes exceptions or modifications to it.

The prevailing church-state situation as we have described it in the United States carries with it three distinct disadvantages or problems. One is the confusion, uncertainty, and even anger that the current state of church-state law and practice engenders. Scholars have used terms such as "incoherent," a "tangled body of law," and "eccentric" to describe current church-state law.[99] No one seems to be happy with the status quo. Steven Smith made a telling point when he wrote that "in a rare and remarkable way, the Supreme Court's establishment clause jurisprudence has unified critical opinion: people who disagree about nearly everything else in the law agree that establishment clause doctrine is seriously, perhaps distinctively, defective."[100] Recall the instance cited earlier, when in 2007 a Michigan high school chorus that wished to sing the Lord's Prayer at their school's May graduation exercise in remembrance of a fellow classmate who had been killed in an automobile accident was told it would not be allowed to do so. One can understand the puzzlement of these students who may have watched on television four days later the National Memorial Day Concert from the U.S. Capitol grounds. It was held on public grounds and partially funded by government agencies such as the National Park Service and the Department of the Army . . . and it featured the singer CeCe Winans singing the Lord's Prayer! The Supreme Court justices themselves issue closely divided rulings on church-state questions, with even the majority and dissenting justices often unable to reach agreement on why they have reached their conclusions.

As a result of church-state confusions and hair-splitting distinctions respect for the law suffers, uncertainty abounds, and government authorities have sometimes taken stances that appear to be at odds with similar practices that elsewhere are accepted without question. The other countries studied in this book seem to have usually handled church-state issues with less controversy and less uncertainty. Perhaps there is something to be learned from them.

A second problem with the American system of strict separation and neutrality living in tension with each other is that it threatens a loss of religious freedom, or autonomy, by religious organizations and endeavors. This is due to the nature of the accommodations that the neutrality, equal treatment standard has had to make to a strict separation, no-aid-to-religion mind-set that still exerts influence. There are political forces today working to accommodate religious symbols and practices in the public realm and to allow faith-based organizations to partner with government in educational, health, and social welfare services, as their secular counterparts do. These efforts reflect the equal treatment approach that is gaining strength in the current era in church-state relations. But for pragmatic reasons efforts to go this route are often combined with attempts to adhere to basic features of the strict separation, no-aid-to-religion approach, which continues to exert its influence. Thus public funding of social services agencies is constitutional, but there are attempts to maintain the legal theory that this is being done without violating the no-aid-to-religion norm. Public funding programs typically—with varying degrees of explicitness—require that the funds may not be used for worship, sectarian instruction, or proselytizing. In legal theory, the money is only going to fund secular services. But, of course, in many of these agencies there is no hard-and-fast line separating the sacred and the secular. Uncertainty abounds. To take just one example: If a counselor at a Christian spousal abuse shelter assures a woman who has been abused and told she is worthless that she in fact is a child of God and precious in His sight, is this "sectarian instruction"?

Also, the strict separation, no-aid-to-religion mind-set affects the key issue of whether or not an agency receiving government funds may take religion into account in its hiring decisions. If, for example, an evangelical Protestant drug treatment center must hire nonbelievers, a Jewish welfare-to-work program must hire Muslims, and a Catholic homeless shelter must hire Wiccans, those evangelical, Jewish, and Catholic programs would virtually cease to be evangelical, Jewish, or Catholic. Yet if the persons they are hiring are providing services with no religious elements or underpinnings, what rationale exists for hiring persons of the faith of the organization? These are the questions that emerge and are hard to answer as the United States attempts to move toward an equal treatment model without surrendering its strict separationist mind-set. Uncertainty and continuing controversy abound.

Under the neutrality, equal treatment model that some other democracies have favored, a pluralism of religious traditions is honored and accommodated. Of course, a Muslim social service agency may hire only Muslims, a Jewish home for the elderly only Jews, and a Christian school only Christians. That is the way the rich religious pluralism of those societies is taken into account. We discuss this more in later chapters.

A third problem in the current American church-state scene relates directly to the vulnerable position that the basic right to the free exercise of religion has been placed in. Religious minorities or adherents of nontraditional faiths face the danger of losing this right. Such faith groups as the Amish, Orthodox Jews, and Native Americans have usually not found much protection for their free exercise of religion in the First Amendment of the Constitution. But the problem extends beyond such nonmainstream religious groups to include more traditional and much larger groups because of the almost total absence of a concept of positive religious freedom in the American setting. Religious freedom is typically seen as a negative freedom: freedom *from* government restraints on one's religious beliefs and practice. Since government in the current American mind-set is largely seen as properly occupying a neutral zone between the various religious groups and between religious and secular belief systems, it is assumed there is no need for government to take certain positive steps to support or encourage religion. After all, government is to be neutral. To give certain religious groups or religion as a whole special support would be to violate neutrality. But a case can be made that a government that recognizes, favors, and aids all sorts of secular enterprises and perspectives is not neutral if it systematically excludes religious enterprises and perspectives. Secular perspectives and belief structures represent a point of view, a worldview, as much as various religious perspectives and beliefs do. Thus, to support secular groups and programs over religious ones is anything but neutral.

Although the United States has moved in the past twenty-five years toward an equal treatment, substantive, positive neutrality approach to church and state, the American mind-set to a large degree is still rooted in the liberal Enlightenment assumption that strictly separating government and religion assures governmental neutrality on matters of religion. In doing so government may violate the very neutrality that liberals are rightly eager to attain. As we view the contrasting approaches to church and state of the other countries considered in this study we will ask whether the assumptions and ideals of Enlightenment liberalism are adequate to assure a genuine religious neutrality on the part of government in today's world.

Notes

1. *Everson v. Board of Education*, 330 U.S. at 16 (1947).
2. *Everson v. Board of Education*, at 18.
3. From the dissent of Justice Robert Jackson, *Everson v. Board of Education*, at 19.
4. Phillip E. Johnson, "Concepts and Compromise in First Amendment Religious Doctrine," *California Law Review* 72 (1984), 817.
5. These numbers are from a 35,000-person survey by the Pew Forum on Religion and Public Life in 2007 and entitled "U.S. Religious Landscape." Available at http://religions.pewforum.org/affiliations.
6. "U.S. Religious Landscape."
7. "Muslim Americans: Middle Class and Mostly Mainstream," Pew Research Center (May 22, 2007), 1. Available at http://pewforum.org/surveys/muslim-american.
8. "Muslim Americans: Middle Class and Mostly Mainstream," 2–3.
9. "U.S. Religious Landscape."
10. "Many Americans Uneasy with Mix of Religion and Politics," Pew Forum (August 3, 2006), 34. The complete survey is available at http://pewforum.org/docs/?DocID=153.
11. Ronald Inglehart, et al., *World Values Surveys and European Values Surveys, 1981–1984, 1990–1993, and 1995–1997* [computer file]. ICPSR version. Ann Arbor, Mich.: Institute for Social Research [producer], 2000. Ann Arbor, Mich.: Inter-University Consortium for Political and Social Research [distributor], 2000.
12. "Trends in Political Values and Core Attitudes: 1987–2007," the Pew Research Center for the People & the Press (March 22, 2007), 30. Available at www.people-press.org/reports/pdf/312.pdf.
13. Sidney E. Mead, *The Lively Experiment* (New York: Harper & Row, 1963), 17.
14. The term "strange coalition" is Mead's. See Mead, *The Lively Experiment*, 35. For more on the role played by these two disparate movements in the disestablishment of the churches in the eighteenth century, see Stephen V. Monsma, *Positive*

Neutrality (Westport, Conn.: Greenwood, 1993), 83–113. Also helpful is Philip Hamburger, *Separation of Church and State* (Cambridge, Mass.: Harvard University Press, 2002).

15. For an account of these events, see Leonard W. Levy, *The Establishment Clause: Religion and the First Amendment*, 2nd ed. (Chapel Hill: University of North Carolina Press, 1994), 58–75.

16. James Madison, "Memorial and Remonstrance Against Religious Assessments," in Robert S. Alley, ed., *The Supreme Court on Church and State* (New York: Oxford University Press, 1988), 19–20.

17. Thomas Jefferson, "Bill for Establishing Religious Freedom," in Alley, *The Supreme Court on Church and State*, 26.

18. See Robert Handy, *A Christian American: Protestant Hopes and Historical Realities* (New York: Oxford University Press, 1984), 24–25.

19. James Bryce, *The American Commonwealth*, rev. ed., vol. 2 (New York: Macmillan, 1911), 769–70.

20. On the Second Great Awakening and its consequences for American Christianity, see Nathan Hatch, *The Democratization of American Christianity* (New Haven, Conn.: Yale University Press, 1989).

21. See Daniel L. Dreisbach, *Real Threat and Mere Shadow: Religious Liberty and the First Amendment* (Westchester, Ill.: Crossway, 1987), 151–55.

22. See George M. Marsden, "The Soul of the American University: A Historical Overview," in George M. Marsden and Bradley J. Longfield, eds., *The Secularization of the Academy* (New York: Oxford University Press, 1992), 11.

23. Charles Leslie Glenn Jr., *The Myth of the Common School* (Amherst: University of Massachusetts Press, 1987), 84.

24. Glenn, *The Myth of the Common School*, 154. Also noting the Unitarian nature of the Christianity of the common schools is George M. Marsden, *The Soul of the American University* (New York: Oxford University Press, 1994), 89.

25. Quoted in Glenn, *The Myth of the Common School*, 164.

26. Carl F. Kaestle, *Pillars of the Republic: Common Schools and American Society, 1780–1860* (New York: Hill and Wang, 1983), 76.

27. Os Guinness, *The American Hour* (New York: Free Press, 1993), 229.

28. Jeffrey Rosen, "Is Nothing Sacred," *New York Times Magazine* (January 30, 2000), 40–42.

29. *Reynolds v. United States*, 98 U.S. at 166 (1879).

30. *Reynolds v. United States*, at 167.

31. See C. Herman Pritchett, *The American Constitution*, 3rd ed. (New York: McGraw-Hill, 1977), 392–94.

32. *Church of the Lukumi Babalu Aye v. Hialeah*, 508 U.S. at 542 (1993).

33. The cases were *Wisconsin v. Yoder*, 406 U.S. 205 (1972), *Sherbert v. Verner*, 374 U.S. 398 (1963), and *Thomas v. Review Board*, 450 U.S. 707 (1981).

34. The cases are *Braunfeld v. Brown*, 366 U.S. 599 (1961), *United States v. Lee*, 285 U.S. 252 (1982), and *Goldman v. Weinberger*, 475 U.S. 503 (1986).

35. *Employment Division v. Smith,* 494 U.S. 872, at 878–879 (1990).

36. *Employment Division v. Smith,* at 885.

37. Public Law 103–141, 103d Congress, Section 3 (b).

38. The case is *City of Boerne v. Flores,* 521 U.S. 507 (1997).

39. For information on this act and its implementation, see www.rluipa.com.

40. See *Report on Enforcement of Laws Protecting Religious Freedom, Fiscal Years 2001–2006* (U.S. Department of Justice, Civil Rights Division), 11, for three such cases.

41. See *Report on Enforcement of Laws Protecting Religious Freedom,* 31–32.

42. On public attitudes toward Muslims, see "Public Expresses Mixed Views of Islam, Mormonism," the Pew Research Center for the People & the Press and the Pew Forum on Religion & Public Life (September 25, 2007), 4–8. Available at http://pewforum.org/assets/files/religionviews07.pdf.

43. The cases are *Engel v. Vitale,* 370 U.S. 421 (1962) and *Abington v. Schempp,* 374 U.S. 203 (1963).

44. *Abington v. Schempp,* at 313.

45. *Abington v. Schempp,* at 313.

46. *Lemon v. Kurtzman,* 403 U.S. at 665 (1971).

47. *Committee for Public Education v. Nyquist,* 413 U.S. at 814 (1973).

48. *Engel v. Vitale,* 421 U.S. at 425 (1962).

49. *Abington School District v. Schempp,* 203 U.S. at 225 (1963).

50. *Abington School District v. Schempp,* at 222.

51. *McCollum v. Board of Education,* 333 U.S. at 210 (1948).

52. See *Zorach v. Clauson,* 343 U.S. 306 (1952).

53. See *Lee v. Weisman,* 505 U.S. 577 (1992), *Wallace v. Jaffree,* 472 U.S. 38 (1985), and *Edwards v. Aguillard,* 107 S.Ct. 2578 (1987).

54. *Epperson v. Arkansas,* 393 U.S. at 106 (1968). Also see a similar statement in *Abington School District v. Schempp,* at 225.

55. See Kenneth D. Wald, *Religion and Politics in the United States,* 2nd ed. (Washington, D.C.: Congressional Quarterly, 1992), 158–61.

56. George Gallup Jr. and Jim Castelli, *The People's Religion: American Faith in the 90's* (New York: Macmillan, 1989), 20.

57. The Pew Research Center for the People & the Press and the Pew Forum on Religion & Public Life, "Religion and Public Life Survey" (July, 2006), 7. Available at http://people-press.org/reports/questionnaire/287.pdf.

58. See *Widmar v. Vincent,* 454 U.S. 263 (1981).

59. *Westside Community Schools v. Mergens,* 496 U.S. at 252 (1990).

60. *Good News Club v. Milford Central School,* 533 U.S. 98 (2001).

61. *Good News Club v. Milford Central School* at 114.

62. See Beth Loechler, "Hyman Yanked from Graduation," *Grand Rapids Press* (May 24, 2007), A1 and A9.

63. See *Roberts v. Madigan,* 921 F.2d 1047 (10th Cir. 1990).

64. See *Settle v. Dickson County School Board,* 53 F.3rd 152 (1995).

65. *O. T. v. Frenchtown Elementary School District Board of Education*, No. 05-2623 (D.N.J. Dec. 12, 2006). In this case the district court supported the right of the student to sing the selected song. For this and other similar cases see *Report on Enforcement of Laws Protecting Religious Freedom*, 9–11.

66. A. James Reichley, *Religion in American Public Life* (Washington, D.C.: Brookings Institution, 1985), 165. Reichley's emphasis.

67. *Lemon v. Kurtzman*, 403 U.S. at 612–613 (1971). The internal quoted material is from *Walz v. Tax Commission*, 397 U.S. at 674 (1970).

68. See *Aguilar v. Felton*, 473 U.S. 402 (1985).

69. *Agostini v. Felton*, 521 U.S. 203, at 231 (1997).

70. *Mitchell v. Helms*, 530 U.S. at 829 (2000). For a book that reprints this decision and has a series of essays by persons that both support and oppose this decision see Stephen V. Monsma, ed., *Church-State Relations in Crisis: Debating Neutrality* (Lanham, Md.: Rowman & Littlefield, 2002).

71. *Zelman v. Simmons-Harris*, 536 U.S. 639, at 662 (2002).

72. *The Williamsburg Charter Survey on Religion and Public Life* (Washington, D.C.: Williamsburg Charter Foundation, 1988), tables. More specifically the academics were a random sample of 155 university faculty members of Ph.D.-granting departments of political science, sociology, history, and English; the media leaders were a random sample of 100 radio and television news directors who were members of the Radio and Television News Directors Association and newspaper editors in cities of over 100,000 population; the government leaders were a random sample of 106 high-level federal executive branch political appointees; and the business leaders were a random sample of 202 executives listed in *Who's Who in Industry and Finance*.

73. *The Williamsburg Charter Survey*, appendix, table 37.

74. *Tilton v. Richardson*, 403 U.S. at 679 (1971).

75. *Roemer v. Maryland Public Works Board*, 426 U.S. at 764 (1976).

76. *Hunt v. McNair*, 413 U.S. at 743 (1973).

77. See *Bowen v. Kendrick*, 487 U.S. at 631 (1988).

78. *Rosenberger v. Rector*, 515 U.S. 819, at 839 (1995).

79. *Rosenberger v. Rector*, at 841.

80. *Rosenberger v. Rector*, at 875.

81. *Rosenberger v. Rector*, at 882.

82. See *Lynch v. Donnelly*, 465 U.S. 668 (1984).

83. *Lynch v. Donnelly*, at 716.

84. *Capitol Square Review Board v. Pinette*, 515 U.S. 753, at 763–64 (1995).

85. *VanOrden v. Perry* 545 U.S. 677 (2005) and *McCreary County v. American Civil Liberties Union of Kentucky*, 545 U.S. 844 (2005).

86. For a thorough consideration of this field, see Stephen V. Monsma, *When Sacred and Secular Mix* (Lanham, Md.: Rowman & Littlefield), 4–10 and 64–80; and Stephen V. Monsma, *Putting Faith in Partnerships: Welfare-to-Work in Four Cities* (Ann Arbor: University of Michigan Press, 2004).

87. On the first two of these organizations, see Sean Mehegan, "The Federal Connection: Nonprofits Are Looking More and More to Washington," *The Nonprofit Times* 8 (November 1994), 43. On the third of these organizations see, *1996 Annual Report* (Chicago: Division of Church and Society of the Evangelical Lutheran Church in America, 1996).

88. Monsma, *When Sacred and Secular Mix*, 68.

89. Monsma, *Putting Faith in Partnerships*, 138, 140.

90. *Bradfield v. Roberts*, 175 U.S. at 298–299 (1899).

91. *Bowen v. Kendrick*, at 615.

92. *Bowen v. Kendrick*, at 610.

93. See Public Law 104–193, section 104. For an excellent description and explication of this section of the law from a supportive perspective, see *A Guide to Charitable Choice: The Rules of Section 104 of the 1996 Federal Welfare Law Governing State Cooperation with Faith-based Social-service Providers* (Washington, D.C.: Center for Public Justice, and Annandale, Va.: Center for Law and Religious Freedom of the Christian Legal Society, 1997). Available at www.cpjustice.org/charitablechoice/guide.

94. For helpful accounts and analyses of what happened, see Amy E. Black, Douglas L. Koopman, and David K. Ryden, *Of Little Faith: The Politics of George W. Bush's Faith-Based Initiative* (Washington, D.C.: Georgetown University Press, 2004); and John Dilulio Jr., *Godly Republic: A Centrist Blueprint for America's Faith-Based Future* (Berkeley: University of California Press, 2007), chaps. 3 and 4.

95. See *Corporation of Presiding Bishops v. Amos*, 483 U.S. 327 (1987).

96. "An Interview with Congressman Robert C. 'Bobby' Scott," August 14, 2002 (The Roundtable on Religion and Social Welfare Policy). Available at www.religionandsocialpolicy.org.

97. *New York Times* (September 28, 2005), A26.

98. See the annual *State of the Law* reports by Ira C. Lupu and Robert W. Tuttle published from 2003 through 2006 by the Roundtable on Religion and Social Welfare Policy of the Rockefeller Institute of Government. Available at www.religionandsocialpolicy.org.

99. See Michael A. Paulsen, "Religion, Equality, and the Constitution: An Equal Protection Approach to Establishment Clause Adjudication," *Notre Dame Law Review* 61 (1986), 317; Reichley, *Religion in American Public Life*, 117; and Johnson, "Concepts and Compromise," 817.

100. Steven D. Smith, "Separation and the 'Secular': Reconstructing the Disestablishment Decision," *Texas Law Review* 67 (1989), 955–56.

~

CHAPTER THREE

The Netherlands:
Principled Pluralism

The Netherlands has a justified reputation as a stable, prosperous democracy with a long tradition of religious liberty. It is also a tolerant—some would even say a permissive—society. Prostitution and the use of marijuana are tolerated in some quarters and under certain conditions euthanasia is permitted. Same-sex marriages have been legal since 2001. Since the seventeenth century the Netherlands has often served as a refuge for persecuted religious groups and, along with Denmark, is often cited as doing much to protect its Jewish citizens during the Nazi occupation. But the famous Dutch tolerance has been pushed to the limit in recent years. In 2002 Pim Fortuyn, a leading anti-immigration politician, was assassinated, and in 2004 the filmmaker Theo van Gogh was killed by a Muslim extremist who, in an especially horrendous act, shot Van Gogh, slit his throat, and left a note with verses from the Qur'an pinned to his body with a knife. Although the Netherlands has been spared the sort of terrorist attacks of 9/11 and those later experienced by Madrid and London, it has been deeply affected by them.

The Netherlands has had one of the most theoretically rooted, thought-out approaches to church-state relations of any of the western democracies. Its study, therefore, should prove particularly enlightening as we explore its historic approach to church-state issues and how it now is working to apply it in a setting marked by a large Muslim minority that contains a small number of extremist, theocratic elements.

This chapter opens with a brief description of the Netherlands and its system of government. It then considers the historical background for the

Netherlands' approach to church-state issues, next it considers the Dutch approach to free exercise issues and questions, and then it does the same for establishment issues as they relate, first, to education and then to nonprofit social service agencies. The last section makes some concluding observations.

The Nation

The Netherlands, with sixteen million people crowded onto 16,000 square miles of land, is one of the most densely populated countries in the world. It is often said that Dutch history and geography have molded people who are, paradoxically, both fiercely independent and strongly committed to cooperation. The independence of the Dutch has resulted in a surprisingly large degree of societal pluralism for so small a country. It was historically fostered by the low-lying, marshy ground of the deltas of the Rhine, Meuse, and Scheldt rivers that resulted in areas developing in relative isolation from one another.[1] This geography kept even the Romans from uniting under their rule the area that is today the Netherlands. During the Middle Ages this area consisted of several autonomous duchies. It was only in the late sixteenth century that a loose confederation of provinces came together to form a single republic. Even today the Frisian language is spoken by 400,000 persons living in the province of Friesland in the northern part of the country.

The Protestant Reformation resulted in the Dutch being further divided between a Catholic south and a Protestant north. The Protestants, in turn, were divided among the dominant Reformed, or Calvinist, group and other Protestant groups such as Lutherans and Mennonites. Meanwhile, the "golden age" of Dutch commercial prosperity developed in the seventeenth century, when truly the business of the Dutch was business. The commercial elites of Amsterdam and elsewhere concentrated more on making money than pursuing theological truth, with the result that the Dutch tolerated a variety of religious traditions when much of Europe was still at war over religious issues. The result is that even today the Dutch are a mosaic of religious, ethnic, and regional groupings, each jealous of its distinct identity and independence.

But this pluralism and independence of the Dutch is only one part of the picture. The other is a strong commitment to cooperation. Many observers of the Dutch scene trace this characteristic to the relentless battle against the sea. Sixty percent of the population inhabits the 25 percent of the land area that is below sea level. This is made possible only by a complex, integrated series of canals, pumps, and seawalls. Dutch survival down through the centuries has necessitated cooperation. As recently as 1953 spring runoff and a series of heavy storms resulted in the drowning deaths of over 1,800 persons. As the population of the Netherlands swelled in the twentieth century from five million to fifteen million and to sixteen million today, cooperation has also been necessitated by the need for urban planning, housing development, and public transportation.

The famous Dutch toleration for differing religious, ethnic, and lifestyle groups is often said to arise out of the combination of these qualities of independence and cooperation. Cooperation in fighting the sea and building a prosperous economy could only be achieved by accepting existing differences and working together in spite of them.

Of the population over twelve years of age 29 percent are Roman Catholic, 21 percent are Protestant, and 42 percent have no religious affiliation.[2] Historically, most Dutch Protestants were Reformed, but in 2004 the two largest Reformed denominations and the Lutherans merged to form the Protestant Church in the Netherlands. There are also about 850,000 Muslims (5 percent of the population), most of whom are immigrants from Turkey or Morocco. The Dutch religious makeup is rounded out by 80,000 Hindus and Buddhists, most of whom are also overseas immigrants, and 25,000 Jews.

Since the 1960s there has been a strong secularization trend in the Netherlands. In 1959 the percentage of the population reporting membership in the Catholic Church was at 37 percent and in the two largest Reformed churches it was at 38 percent (compared, as just seen, to 29 and 21 percent in 2007).[3] In 1959 only 21 percent reported no religious affiliation, compared to 42 percent in 2007. Some 71 percent of the population report hardly ever or never attending worship services.

Despite this secularization trend, strong religious belief also remains among a minority of the population. As one scholar reports: "Although the degree of secularization in the Netherlands is high compared to other Western European countries, the degree of active participation of church members in the church is also comparatively high."[4] In 2007, 11 percent of the population reported attending church weekly and 19 percent reported attending church monthly or more, both of which are higher than in most other west European countries.[5] The World Values survey of 1990 showed weekly church attendance in the Netherlands at 20 percent, higher than in France, Britain, Germany, and the Scandinavian countries, yet it was either at the same level or at higher levels in the percentages reporting rarely or never attending church.[6]

A 2005 government report estimates that among the Muslims only several hundred persons are hard-core radicals. But it also reports there are several thousand who sympathize with the hard-core radicals, a number that "is currently growing in size."[7]

Politically, the Netherlands is a constitutional monarchy, with Queen Beatrix serving as the head of state.[8] It has a parliamentary form of government with a bicameral legislature called the States-General. The upper house has seventy-five members elected indirectly by the members of provincial councils and the lower house has 150 members elected directly by the populace by a strict system of proportional representation. Most legislation originates with the cabinet and must be passed by both houses of the States-General, but only the lower house may amend or introduce bills. There are four major political parties: the Christian Democratic Appeal (CDA), the Labor Party (PvdA), the Socialist Party (SP), and the People's Party for Freedom and Democracy (VVD)—a right-of-center, business-oriented party. The current government, formed after the 2006 elections, is a coalition of the CDA, PvdA, and the Christian Union (a small Protestant party). The prime minister, Jan Peter Balkenende, is a member of the CDA and has been the prime minister since 2002. The Christian Democrats have been a part of every government since 1918, except from 1994 to 2002.

The Dutch political system has been described as corporatist and consociational.[9] The former term emphasizes the tendency for institutionalized representatives of key societal organizations to make public policy through a process of negotiation and compromise among themselves and with governmental officials. Consociational democracy emphasizes the tendency in segmented, or sharply divided, societies for the elites of the various segments to replace the incompatible demands of their constituent groups with pragmatic compromises that maintain the unity of society.

Although the Dutch political system has been undergoing significant change in the past ten to twenty years, the corporatist concept of the Dutch political system is still accurate. Rudy Andeweg and Galen Irwin have written that "obituaries of neo-corporatism seem premature. . . . [T]he incorporation of interest groups into the decision-making process . . . is still characteristic of Dutch policy-making in many fields."[10] Recently the Dutch concluded that the number of advisory bodies had gotten out of hand and in 2005 to 2006 their number was sharply reduced. Most executive departments, however, continue to have three or four permanent advisory councils and additional ad hoc ones. The Department of Health Care, for example, now has four and the Department of Education three.

Questions have also been raised concerning whether the consociational concept is still applicable to the current Dutch scene.[11] But whatever one's position on that issue, it is clear that the Dutch political system continues to be marked more by negotiation, discussion, and compromise than by adversarial confrontations with outright winners and losers.

All these are themes to which we will return later in the chapter as we seek to understand Dutch church-state principles and practices. But first it is important to gain insight into the historical forces that have shaped the distinctive Dutch church-state practices and the assumptions and perspectives that underlie them.

The Historical Background

In the nineteenth century, liberal Enlightenment thinking then ascendant in the western world confronted both the United States and the Netherlands with a similar challenge. The United States took one road; the Netherlands another. As a result the two countries' approaches to church-state issues have sharply diverged down to today. The story of this challenge, how the Dutch responded to it, and the consequences for church-state relations largely revolve around the issue of education. The Dutch liberals in the nineteenth century reacted against the old conservative order that had featured a semi-established Reformed Church (*Hervormde Kerk*) and a host of privileges for the aristocratic classes. In contrast, the liberals worked for more popular participation in government, a more limited role for the state, and no state favoritism toward religious groups.

Underlying the reforms advocated by the Enlightenment liberals was a particular view of the ideal society, which explains why they believed there could be more popular participation in the political system without societal divisions and greed destroying societal stability as the conservatives feared. Dutch scholar Siep Stuurman has described this basic liberal view of that time: "Through education and propagation of (Liberal) 'culture' among all classes the circle of citizens could be broadened and the basis of the state as well. On this course a homogeneous Dutch nation would come into being, and would naturally take on a liberal coloration."[12] The liberal goal was a society marked by a consensus of values that were common and nonsectarian. Such a society would make possible broad democratic participation and a removal of the old prerogatives of the aristocratic classes without creating the social and political chaos the conservatives were predicting. The public schools were to play an especially important role in the teaching of a common, liberal culture of national unity, tolerance, and virtue.

Therefore, at the beginning of the nineteenth century a strong movement developed in the Netherlands to create publicly funded common schools that all children would be required to attend. Stuurman also wrote that the homogenization of the nation was "the political core of the liberal school policies. The school as a nation-forming institution must not be divided among competing 'sectarian schools' or left in the hands of an exclusive political or church party."[13] In the liberal view religion and morals were not to be ignored; instead, children ought to be taught a "Christianity above doctrinal differences."[14] This was the core of the liberal view of education and was very similar to the view of education advocated in the United States by Horace Mann and his supporters, as we saw in chapter 2. Education ought to be universal and carefully regulated by the government to make sure that divisive, parochial Christian doctrines were eliminated in favor of broad moral themes that would produce national unity and responsible citizens.

But where did that leave the diverse religious communities of the Netherlands? The answer is that in the liberal scheme of things particularistic, divisive religious beliefs were to be relegated to the purely private sphere. As a result schools outside the common school scheme of things were at best viewed with suspicion, and at worst simply banned.

As the nineteenth century wore on, increasing opposition to this concept of education grew among Catholics and especially among a number of orthodox Reformed groups within the large, semiestablished *Hervormde Kerk* and from some who had seceded from it, believing it was deserting traditional, orthodox Calvinist theology and practice.[15] From out of this opposition both the orthodox Reformed and the Catholics started to develop their own political movements in the 1860s.

Meanwhile liberalism was also changing, leading to a hardening of the lines. It was becoming more anticlerical and more committed to a secular philosophy. Political scientist Stanley Carlson-Thies summarizes the changes in Dutch liberalism in the 1870s: "Progress, advance through science, . . . liberation from outmoded dogmas—these were the watchwords of the younger generation. Simple dismissal of the benighted, who clung tenaciously to outmoded Christian beliefs, was no longer enough; those beliefs, and the schools and political initiatives embodying them, had to be confronted and defeated."[16]

The tensions that had been building for some time between the Enlightenment liberals, who were dominant in parliament, and the more orthodox Reformed groups both within and outside the large *Hervormde Kerk* and the Catholic forces came to a head in reaction to the passage of a new school law in 1878. Led by Kappeyne van de Coppello, the liberals pushed through parliament a new education law. It mandated new and higher standards for all schools—public schools run by municipalities, as well as alternative schools being run by Catholic and orthodox Reformed groups. It then provided generous financial subsidies from the central government to pay for these mandated improvements for the public schools, but not for the religious alternative schools. The alternative schools would have to come up with the additional funds, and if they could not, they could be closed by the education authorities. In the context of the times, the Catholics and orthodox Reformed viewed this law as an all-out attack on the religiously based schools and as reneging on the freedom of education liberals had earlier supported in the 1848 constitution and a 1857 school law.

The law ignited a firestorm out in the country. It led to a mass political movement and drove the orthodox Reformed and Catholics—two groups with long histories of antagonism and distrust—into a formidable, politically active alliance. In only five days the orthodox Reformed groups collected over 300,000 signatures in opposition to the new education law and the Catholics over 160,000. As Carlson-Thies has written, "Compared to the total population of only some four million and an electorate of 122,000, this was an outpouring of popular sentiment of startling size."[17] Within a year the Reformed groups had established the Anti-Revolutionary Party (ARP), which, Hans Daalder has reported, "pioneered modern mass-party organization techniques in the Netherlands."[18] By 1883 a program for a Catholic party had been written and was receiving wide circulation among Catholics, although it was several decades before the formal establishment of a Catholic party.

The 1878 school law led to a "monstrous alliance," as one Dutch observer termed it,[19] between the orthodox Reformed groups and the Catholics. The ARP-Catholic alliance quickly became a major political force, winning an absolute majority of the lower house in 1888. Over a period of forty years and in a series of stages it won total approval of its vision of education: religiously based schools of various types and public schools espousing a "neutral," consensual philosophy all sharing fully and equally in public funding. This concept was enshrined in the Dutch Constitution in 1917, where it remains today. This constitutional victory was made possible by a pragmatic coalition among the ARP-Catholic forces, which wanted equal funding for their schools; the social democrats, who wanted universal male suffrage; and the Liberal Party, which wanted a proportional representational electoral system. All three received what they wanted in what has been termed "the pacification of 1917."

The powerful Catholic-Reformed alliance has continued to play a prominent role in Dutch politics. The Catholic People's Party, the ARP, and the Christian Historical Union (a second Reformed party formed in 1908) in 1980 merged to form the Christian Democratic Appeal (CDA). This party continues to be a major force in Dutch politics. It is the largest party in the lower house today, its leader, Jan Peter Balkenende, is the prime minister, and, except for 1994 to 2002, it (or its forerunners) has been a part of every government since 1918.

Equally important, however, is the fact that this alliance prevailed over the liberals on the intellectual front. Led by several Reformed thinkers, but also supported by the Catholic leadership, explicit, well-worked-out theories based on a pluralistic view of society were developed to uphold its position of government support for all education, public and private alike. Those theories were also applied to areas of society other than the schools, and gained broad acceptance in Dutch society. In conducting interviews in 1996 and again in 2006 with many Dutch government, church, education, and social service leaders, we were often struck by the extent to which these concepts have become part of the Dutch mind-set on issues of church and state. It is important to understand them well. They form the heart of the principled pluralism we have noted in the title of this chapter.

In the Netherlands the orthodox Reformed groups and the Catholics came together to advocate a pluralism that respects and gives room for a variety of religious-intellectual movements. The pragmatic situation both groups found themselves in may have encouraged this response, since both were minority groups that were unlikely to be able to impose their beliefs on the nation as a whole. Nevertheless, they developed a principled rationale for the positions they took and this rationale has had a lasting impact in Dutch society. Two persons—a Calvinist and a Catholic—are especially important in understanding how this came about.

The central figure in the path taken by the orthodox Dutch Calvinists was Abraham Kuyper (1837–1920), theologian, journalist, and, from 1901 to 1905, prime minister. Michael Fogarty has written that Kuyper was "the greatest leader whom Dutch Protestantism in modern times has produced."[20] Even today "Dr. Kuyperstraat" in The Hague is the street on which one finds the headquarters of the CDA. In it there is an Abraham Kuyper room containing various historical memorabilia from his long career. The influence of Kuyper and the orthodox Reformed party he founded, the ARP, is hard to overestimate.

Kuyper decisively, explicitly rejected the creation of a theocracy where the state would promote Christian beliefs and values. Time and again he spoke in favor of, and when in political power worked for, a political order that recognized and accommodated the religious pluralism of society. His goal "was not a theocratic recasting of the public order as a substitute for the liberals' project of privatizing religion. As cabinet head and leader of the confessional bloc, Kuyper forcefully reiterated as the confessional goal a system in which all views would be accorded equal rights in state and society."[21] When in 1898 Kuyper was invited to give the Stone Foundation lectures at Princeton University, one of his lectures was on "Calvinism and Politics." In it he stated that government should allow "to each and every citizen liberty of conscience, as the primordial and inalienable right of all men."[22] He also praised the concept of "a free Church, in a free State" and criticized czarist Russia and the Lutheran concept of secular rulers determining the religion of their kingdoms as violating this ideal. But—and this is highly significant—he also criticized "the irreligious neutral standpoint of the French revolution" as violating the ideal of a free church in a free state.[23] Kuyper often spoke in support of "parallelism," that is, the right and freedom of differing religious and philosophical perspectives and movements to develop freely on separate, parallel tracks, neither hindered nor helped by the government.

The Canadian political scientist Herman Bakvis has concluded: "It was the example of the Calvinists under the leadership of . . . Abraham Kuyper that gave the Catholics impetus towards developing some sort of party organization."[24] The person who emerged to lead this drive was a Catholic priest, journalist, and member of parliament, Herman Schaepman (1844–1903). In 1883 he called for a Catholic political party and outlined in a journal he coedited the program such a party would pursue. Much in Schaepman's thinking paralleled Kuyper's. The Catholic party he desired, according to Carlson-Thies, "would seek only equality for the Catholic church, not predominance, and would promote freedom of religion, independence of the churches from the state, and equal rights for all citizens and all religious bodies. . . . No special rights were needed, but there must be acceptance of the special character of Catholic desires and demands."[25] He also argued there was "a common cause to be made between Catholics and Anti-Revolutionaries on the schools issue; both groups wanted control of their own educational system."[26]

It was these pluralistic principles—tolerant, yet insisting that a variety of religious views and perspectives had as much right to sit at the public policy table as their secularly based counterparts—that triumphed over liberal thinking in the early twentieth century. When this victory was ensconced in the Constitution in 1917 by the guarantee of full funding for schools of all faiths on par with the public schools, the principles of pluralism came to dominate public thinking and to be copied in many other areas of public life. From the 1920s to the 1960s—and some would say down to today—a system referred to as pillarization (*verzuiling*) came to mark Dutch society.

Under pillarization most areas of group human activity—political parties, labor unions, education, television broadcasting, retirement homes, social service agencies, and recreation clubs—were marked by separate organizations representing the different religious and secular points of view.[27] There were four main pillars: Reformed, Catholic, socialist, and neutral (that is, liberal). This meant, for example, that there was a Catholic political party, a Catholic labor union, Catholic schools from primary to university, a Catholic television network, Catholic newspapers, various Catholic recreation clubs, and more. These organizations would constitute the Catholic pillar. A person growing up in a Catholic household would largely live his or her life in the context of Catholic organizations (the Catholic pillar). A person growing up in a Reformed home or in a home without particular religious commitments but of a socialist (for the working class) or liberal (for the business and small entrepreneur) bent would face a similar situation. This social structure fit well with the principles articulated by Kuyper and adopted by Catholics. If all of life is touched by religion, one's religious beliefs (or their secular counterparts) would be relevant to what one reads, how one votes, how one seeks an education, and even how one recreates. As foreign as such a system seems to the American observer, it worked well in the Netherlands in the 1920–1960 period. In contrast to nearby continental European nations such as Germany, France, Spain, and Italy, the Dutch lived and prospered in social and political stability.

In recent years this system has faced two very basic challenges that have fundamentally altered it, even while not doing away with it. One is the strong secularization trend noted earlier and the second is the influx of large numbers of Muslims from overseas, including a small number of radicals who have no wish to assimilate into Dutch society. We discuss each of these in turn.

The strong secularization trend from the 1960s onward has undercut much of the meaning that the religious pillars had. In fact, pillarization in the Netherlands today has a negative connotation—something that is in the past and referring to an era of religious exclusiveness and division. Voting by religion has fallen precipitously. Although 70 percent of Dutch children still attend private schools today, parents now select schools largely in terms other than their religious character. Many Protestants attend Catholic schools, Catholics attend Protestant schools, and nonbelievers attend both. Support for other forms of pillarized organizations has dissipated. As a result, many of the formerly pillarized organizations are combining: Protestant with Catholic, and both with secular. The Dutch no longer live most of their lives within a single pillar, but pick and choose. Members of a family may belong to the newly formed Protestant Church in the Netherlands, yet send their children to a Catholic school. Meanwhile, the wife may work at a secular drug treatment center, the husband may belong to the CNV (a Christian—Catholic and Protestant—labor union), they may largely listen to the new commercial television channels, and in the last election they may have voted for the nonreligious, right-of-center VVD.

Is then pillarization dead? Some would say yes. But others say pillarization is not dead, but changed from forty or fifty years ago. When in 2006 we asked Sophie van Bijsterveld, who is a member of the upper house of the States-General and probably the foremost church-state scholar in the Netherlands, whether or not pillarization was dead she responded:

> It is pillarization and it still exists. Many of the organizations still continue to exist, but of course society has changed and we have become a post-modern, secularized, individualized society, as a lot of societies in Europe have. But these organizations to a large extent continue to exist; the legal framework is still the same. . . . Pillarization was a very closed sort of society with everybody living in his or her own pillar. . . . That sort of a closed society of course is long gone. But that doesn't mean those institutions have disappeared.[28]

She went on to make the point that recently many organizations, rather than ignoring or relegating to the dustbin their religious or philosophical roots, have been self-consciously reexamining those roots in an effort to establish a religious or philosophical identity suited to the present-day setting.

In many fields, organizations rooted in religious or secular principles still exist and are recognized and allowed for by official government policy as organizations reflecting a particular religious or secular point of view. And in corporatist fashion the leaders of these groups are often called upon to advise the government on issues of concern to them. It is not assumed that a neutral, secular organization representing a segment of the population can speak for all. In short, the continuing Dutch mind-set recognizes and seeks to accommodate the religious-belief-ethnic pluralism of society. This aspect of the old pillarization system is still alive.

A second major factor affecting the pillarization model is the presence of a large Muslim minority—some 850,000 persons constituting 5 percent of the population. A small number of Muslims are not assimilating into Dutch society and a very small number are radical theocrats who resist assimilation and reject democratic norms. Today, some 18 percent of the population comes from a non-Dutch background and 9 percent from a nonwestern background.[29] In the six years since the assassinations of Pim Fortuyn and Theo van Gogh and terrorist attacks elsewhere in the West, the Dutch political scene has been roiled by sharp debates over immigration, religious freedom, and assimilation. An official 2004 government document raised key questions now being asked:

To what extent can a school or association propagate its own identity without discriminating against others or being banned? Just how different can you be in the Netherlands? How tolerant are we? These are questions that go straight to the heart of the Netherlands as a democratic state under the rule of law, the individual as democratic citizen and the question of social cohesion with the Netherlands.[30]

Such questions go straight to the heart of the Dutch model of pillarization as it still exists today: recognizing and accommodating a plurality of associations and organizations, based on religious or philosophical underpinnings. There is a renewed emphasis in the Netherlands today on integration, that is, on means and ways to integrate immigrant communities into the common values of a tolerant, democratic polity. And there is a parallel de-emphasis on maintaining and making allowances for distinctive religious and ethnic communities.

Just as with the recent secularization process, however, this does not mean that pillarization is dead. As we will shortly see there are more than forty-eight separate Muslim schools, fully funded by the government, television programming time has been allotted for Muslim programming, and there are two government-funded programs for training imams (at Leiden University and the Free University in Amsterdam). Two scholars describe the current situation in these words:

> Minority groups are provided instruction in their own language and culture; separate radio and television programs; government funding to import religious leaders; and subsidies for a wide range of social and religious organizations; "consultation prerogatives" for community leaders; and publicly financed housing set aside for and specifically designed to meet Muslim requirements for strict separation of "public" and "private" spaces.[31]

The religious-belief-ethnic pluralism of society—including the Muslim sector—is still being recognized and accommodated.

All this is not without controversy. To some, the traditional emphasis on separate organizations representing religious and philosophical traditions, including now the Muslim tradition, is divisive and is being used by radical Muslims to resist assimilation and to spread their radical doctrines. Veit Bader has argued, however, that in the case of separate schools such fears "are theoretically implausible and empirically untenable."[32] He goes on to argue that under what he terms "associational democracy" ethnic-religious minorities "are more likely to create fair and stable forms of cohesion and political unity, to create toleration and the appropriate civic virtues and bonds, and at least help to reduce the chances of violent conflicts and terrorism."[33]

Others have also argued that the traditional emphasis on separate organizations will help ultimately in integrating Muslims fully into Dutch society. As Muslims form their own schools and other organizations, as they receive public subsidies, and as they are drawn into negotiations over public policies and their implementation, they will feel more accepted as a part of Dutch society and will come to accept more fully the norms of individual freedom and democratic governance. George Harinck told us that ten years ago Jan Peter Balkenende, the Dutch prime minister,

> would have said "Well, we are against an Islamic pillar because it means you lock these people in their own tradition and don't make them Dutch." Nowadays his party [the CDA] and he have changed their opinion and they say, "Well, we support Islamic organizations because we have learned in the last ten years that these people don't integrate into society just by living here. So, you want to tell them . . . [to] found an Islamic political party, and your leaders will learn to deal with the other Dutch in parliament and they will learn that they need to negotiate." The Netherlands is a country with all kinds of minorities and no majority, so if you want to form a majority you have to make coalitions. . . . Well, the best way to support it [Muslim integration into Dutch society] we think now is by supporting them in founding their own organizations.[34]

In summary, pillarization has changed since the 1960s, but it is still a part of the Dutch way of governing and thinking about societal organizations. The term itself is no longer very descriptive or widely used. What is still in existence are societal-political organizations segmented by religious-philosophical orientations, and a society and a government that accept the legitimacy of and seek to accommodate such organizations in a wide variety of fields. They are seen as reflecting points of view of significance in the populace and as serving segments of the taxpaying populace, and for both reasons deserve recognition and support. In the following sections the significance of this pluralistic view of society for church-state relations is developed.

The Free Exercise of Religion

The basic right to the free exercise of one's religion is laid down in Articles 1 and 6 of the Dutch Constitution, as revised in 1983. Article 1 states:

> All persons in the Netherlands shall be treated equally in equal circumstances. Discrimination on the grounds of religion, belief, political opinion, race or sex or on any other grounds whatsoever shall not be permitted.[35]

And Article 6 reads:

1. Everyone shall have the right to manifest freely his religion or belief, either individually or in community with others, without prejudice to his responsibility under the law.
2. Rules concerning the exercise of this right other than in buildings and enclosed places may be laid down by Act of Parliament for the protection of health, in the interest of traffic and to combat or prevent disorders.

In seeking to understand these constitutional provisions it is important to realize that the Dutch judiciary does not have the power of judicial review over acts passed by parliament. Article 120 clearly states that "The constitutionality of Acts of Parliament and treaties shall not be reviewed by the courts." The courts, however, can find and sometimes have found acts of municipal and provincial councils and executive branch agencies to be unconstitutional. In addition, Article 94 provides that acts of parliament and other statutes that conflict with treaties—such as the European Convention on Human Rights—are not applicable. The Dutch courts have historically been hesitant to hold acts of local councils and executive agencies unconstitutional or to enforce Article 94 against acts of parliament, although they have become somewhat more activist in doing so in recent years. Also relevant is the fact that Dutch citizens and groups, when compared to Americans, are slower to assert their perceived constitutional rights in the courts. The Dutch culture is more committed to negotiation and working situations out through discussions than to legal confrontations. Therefore, judicial interpretations have not been a dominant influence on the development of free exercise rights, as they have in the United States. Nevertheless, the constitutional provisions are important, both as a reflection of Dutch thinking and as legally enforceable provisions.

There are four aspects of the religious freedom language contained in Articles 1 and 6 that are important to note. One is that Article 6 provides for the free exercise of both religion and "belief." Protection of "belief" as well as religion was a change made in the 1983 revisions to the Constitution in order to make clear that secularly based beliefs were to have the same legal protection as religiously based beliefs. This is fully in keeping with the Dutch concept of pluralism discussed earlier—that all religions, as well as their secular equivalents, deserve respect and protection. The Dutch word translated as "belief" is *levensovertuiging* and more literally could be translated as "life conviction." It is not just any belief that has constitutional protection, but firm convictions that guide one's life, even though they are not rooted in religion in the traditional sense.

Second, Article 6 makes clear that one's freedom to manifest religion or belief is protected whether one exercises it as an individual or "in community with others." Individual rights are protected, but so are the rights of people to act as part of a larger community or group. This communitarian emphasis can also be traced back to Dutch pluralism, with its emphasis on a plurality of religious and "life conviction" groups and associations and the important, legitimate role they play in society. It contrasts with the approach of Enlightenment liberalism that tends to assume the protection of individual, private religious belief is sufficient and to downplay the importance of the fact that religion is almost always lived within faith communities.

Third, the second section of Article 6 contains an exception similar to the American "compelling state interest" test. The exercise of the right to religious freedom may be regulated in the interest of public health, the free flow of traffic, or the prevention of civil disorder.

A fourth point to note is especially important. Article 1, by stating that all people are to be "treated equally in equal circumstances," lays the groundwork for the free exercise right of religious organizations to receive the same sort of governmental assistance that their secular counterparts receive. Legal scholar Van Bijsterveld has written:

> It [Article 1] guarantees equal treatment in equal circumstances to all persons. . . . It is clear that under the Constitution public-authorities in the Netherlands shall be neutral with respect to the various religious and non-religious denominations. . . . [I]t is clear that once authorities subsidize or support certain activities, religious counterparts cannot be excluded for that reason. Article 1 forbids this.[36]

Elsewhere she has written, "No *general* state support to churches exists." But then she goes on to note that "financial support to churches and religion is allowed under special circumstances in order to prevent the free exercise of religion from becoming illusory."[37] In an interview Van Bijsterveld gave an example of what she had in mind when she explained that government should enable the free exercise of religion, not make it impossible. "So [it means] the positive protection of religion, so to say. In the case of ancient church monuments, we say the government supports old castles and other old buildings, so it should also protect ancient church monuments. They should not be excluded. That is what equal treatment means."[38]

In the Dutch mind-set, nondiscrimination and equal treatment in equal circumstances means that general programs of aid or support may not exclude religiously based beliefs and organizations. One sees the application of the basic concept of pluralism discussed in the previous section. A variety of religious and secular beliefs and their organizations and programs are to be treated equally by government. This principle is basic to the Dutch approach to church-state issues.

Also key to understanding the Dutch implementation of religious freedom is the Equal Treatment Act and the decisions of the Equal Treatment Commission created by this act.[39] It was enacted in 1994 and amended in 2004. It provides "protection against discrimination on the grounds of religion, belief, political opinion, race, sex, nationality, heterosexual or homosexual orientation or civil status."[40] It forbids both direct and indirect discrimination, the latter being actions which, while not intending to discriminate, have the effect of discriminating.

Three concrete issues that have arisen help to illustrate how the Netherlands has dealt with the free exercise rights of minority religions in an increasingly pluralistic society. An issue with which the Netherlands, as well as other European countries, have had to deal is the wearing of religious clothing and especially the wearing by Muslim women of headscarves, or *niqaabs,* and burqas (which cover the entire body, including the face). In almost all cases the Equal Treatment Commission has ruled Muslim women may not be denied employment or schooling due to wearing headscarves or *niqaabs* and burqas. Van Bijsterveld has summarized the position the Commission has developed: "When an applicant is refused a job because she wears a headscarf *as an expression of religion,* this constitutes a *direct* distinction on the basis of religion and contravenes the Equal Treatment Act."[41] On this basis the commission held in two different cases that a Muslim court registrar and a Muslim cashier at a private bank must be allowed to wear a headscarf.[42] That such cases are pushing the limits of Dutch tolerance, however, is revealed by the fact that in the case of the court registrar, the commission's decision was publicly condemned by the Minister of Justice who announced he would seek a change in the law in order to ban the wearing of any religious symbols during court hearings.[43] It should be noted, however, that this change in the law was not enacted.

The commission also decided that students must be allowed to wear headscarves in public schools if they are doing so out of religious motivations, and ruled against two public schools that were seeking to bar teachers from wearing headscarves.[44] It also went further and ruled in one case that a pupil must be allowed to wear clothing that almost completely covered her face, although it ruled the opposite way in a case involving students who were preparing for teaching careers.[45] Van Bijsterveld explains these decisions on the basis of the Dutch understanding of state religious neutrality: "In the Netherlands, state schools are neutral with respect to religion or belief. Unlike in France, this is a positive neutrality. The neutrality does not aim at banning religion or belief from the public school altogether."[46] Equal treatment of all religious and secular beliefs systems is key in the Dutch mind-set. Thus the Dutch do not have the same problem with pupils and even teachers wearing religious garb as have some other countries, as long as all religions and secular belief systems are treated equally. If that is done, there is no favoritism, there is no discrimination.

The wearing of the traditional burqa in public has also proven to be controversial in recent years. Under the previous government the lower house twice voted to ban the wearing of them in public and shortly before the November 2006 elections the government itself announced plans to seek passage of legislation to this effect. But after protests from the Muslim community and elsewhere and after the election resulted in a slight shift to the left, the government dropped plans to ban the burqa. Its wearing in public remains legal. Traditional Dutch tolerance won out—but just barely.

A second free exercise issue the Netherlands has been dealing with involves religious groups that do not accept the Dutch society's consensus on gay rights and the role of women in society. The Dutch criminal code makes it a felony to incite hatred or discrimination against others by way of written or oral expression.[47] Some charges have been brought against Muslims as well as theologically conservative Christians who have spoken out against homosexuality or a liberated role for women. Their claims of protection under the free exercise of religion have usually prevailed, as explained by an official in the Ministry of the Interior and Kingdom Relations:

> We've seen that in the Netherlands, in recent years, people from different religious communities, both Christian and Muslim, have made hurtful remarks about homosexuality and the social status of women. Homosexuality has been described as damaging to Dutch society and labeled an infectious disease. *In every case* where one of these people was charged with discrimination, the result was acquittal. The main reason was the religious context of their statements, which allowed them to appeal to freedom of religion.[48]

Again, the Dutch understanding of pluralism led to the protection of religious minorities to speak their minds.

A third free exercise issue grows out of the greater visible presence of Muslims. Periodically, questions have arisen over such issues as the frequency and allowable volume of Muslim calls to prayer and the building of large mosques that in the view of many do not fit in with prevailing architectural styles. Especially controversial was the Essalaam mosque in Rotterdam, a large building that holds 1,200 worshippers and has minarets soaring forty-four meters into the air.[49] It was initially approved by the Rotterdam municipal council, but after a change in the political composition of the council there were attempts to block its construction or, at the least, lower the height of the minarets so they would no longer tower over the surrounding area. There have been similar controversies elsewhere. Some mosques have been attacked and set afire by right-wing ruffians.

These controversies and conflicts, however, are a sign of shifting attitudes among the Dutch populace, not changes in the legal status of Muslims or other religious minorities. The Essalaam mosque was built and is open today. Other mosques in other cities have been built, even though protests have sometimes attended them. But one must be careful not to exaggerate shifting Dutch attitudes. As the recent 2006 general election demonstrates, the picture is mixed. The strongly anti-immigration—many would say anti-Muslim—party of the assassinated Pim Fortuyn gained only 0.2 percent of the vote, and the conservative, more moderately anti-immigration—again many would say somewhat anti-Muslim—party, VVD, lost six seats in the lower house and garnered only 15 percent of the vote (down 3 percentage points from the previous election).[50] Meanwhile, the Socialist Party, with a more open attitude toward immigrants, gained sixteen seats. But one must also note that a new right-wing party marked by anti-Muslim attitudes, the Freedom Party (PVV), garnered nine seats and 6 percent of the vote.

In summary, the Netherlands has a more expansive understanding of the free exercise of religion than does the United States. This free exercise is interpreted to include the equal treatment of religious and nonreligious organizations and programs, and protects most practices of minority religious groups. Nevertheless, the Netherlands continues to struggle with free exercise questions in the face of increasing religious pluralism resulting from the increasing numbers of non-Christians—and especially of Muslims. In dealing with minority religions and their practices, accommodation is the norm, but more questions are being raised whether the complete freedom of religious expression sometimes needs to yield to a perceived need for greater integration into the values and norms of Dutch society. The Dutch proclivity for toleration and flexibility is being stretched to the limit, but with a few exceptions it is still dominant, both legally and in the public's attitudes. The Dutch continue to have a broad, expansive understanding of the free exercise of religion.

Church, State, and Education

The Dutch concept of pluralism translates, when applied to education, to a deep and lasting commitment to freedom of choice. There is strong support for the proposition that parents should be able to choose the sort of education their children receive, whether that be Catholic; Protestant in a genial, broad sense; Reformed in a strict, orthodox sense; Jewish; Muslim; Hindu; secular; or secular with certain special teaching techniques or philosophies such as Montessori. A study by the Organization for Economic Cooperation and Development (OECD) concluded that "'the central value of freedom of choice' was an aspect of Dutch education 'beyond debate at the present time.'"[51] One official with a national organization representing the boards of Protestant schools told us: "We are so much for freedom of education. . . . This is a part of the Dutch way of thinking." He went on to state that the potential problem of separate schools dividing Dutch society rarely comes up, but that "if it is discussed the desire for freedom always prevails."[52] Since that interview questions have been raised concerning the funding of Muslim schools amid fears they may be stifling the integration of Muslim immigrants into Dutch society and values or even teaching violence. One Dutch politician has called for the forced closure of all Islamic schools.

Nevertheless, about 70 percent of the primary and secondary school students attend nonpublic schools, by far the highest level of the five countries considered in this study. As of 2002, there were almost 8,000 primary schools, and of these 33 percent were public schools, 30 percent were Catholic schools, 30 percent were Protestant schools, and 7 percent were other private schools. There were 650 secondary schools, and of these 29 percent were public, 25 percent Catholic, 22 percent Protestant, 13 percent were secular, and 11 percent were interdenominational.[53] There are about forty-six Muslim primary schools and two Muslim secondary schools, as well as three Jewish schools (one of which is strictly orthodox) and four Hindu schools.[54] All of these schools are fully funded by the government.

This pattern of multiple types of schools, all funded by the government, is enshrined in Article 23 of the Constitution, which provides: "All persons shall be free to provide education . . ." and "Private primary schools . . . shall be financed from public funds according to the same standards as public-authority schools." It also states that private secondary schools shall receive public funding, as determined by the States-General. L. S. J. M. Henkens, who served as the director of secondary schooling in the Ministry of Education and Science, has written that Article 23 protects three distinct freedoms: the freedom to found schools, the freedom to determine the principles on which schools are to be based, and the freedom to organize the instruction. The second of these freedoms "entitles the competent authority of a school to choose the ideological or philosophical principles on which teaching at the school is to be based. The third . . . [entitles] the competent authority to decide on the content of teaching and the teaching methods to be used in the school."[55] Later he writes that "these freedoms remain untouched eighty years after they were first enshrined in our Constitution."[56] This means that whenever there are sufficient numbers of parents who want a new school that incorporates a certain distinctive religious or secular philosophy (*richting*, or direction), the government is committed to fund it as fully as it does the public schools. This includes the construction of facilities.

In this section we consider how this freedom of educational choice— enshrined in Article 23 of the Constitution and rooted in the Dutch concept of pluralism—works out in practice and how it affects church-state relations.

In practice the Netherlands' basic policy of fully funding all schools still leaves many unresolved issues. One issue is how many parents and pupils asking for a new school are sufficient for the government to accede to their request. The numbers of students needed to found a new, publicly funded school are set by national standards that vary based on pupil density in the area. In rural areas as few as eighty pupils may be enough, while two to three hundred are generally required in urban areas. Whether a school of the same or similar orientation is nearby is also considered, as well, of course, as what constitutes "nearby." If there already is a school of the same religious or secular orientation in the area, the authorities may require 350 or more pupils before they approve a new school, even though attending the existing school may require a lengthy trip. The Netherlands' compact size, excellent public transit system, and ever-present system of bicycle paths make lengthy trips to reach school less onerous than might be supposed.

A second issue is determining exactly what constitutes a new or distinctive religious or secular direction. If there already is a Protestant school in a community, but some parents believe it is too modern or contemporary in its theology, is that a sufficient basis for the government to fund a new school? Some Muslims have thought that the government has been insensitive to the differing groups within Islam. On the other hand, the principal of an Islamic school has reported that his school's Muslim character made it easier for it to receive approval of the government officials, since it clearly marked it as having a distinctive religious direction or *richting*.[57]

A third issue is when must a school close as the number of its students declines. If the number of pupils falls to less than thirty in a rural area or less than 150 in an urban area, the school faces the possible loss of government funding. Or there may be pressure for such a school to merge with a school of a similar nature. Again, there are no hard and set rules; public authorities must make many judgment calls. In recent years the government has been seeking economies of scale by avoiding very small schools. It has been slower to fund new schools and quicker to encourage small schools to combine or merge with others. Sometimes two small schools meet in the same building, with most of their classes held separately.

Two factors seem to make a system with as much potential for conflict and abuse in fact work with a manageable number of tensions and conflict. One is that Dutch society as a whole—including the public authorities—is genuinely committed to a pluralistic education system. Thus groups of parents wishing to maintain or start a school—while not automatically granted their request—are received with respect and given serious consideration. Second, the famous Dutch system of governing by discussion, negotiation, and consensus-building comes into play. There are umbrella organizations representing the various religious and secular groups active in education, and thus active discussions and negotiations ensue when an issue arises over the founding or closing of a school of a particular group.

Although this system works well for most of Dutch society it poses some problems for the 850,000 Muslims. First, the attacks of 9/11, subsequent terrorist attacks by Muslim extremists, and the murder of Theo van Gogh in 2004 have all worked to create a spirit of suspicion and distrust that was previously unknown in Dutch society, or at least limited to the fringes of society. Second, Muslims themselves are sharply divided among different national origins—largely Moroccan, Turkish, Indonesian, and Surinamese—and between more radical and more moderate elements. There are few Muslim umbrella organizations that can discuss and negotiate with public authorities on behalf of large segments on the Muslim community.

As a result, although the pluralism of the Dutch—including the old pillarization model—would seem ready-made for dealing with the needs of a minority religious community such as the Muslims, all has not gone smoothly. The principal of the Muslim school we cited earlier commented on this: "The period of Pillarisation is now often being condemned as a bad period in Dutch history, but Pillarisation and religion at that time gave clear direction as to morals and values in the society, which now seem to have disappeared. Diversity in society is a good thing and an Islamic pillar in Dutch society may contribute to the emancipation of Muslims in this society as well."[58] As a result there are those who are looking to the traditional Dutch system of full government funding for a variety of religiously and philosophically based schools as a means not to divide Dutch society and to alienate its Muslim minority, but as a means to emancipate the Muslim minority and to serve as a basis to integrate them into Dutch society. This position is reflected in the comments of two observers:

> From our interviews we can conclude that Islamic schools . . . just want to be normal Dutch schools. But instead of offering public or Christian education they give their students the opportunity to develop an Islamic identity.
>
> These schools are different in that they see their existence as separate Islamic educational institutions essential for the emancipation of Muslims in Dutch society. Consequently, they draw clear parallels between the period of Pillarisation in the Netherlands, in which religious and political groups openly segregated themselves from Dutch society in order to strengthen their position and increase their acceptance.[59]

The exact form the funding of private schools takes is both complex and in a state of flux. Traditionally, the central government pays all salaries directly. This means that all teachers, no matter in what type of school they teach— public or private—are on the same pay scale. Every school receives a certain amount annually from the central government. In recent years there has been a move to give schools greater financial autonomy by way of making lump-sum grants. These payments are determined by a formula, based on the number of pupils in a school, the type of building it has, and other relevant factors. This change was instituted because government officials thought the education budget was too open-ended and desired a more predictable—and more manageable—budget.

Schools are not allowed to charge additional fees, although most request parents to make voluntary contributions. Most private and some public schools request such contributions and there are expectations that parents will make them. The contributions vary with the parents' income and average from 200 to 600 euros a year ($300 to $900).

Relevant to the issue of church-state relations is the fact that the vast majority of the private schools receiving full public funding are religious in nature—Catholic, Protestant, Jewish, Muslim, and Hindu. One of the Jewish schools receiving funding is orthodox in nature. When pressed as to the nature of the Catholic schools, Dominique Majoor of a Catholic umbrella education organization acknowledged that some Catholic schools are Catholic only in name, but then went on to state: "But I think still a lot of schools are Catholic not only in name but also by what they are doing and how they are doing it. The ideal within my organization is that we should work on it and improve it. . . . But I look at my own schools—the schools I've seen—and you can really recognize them as being Catholic."[60]

Even more telling, about 5 percent of the Dutch population belongs to several strictly Reformed, or orthodox, Protestant denominations.[61] About 90 percent of their children attend schools sponsored by these churches and these schools are marked by an integration of religious perspectives into all subject fields. They are free to hire only teachers in agreement with their religious commitments and to accept students based on the religion of their families. In the term used by the American Supreme Court, they are "pervasively sectarian" schools. They are also fully funded by the government. Even though they clearly are based in a minority religious community that runs counter to the strong forces of secularization dominant in Dutch society, they have experienced minimal problems in obtaining governmental approval for opening new schools, obtaining full government funding, and maintaining the freedom to teach their beliefs in the classroom.

In short, although most of the religious schools receiving full public funding are religious in a very general sense—as one would expect in a very secularized society—some are also very specifically, distinctively religious in nature. They too receive full funding from the government.

The Dutch typically characterize their system as one of church-state separation. "The system of church and state relationships is characterized throughout as one of separation of church and state."[62] When we asked the author of these words how church-state separation can be squared with financial support for religious organizations, including deeply religious schools, she replied that the Netherlands has no established church and that the state does not directly finance the churches, but if the state subsidizes education and social work, it must not discriminate against religion. If it funds neutral organizations, funding religious ones does not violate church-state separation.

> There have also been court decisions [ruling] that government doesn't have to subsidize social work, charitable work, or youth work, but when it subsidizes this type of work it should make no discrimination on the basis of religion or belief. So if a "neutral" organization applies for this work it may receive it, but if a church or religious organization wants to carry out this work, it should not be excluded because that would not be equal treatment.[63]

It is on the basis of equal treatment—of making funds available neutrally for all types of religious schools and for religious and secular schools alike—that funding of religious schools and church-state separation are seen as being compatible.

This leads to the question of how much freedom or autonomy is granted religious schools. Are they fully free to be as religious as they wish? Or are there overt or subtle pressures to conform and to water down their religious message? First, it is clear that all schools—public and private, religious and secular—are under numerous limitations and constraints. The Netherlands is a highly regulated society, with government regulations affecting almost all areas of life. Education is no exception. Much of the curriculum is set on the national level, as are the certification standards and the working conditions for teachers. All students from all schools take the same comprehensive exams. Schools clearly are not free to have whomever they want, teaching whatever they want them to teach.

Nevertheless, schools are, in a formal sense, completely free to be as religious as they wish to be. Article 23 of the Constitution seeks to protect this religious freedom when it states that government standards shall give "due regard, in the case of private schools, to the freedom to provide education according to religious or other belief." It later goes on to state that the funding "provisions shall respect in particular the freedom of private schools to choose their teaching aids and to appoint teachers as they see fit." In this context "teaching aids" refer to such learning supports as textbooks, maps, and films. The director of an umbrella Catholic school association has written that "educational institutions at all levels are permitted to teach in the manner they please. They can choose their own texts and their own teachers, including the possibility of using religion and lifestyle as a criterion for hiring."[64] Chris Janse, who is from one of the small, strictly orthodox Protestant groups, discussed some tensions they had experienced with government officials over the teaching of evolution and some other curriculum matters, but then he concluded: "In general, you can't say that the government makes it very difficult for us."[65]

This is not, however, the entire story. There are two sources of pressures or constraints on the religious character of the schools. First, in reaction to fears that some of the Muslim schools might be teaching violence or hatred, a system of school inspections now looks more closely than it did earlier on what is being taught in the schools. It is still the case that "confessional schools are subject to state inspections, but the teaching of religion itself is not."[66] An attempt to include the content of religion courses being taught in the schools in the inspections was rejected by parliament. Nevertheless, school inspections can reach conclusions concerning the general atmosphere or teachings of a school. As an official in the Ministry of Justice, Kees Klop, stated: "They [the inspectors] do not look at the content of the religion being taught, but only if the schools are teaching students to hate others."[67]

Veit Bader of the University of Amsterdam reported to us that a 2005 official report on fifty-two Muslim schools found only two where serious concerns over the teaching of hatred and violence existed.[68] Some schools in the strict, orthodox Reformed tradition have felt under some new pressures over what they are teaching, since they feel that in the public mind they are being lumped in with the Muslim schools.[69] But these concerns and pressures must be viewed in the context of Dutch pluralism, which has traditionally given religiously based schools a great deal of freedom.

A second way in which government pressures can be brought to bear on religious schools relates to their hiring practices. When there is a vacancy, schools are legally free to hire any qualified applicant, but there are certain financial advantages in hiring a currently unemployed teacher, whether or not he or she agrees with the religious character of the school. As the principal of one Protestant school has written: "At the moment we are forced to give precedence to teachers from other schools who have, for some reason or other, lost their jobs, unless there are very clear and relevant reasons for not doing so."[70] These pressures can be resisted, but they are there. Also, the right to make hiring decisions based on religion is not automatically accorded all religiously based schools. Rather, they need to demonstrate that doing so is necessary in order to preserve the school's religious identity.[71] As a result, ironically, it is easier for the more pervasively religious schools to justify hiring decisions based on religion than it is for the more nominally religious schools.

In short, the Netherlands is a highly regulated society, and this also extends to the schools. The schools face significant pressures on their religious character and they need to have a clear and distinct understanding of their own religious nature, if they are to resist these pressures. Without that understanding, the danger is great that they will not successfully resist the pressures on them and the formal freedom they are promised in the Constitution will not be realized in practice.

This leaves the question of the role of religion in the public schools. Article 23 stipulates: "Education provided by public authorities shall . . . [pay] due respect to everyone's religion or belief." This has been "interpreted as a neutrality clause which requires a positive attitude towards religion. . . . Provision is made for [voluntary] religious education in public-authority schools. . . . A whole series of court rulings established that instruction in non-religious (humanist) belief should be offered and subsidized on the same basis as religious instruction."[72] Exactly how these requirements are met varies from one locality to another. Usually they are met by some form of objective teaching about religions and the role they play in society. Sometimes released time programs have been adopted, where students are taught by representatives of the various faiths after normal school hours. Prayer and other devotional activities are very rare in public schools, but have never been explicitly outlawed by either court decision or parliament. There is no attempt to encourage or promote consensual religious beliefs and traditions in the public schools. Such efforts would run counter to the principle of religious pluralism embraced by the Dutch.

There is, however, little educational choice on the university level. Over 75 percent of the university students are in public universities, with only 9 percent in one Reformed university, and 14 percent in two Catholic universities.[73] But this is only a part of the story. The Protestant and Catholic universities are almost indistinguishable from their public counterparts. In fact, the universities are so similar that students are centrally assigned to the various universities, with a lottery system used in cases of excess demand. All universities, including those with a religious tie, are funded by the central government. Theological schools are also funded by the government, and here distinctive religious differences, of course, still exist. Since 1962 the education of humanist counselors has also been included in the system of government support. And currently there are two government-funded programs for training imams, one at the Free University of Amsterdam and one at Leiden University. Again, one sees the Dutch understanding of governmental religious neutrality, a neutrality gained not by failing to fund any theological education, as is the case in the United States, but by funding theological training for all religions and for secular, humanist counselors as well.

Educational choice, as we said at the beginning of this consideration of education, is the cornerstone of the Dutch approach to education. Religious schools are fully funded, and this is seen not as a violation of church-state separation and religious neutrality, but as a necessity if government is to be truly neutral among competing religious and nonreligious belief systems. To do otherwise would be to pick sides and thereby violate the free exercise rights of those left out.

Church, State, and Nonprofit Service Organizations

The struggle over the financing of private religious schools and the settlement reached on that issue historically did much to shape the Dutch approach to the role nonprofit service organizations play in society and their funding by the government. The field of education established the pattern of relying upon private nonprofit organizations to provide a vital public service, with the government providing the funding. That pattern is the one that has been followed in the health care, social service, broadcasting, and other public service areas. Private—sometimes religiously based—agencies provide the services and government provides most of the funding. Herman Aquina has pointed out that "about 70 percent of GNP is allocated by government in some way, but only 10 percent of GNP is directly controlled by core government: the other 60 percent is accounted for by PGOs [Para-Government Organizations]."[74] A recent study found that 59 percent of the revenues of Dutch nonprofit organizations come from the government, with fees they charge for their services being the only other significant source of revenue.[75] The number is even higher in the social services field, with 66 percent of the revenues coming from the government.[76] This pattern shows no sign of reversing itself. In fact, two observers have noted that in recent years the government "privatized some of its agencies and transformed them into private nonprofits."[77] These same two observers concluded: "Still today this intertwinement of the state and private initiative in the nonprofit sector remains a vital factor in its functioning."[78]

The situation that exists in the field of treatment for drug addiction is typical: "About 3,000 people, spread over 70 institutions at 200 addresses are working in specialized addiction care in the Netherlands. On an annual basis there are some 80,000 clients. Apart from a few municipal methadone programmes, the entire service is of a private character."[79]

Historically, "religion was a major factor in the creation and development of the Dutch nonprofit sector."[80] The same pillarization system that we noted in the case of schools and other voluntary organizations existed in the area of social services.

> During the last part of the nineteenth century and the first half of the twentieth century, . . . the diversity of religious motives and political ideologies led to the formation of Roman Catholic, Protestant (Calvinistic), socialistic, and nonsectarian humanistic organizations like separate pillars in an edifice. Thus, the whole society was structured by these religious and ideological organizations. This "pillarization" was for the most part as true in politics as in the sphere of delivering nonprofit services.[81]

The nonprofit service sector has, however, been deeply affected by the more general "depillarization" and secularization trends that swept through the Netherlands—more so than education. The secularization trend means that many faith-based social service agencies have lost the constituency or base that in the past had supported them and provided a rationale for their existence. Meanwhile government cost-saving pressures have forced many agencies to merge with other agencies, including Protestant or Catholic agencies with secular agencies. With their constituencies melting away, the religious agencies possess weak means with which to resist such pressures. When this occurs, nonprofit service organizations do not even have the same protections that schools have by way of Article 23 of the Constitution. Stavros Zouridis, an official in the Ministry of Justice, explained to us that if one agency is spending more money for a certain item or service than others, it is called upon by government officials to explain why. They are thereby forced to adopt the lower-cost practices of other agencies—and in the process lose more of their autonomy.[82]

Jaap Doek, a professor of family law at the Free University of Amsterdam, reached this conclusion in the area of child protection services:

> [T]he government has strengthened its influence and control over the non-governmental organizations in the field of child protection. These organizations are in fact instruments of the government in carrying out her responsibility for children in need of care and protection. These organizations can only operate as child protection services if they are recognized by the government and this recognition is only possible if they meet the conditions set by the government.[83]

This same conclusion has been echoed by many others in other areas. For example, Zouridis told us that the private social service agencies "are now controlled by the state. The welfare agencies have lost their autonomy."[84] In short, the control of the Dutch government over nonprofit service organizations that receive public funding is great.

Nevertheless, many religiously based nonprofit service organizations still exist and take part in government funding programs just as their secular counterparts do. Many of these are clearly religious in more than name. In our interview with Chris Janse, a leader in one of the small, strictly orthodox Reformed groups, we asked if his church had its own distinctively Reformed social service agencies. He replied:

> Yes we have several homes for elderly people. There are homes for children and older people who are mentally retarded, who are handicapped . . . Also, for people with psychological problems. There are also advisory institutions you can go when you have problems in your family or with children, with . . . broken marriages. These are not all subsidized by the government, but most of them are 100 percent or 90 percent subsidized by the government.[85]

He also reported that these agencies are able to restrict hiring to persons in agreement with their religious beliefs: "You can ask for people who accept the basis—the doctrinal basis—of the institute; no problem." He went on to relate that several years ago the issue arose of their practice of not hiring practicing homosexuals. The outcome was that they are not allowed to openly state or advertise that they do not hire homosexuals, but they can ask job candidates if they agree with the moral standards of the agency. And since homosexual practices go against their moral standards they can in this way indirectly avoid hiring practicing homosexuals.

Other examples can be cited. There are six international aid and relief agencies—one Catholic, one Protestant, and four secular agencies. Much of the Netherlands' foreign assistance money is funneled through these six agencies, including the two religiously based ones. A rabbi reported to us that there are three Jewish homes for the elderly, a Jewish social welfare organization, and a Jewish child welfare agency, among other Jewish organizations. When pressed on whether Jewish organizations receive public funds just as Christian organizations do, or if there is some subtle discrimination against them, he responded unambiguously that Jewish organizations receive public funding just as their Christian and secular counterparts do.[86]

There are Muslim social service agencies that also receive government funding, such as several Islamic homes for the elderly that are government funded. According to one team of scholars Muslim agencies have "achieved a strong position in civil society, thanks to the existing legislation and the protection of freedom of religion."[87] There is government-subsidized Muslim television programming. Nevertheless, problems remain and Muslim organizations do not take part in the system we have been describing as fully as do Christian, Jewish, and secular agencies. The key problem is that even when Muslims develop social service programs, questions of stability, openness, and organizational strength that the Dutch system expects are often not there. As one Muslim who works for the Platform of Islamic Organizations in Rijnmond (SPIOR) in the Rotterdam area has put it: "No professional organization and also no financing!"[88]

In brief, the Dutch make extensive use of nonprofit organizations to deliver a wide variety of public services and many of these organizations possess—to greater and lesser degrees—religious orientations. The system has been battered by the secularization of Dutch society, not-always-successful moves to incorporate Muslims and other religious minorities into the system, and governmental moves to enforce cost savings and regulations. But the system still exists.

To many Americans such practices would seem to be a denial of religious freedom. After all, tax money from nonbelievers is going to fund Jewish homes for the elderly, money collected from Jews is going to support Christian family counseling programs, and taxes paid by Christians are going to fund Muslim television broadcasts. But the Dutch response is to insist that not to fund such religious organizations would be a denial of religious freedom. This came out in our interviews time and again. Frans Koopmans, of De Hoop (The Hope) drug treatment center, made a point that is fundamental to the Dutch mind-set in regard to state funding of religious service organizations when he stated, "Every hospital, every helping facility has its principles, its priorities, its fundamentals. Even though they are perhaps not Christian. Everyone is working out of a philosophy. We are working out of a Christian philosophy because we are wholeheartedly convinced it is the truth."[89] As a result of this perspective, equal treatment demands that religious and nonreligious organizations be funded in the same manner. As Koopmans also said, "We have Christians in the Netherlands and we should have facilities to help that specific part of our population. If people are humanistic, you should have a humanistic hospital."[90] This reasoning is firmly rooted in the Dutch concept of pluralism noted throughout this chapter.

Similarly, when asked concerning possible negative reactions of nonbelievers, Jews, or Muslims over their taxes going to fund his explicitly Christian organization, Martin de Jong, of a distinctively Christian agency serving retarded children and their families, responded:

> We almost never have that kind of discussion, because they can get money for the same kind of activities in their interpretation of life. It's a right for everyone to get money for such kind of activities. . . . They have a right to get money for such kind of activities; we have the right to get money for such kind of activities. So when they say that to me I can say that is a common right, it is not only my right. . . . It's not a right especially for Christians, or for the Jewish; it's a common right.[91]

Maria Martens of VKMO (an umbrella organization of Catholic social service organizations) defended her agencies' receiving public funds with these words: "When the government gives money for housing for the elderly, why not to Catholics? . . . When we are all paying our taxes, for these kinds of initiatives, and we have our [initiatives], why should we be left out?"[92]

Koopmans, De Jong, and Martens were appealing to a basic sense of governmental neutrality or evenhandedness based on the concept of a pluralistic society, whose various elements have distinctive philosophies or approaches and are deserving of the same support. This is the same concept to which Van Bijsterveld made reference in the words quoted earlier when she said that "government doesn't have to subsidize social work, charitable work, or youth work, but when it subsidizes this type of work it should make no discrimination on the basis of religion or belief . . . [I]f a church or religious organization wants to carry out this work, it should not be excluded because that would not be equal treatment."[93] In the dominant Dutch mind-set public funding of social service organizations does not violate church-state separation or governmental religious neutrality, as long as such funding goes to the organizations of all religious traditions and to those of nonreligious secular groups as well. In fact, to do otherwise is seen as discriminating against religion. Undergirding this mind-set is the rejection of an assumption often made in the United States, namely, that religious organizations have a bias or a distinctive ax to grind, while nonreligious secular organizations are neutral. In the Netherlands secular and religious organizations alike are seen as operating out of certain distinctive philosophies or beliefs.

This leads to the question of the amount of religious freedom possessed by religious nonprofit service organizations that receive public funds. On the one hand, there are strong and convincing claims to the effect that government funding has led to an enormous amount of government control over nonprofit organizations.

On the other hand, there is persuasive evidence that the control exercised by government officials usually does not extend to the religious activities and identifications of nonprofit organizations. Koopmans of the evangelical drug rehabilitation program De Hoop gave this issue of government control following government funding the proper balance when he said: "What we do have, of course, are regulations for every psychiatric hospital—Christian or non-Christian, humanistic, anthroposophic—which we have to subscribe to. But they are not anti-Christian regulations or something like that. . . . The Netherlands always has been known as a very tolerant country in which everyone could believe whatever you wanted as long as you did not hurt anyone else. Well, it's still so."[94]

In fact, more than one observer told us that those agencies that are more distinctively religious are in a better position to resist governmental pressures to merge with other agencies or to alter their practices than those with a more nominal religious or a fully secular character.[95] Van Bijsterveld stated that "it is easier for organizations to resist pressure to merge with other organizations if they are very distinctively Christian, and harder if they are more generally Christian. Then it is harder for them to document a distinct identification or direction—we say *richting*—that is lost if they would merge with another."[96] In the pluralist mind-set, an agency's distinct religious or philosophical orientation is something to be respected and allowed for, not something looked down upon or ignored. That is why distinctively religious agencies are still allowed to make hiring decisions based on religion, something that we saw in chapter 2 is highly controversial in the United States.

In summary, Dutch policies in regard to religiously based social service organizations are similar to those in regard to schools. In both cases the government—supported by attitudes prevalent in Dutch society—provides generous levels of funding to a wide variety of service organizations, religiously and secularly based alike. This public policy is rooted in a pluralistic concept of society that recognizes a variety of religious and secular belief systems present in society, all of which are held to be legitimate, contributing forces and therefore possessing an equal right to expect an appropriate share of public support. This system has, however, had some difficulties accommodating itself to the various immigrant Muslim communities, and therefore Muslims, while taking part in this system, do not do so to the same extent as other religious and secular groups. As is the case throughout Dutch society, there are many government regulations affecting the service organizations receiving public funds, a situation reinforced by recent government efforts to achieve economies in the delivery of social services. The general secularization of Dutch society—and therefore of many of its previously religiously based non-profit organizations—has made it harder for many agencies to resist the homogenizing influence of government regulations. Nevertheless, the religious missions of religiously based agencies appear largely to be respected, at least when those religious missions are clearly in evidence and articulated.

Concluding Observations

The Netherlands is a clear example of the third model of church-state relations presented in chapter 1, the pluralist model. The Dutch seek to attain governmental neutrality on matters of religion, not by a strict church-state separation that sees all aid to religion as a violation of the norm of neutrality, but by a pluralism that welcomes and supports all religious and secular structures of belief on an equal, evenhanded basis. This is a system of principled pluralism—as we put it in the title of this chapter—in that the Netherlands' pluralist approach to church and state is rooted in certain self-consciously held beliefs.

The principled nature of the Dutch church-state pluralist system can be seen in two basic beliefs or assumptions that undergird it. One is a pluralistic view of society that sees a variety of religious and philosophical movements—even when they are full participants in the public life of the nation—as normal and no threat to the unity and prosperity of society. Such movements do not have to be relegated to the private realm, with only consensual civil religious beliefs and values allowed into the public realm. This perspective has been seriously questioned in recent years due to debates over the role of immigrant Muslim groups in Dutch society. Many have questioned whether or not Muslims are—or even are capable of—fitting into the Dutch system of religious pluralism. That system is based on tolerance and a willingness to live side by side with persons of sharply different religious and philosophical beliefs. There also needs to be some glue—some shared traditions and values— that bind the Dutch into a single people. Some have questioned whether Dutch Muslims share enough traditions and values with the rest of Dutch society to make the system of pluralism work.

For our purposes the important point is that the traditional pluralistic legal forms and—even more importantly—mind-set continue to be dominant. True, pluralism has, in the past ten years, been battered in a way it had not since the "pacification" of 1917. Especially some of the political parties on the right, such as the VVD and the PVV, are—in part due to concerns over the Muslim minority—raising new questions about how far the state should go in recognizing and funding the schools and social service agencies of religious groups.

Nevertheless, a commitment to religious pluralism is still enshrined in the legal structure and is the dominant mind-set. We have repeatedly seen this. As Veit Bader of the University of Amsterdam related to us:

> The system for financing religious schools in the Netherlands is entrenched. . . . And in a comparative perspective, this opened more opportunities for Muslims to have their own schools in the Netherlands compared to all other European countries. In the UK there is now after a long battle two publicly financed schools—directly recognized Muslim schools—France has none, and in the Netherlands we have some 50 Muslim schools, in a much smaller country, with many fewer practicing Muslims.[97]

A second underlying belief or assumption is that nonreligious, "neutral" organizations and movements are not truly neutral—as is often assumed within the liberal Enlightenment view of society—but are yet another *richting*, or direction, equally legitimate but no more legitimate than a host of other religious and nonreligious philosophies or directions.

Public policies that respect, accommodate, and support public roles for a plurality of religious and secular belief structures emerge out of these beliefs. The comments Bob Goudzwaard, a retired professor of economics at the Free University of Amsterdam, made to us in 1996 still hold true in understanding Dutch policies in regard to church-state issues: "Nondiscrimination, when it comes to religion, always also means in the Dutch mindset that if you have an organization that thinks it good to have a Christian approach, that cannot be a reason in itself to withhold subsidies because that would be discrimination. That is still very often present in the mindset."[98] This is a basic point that has emerged at various points throughout this chapter. What is often viewed in the United States as discriminating in favor of religion, and thereby a form of establishing religion, is viewed in the Netherlands as necessary in order not to discriminate *against* religion. On this basis the government funds a wide variety of private religiously based schools, universities, theological schools, and social service and health agencies. To do otherwise would violate the free exercise rights of those not recognized or accommodated on a basis equal to other religious or secular movements. As Van Bijsterveld said, "Freedom of religion is not only a negative freedom in the sense that the government not infringe upon it, but also the structure of the law must create an atmosphere so that religion can really be exercised."[99] If religion is to be fully free, government must take certain positive steps to accommodate it so that religion, along with secular beliefs, can in practice be freely exercised.

By following this concept of pluralism the Netherlands has created an approach to church-state issues that appears to have achieved the traditional liberal goal of governmental neutrality on matters of religion.

There is a paradox here. In the name of opposing the liberal vision of society based on privatizing particularistic religious beliefs and favoring a generic moral consensus, the Dutch have forged an approach to church and state that achieves the liberal goal of religious freedom for all. It does so by allowing the recognition and support for the full range of particularistic religious beliefs, a practice that liberalism traditionally had assumed inevitably would lead to divisiveness and religious repression of one group by another. Once one accepts the fact that consensual moral-religious beliefs that are accepted by most but not all of the population and that public institutions and programs purged of all religious elements are not truly neutral, but reflect certain philosophical or moral perspectives, it is hard to disagree with the basic Dutch contention that true governmental neutrality can only be attained by treating people and organizations of all religious and nonreligious perspectives and beliefs equally—not by favoring one over the other.

In seeking to understand how the Netherlands successfully arrived at its commitment to a principled pluralism, the role played by Catholic-Protestant cooperation must be recalled. It was the "monster alliance," forged in the 1870s between Catholics and the more orthodox among the Reformed Protestants, that was able to overcome the previously dominant liberal forces and carry the day politically. In the United States, as seen in the previous chapter, Protestants largely made common cause with liberals in opposition to the Catholic Church. Yet it is important to note that the theories of religious pluralism that were developed by this alliance were much more than a rationalization for the advancement of its members' own causes. It was an ideology to which they were in reality committed. Jews, socialists, and secular humanists were early included within it, and today Muslims and Hindus—with some difficulties—are as well. It was a genuine, not a sham, commitment to pluralism.

Finally, it is helpful to note that in part this system may work as well as it does in the Netherlands because of certain unique Dutch conditions. Even the small, compact size of the country enters in, served as it is by excellent public transportation and an amazing system of bicycle paths. This means schoolchildren can safely ride to schools some distance from their homes, thereby making it easier to sort out the children by religious or philosophical conviction. The public transportation system makes it possible for citizens to reach the social or health service agency they wish to use. The sense of cooperation and national unity forged by a common history and language (except for a small minority of Frisian speakers) may also play a role. Countries without the same long tradition of working together may have a harder time maintaining a sense of national unity and purpose than has the Netherlands. Nevertheless, the Netherlands stands as a testimony to the possibility of combining genuine governmental religious neutrality, a broad system of recognition and support for religious and secular private schools and social service organizations, and national purpose and unity. There is much to learn from the Dutch experience.

Notes

1. For a brief, readable account of the historical background of Dutch pluralism, see Robert C. Tash, *Dutch Pluralism* (New York: Lang, 1991), chap. 2.

2. *Statistical Yearbook of the Netherlands, 2007* (Voorburg: Statistics Netherlands, 2005), 116. Available at www.cbs.nl. Also see Sophie C. van Bijsterveld, "State and Church in the Netherlands," in Gerhard Robbers, ed., *State and Church in the European Union*, 2nd ed. (Baden-Baden, Germany: Nomos Verlagsgesellschaft, 2005), 368; and, on the number of Muslims, "More than 850 thousand Muslims in the Netherlands" (available at www.cbs.nl/en-GB/menu/themas/vrije-tijd-cultuur/publicaties/artikelen/archief/2007/2007-2278-wm.htm).

3. See G. A. Irwin and J. J. M. van Holsteyn, "Decline of the Structured Model of Electoral Competition," in Hans Daalder and Galen Irwin, eds., *Politics in the Netherlands: How Much Change?* (Totowa, N.J.: Cass, 1989), 34; and *Statistical Yearbook of the Netherlands, 2007*, 116. On the recent secularization trend also see James

Carleton Kennedy, *Building the New Babylon: Cultural Change in the Netherlands During the 1960s* (Ph.D. dissertation, University of Iowa, 1995).

4. Van Bijsterveld, "State and Church in the Netherlands," 368.

5. *Statistical Yearbook of the Netherlands, 2007*, 116.

6. European World Values Survey, Four-Wave Integrated Data File, 1981–2004, v.20060423, 2006. The European Values Study Foundation and World Values Survey Association.

7. "Radicalism and Radicalisation" (Report of the Directorate of General Judicial Strategy to the Speaker of the Lower House of the States General, 19 August 2005, Ref no. 5358374/05/AJS), 33.

8. For an excellent introduction to Dutch government, see Rudy B. Andeweg and Galen A. Irwin, *Dutch Government and Politics* (New York: St. Martin's Press, 1993).

9. See Andeweg and Irwin, *Dutch Government and Politics*, chaps. 2 and 7. On consociational theory see Arend Lijphart, "Consociational Democracy," *Comparative Political Studies* 1 (1968), 3–44.

10. Andeweg and Irwin, *Dutch Government and Politics*, 175.

11. See the discussion in Andeweg and Irwin, *Dutch Government and Politics*, 33–44. Also see Arend Lijphart, "From the Politics of Accommodation to Adversarial Politics in the Netherlands: A Reassessment," in Daalder and Irwin, eds., *Politics in the Netherlands*, 140–53.

12. Quoted by Charles L. Glenn Jr., *The Myth of the Common School* (Amherst: University of Massachusetts Press, 1987), 46.

13. Quoted by Glenn, *The Myth of the Common School*, 46. Emphasis removed.

14. Quoted by Glenn, *The Myth of the Common School*, 47.

15. Especially able accounts in English of this struggle are found in Glenn, *The Myth of the Common School*, 244–49; and Stanley Carlson-Thies, *Democracy in the Netherlands: Consociational or Pluriform?* (Ph.D. dissertation, University of Toronto, 1993), 44–231. Much of what follows is based on these accounts.

16. Carlson-Thies, *Democracy in the Netherlands*, 138.

17. Carlson-Thies, *Democracy in the Netherlands*, 144.

18. Hans Daalder, "The Netherlands: Opposition in a Segmented Society," in Robert A. Dahl, ed., *Political Opposition* (New Haven, Conn.: Yale University Press, 1966), 201. The revolution the party was against was the French Revolution, and more particularly the liberal principles in which the Reformed groups saw it being grounded.

19. The term is from G. J. Rooymans, used in a publication put out by the Catholic party in 1948. See Carlson-Thies, *Democracy in the Netherlands*, 175.

20. Michael P. Fogarty, *Christian Democracy in Western Europe, 1820–1953* (London: Routledge & Kegan Paul, 1957), 172. On Kuyper and his influence also see John Bolt, *A Free Church, a Holy Nation: Abraham Kuyper's American Public Theology* (Grand Rapids, Mich.: Eerdmans, 2001); James Bratt, ed., *Abraham Kuyper: A Centennial Reader* (Grand Rapids, Mich.: Eerdmans, 1998); Johan D. van der Vyver,

"Sphere Sovereignty of Religious Institutions: A Contemporary Calvinistic Theory of Church-State Relations," in Gerhard Robbers, ed., *Church Autonomy: A Comparative Survey* (Frankfurt am Main, Germany: Peter Land, 2001), 645–81; and Cornelius van der Kooi and Jan de Bruijn, eds., *Kuyper Reconsidered: Aspects of His Life and Work* (Amsterdam: VU Uitgeverij, 1999).

21. Carlson-Thies, *Democracy in the Netherlands*, 229.

22. Abraham Kuyper, *Calvinism: Six Stone Foundation Lectures* (Grand Rapids, Mich.: Eerdmans, 1931), 108.

23. Kuyper, *Calvinism*, 106.

24. Hennan Bakvis, *Catholic Power in the Netherlands* (Kingston, Ontario: McGill-Queen's University Press, 1981), 61.

25. Carlson-Thies, *Democracy in the Netherlands*, 168–69.

26. Bakvis, *Catholic Power in the Netherlands*, 62.

27. On pillarization, see Erik H. Bax, *Modernization and Cleavage in Dutch Society* (Aldershot: Avebury, 1990), chaps. 5 and 6; and Harry Post, *Pillarization: An Analysis of Dutch and Belgian Society* (Aldershot: Avebury, 1989).

28. Interview with Sophie C. van Bijsterveld (September 25, 2006).

29. "Policy Document on Fundamental Rights in a Pluralistic Society" (Ministerie van Binnenlandse Zaken en Koninkrijksrelaties, May, 2004), 7.

30. Ibid., 3–4.

31. Paul M. Sniderman and Louk Hagendoorn, *When Ways of Life Collide: Multiculturalism and Its Discontents in the Netherlands* (Princeton, N.J.: Princeton University Press, 2007), 15.

32. Veit Bader, *Secularism or Democracy? Associational Governance of Religious Diversity* (Amsterdam: University of Amsterdam Press, 2007), 297.

33. Ibid.

34. Interview with George Harinck, director of the Historical Document Center for Dutch Protestantism, Free University, Amsterdam (September 20, 2006).

35. This and the following quotations from the Netherlands Constitution are taken from the English translation of the Constitution published by the Constitutional Affairs and Legislative Division of the Ministry of Home Affairs (October 1989).

36. Sophie C. van Bijsterveld, "The Constitutional Status of Religion in the Kingdom of the Netherlands," *The Constitutional Status of Churches in the European Union Countries* (European Consortium for Church-State Research, proceedings of the 1994 meeting, University of Paris), 207 and 211.

37. Sophie C. van Bijsterveld, "State and Church in the Netherlands," in Robbers, ed., *State and Church in the European Union*, 384. Italics added.

38. Interview with Sophie C. van Bijsterveld (February 9, 1996).

39. For a helpful report on the activities and decisions of this Commission in 2002 see Sophie C. van Bijsterveld, "Church and State in the Netherlands, 2002," *European Journal for Church and State Research*, 10 (2003), 80–91.

40. Equal Treatment Act (Commissie Gelijke Behandeling). Available at www .cgb.nl/cgb170.php.

41. Bijsterveld, "Church and State in the Netherlands, 2002," 81. Italics present.

42. Ibid., 83–84.

43. See the speech by A. Nicolai, the Dutch state secretary of Foreign Affairs, in *Report of the International Conference on Fundamental Rights in a Pluralistic Society* (The Hague: Ministry of the Interior and Kingdom Relations, 2004), 60.

44. See "Advisory Opinion of the Dutch Equal Treatment Commission on Niqaabs and Headscarves in Schools" (CGB Advisory Opinion/2003/01, 16 April 2003). Available at www.cgb.nl.

45. On these cases, see Sophie C. van Bijsterveld, "The Permissible Scope of Legal Limitations on the Freedom of Religion or Belief in the Netherlands," *Emory International Law Review* 19 (Summer, 2005), 974–76.

46. Ibid., 974.

47. See Bijsterveld, "State and Church in the Netherlands," 387.

48. H. P. Heida, "Introduction to the Workshops," in *Report of the International Conference on Fundamental Rights in a Pluralistic Society* (The Hague: Ministry of the Interior and Kingdom Relations, Constitutional Affairs and Legislation Department, 2004), 59. Italics added.

49. A helpful summary of this controversy can be found at Michael Z. Wise's web site: www.michaelzwise.com/articleDisplay.php?article_id=80.

50. The exact 2006 election results can be found at www.nlverkiezingen.com/TK2006.html.

51. Organization for Economic Cooperation and Development, *School: A Matter of Choice* (Paris: OECD, 1994), 68. The quotation is from an earlier OECD study.

52. Interview with W. Bos (January 26, 1996).

53. "The Education System of the Netherlands, 2006" (The Hague, Ministry of Education, Culture and Science, 2006), 27–28. Available at www.minocw.nl/documenten/eurydice_2006_en.pdf.

54. See Froukje Demant, Marcel Maussen, and Jan Rath, *Muslims in the EU: Cities Report, the Netherlands* (Open Society Institute, EU Monitoring and Advocacy Program, 2007), 20; and Theo van Miltenburg and Frank Blom, "Most Children Go to Special Schools," Web Magazine of Statistics Netherlands (September 27, 2004). Available at www.cbs.nl/en-GB/menu/themas/onderwijs/publicaties/artikelen/archief.

55. L. S. J. M. Henkens, "The Development of the Dutch Education System," in Tymen J. van der Ploeg and John W. Sap, eds., *Rethinking the Balance: Government and Non-Governmental Organizations in the Netherlands* (Amsterdam: VU University Press, 1995), 52. Sophie van Bijsterveld has more recently reiterated these three freedoms. See Bijsterveld, "The Permissible Scope of Legal Limitations on the Freedom of Religion or Belief in the Netherlands," 941.

56. Henkens, "The Development of the Dutch Education System," 55.

57. The person referred to is Abdulqadir Jarmohamed, principal of Het Nieuwe Western School in Rotterdam. See Robert Lavies and Amanda Wetzel, "Islamic Schools in the Netherlands: A Catalyst for Integration into Dutch Society?" in *Reports of the 2002 Fellows in Denmark, Germany and the Netherlands* 4 (September, 2002), 77. Available at www.humanityinaction.org/docs/Lavies__Wetzel,_2002.pdf.

58. Quoted in Lavies and Wetzel, "Islamic Schools in the Netherlands," 78.

59. Ibid., 80.

60. Interview with Dominique Majoor of the General Bureau for Dutch Catholic Education (January 26, 1996).

61. This paragraph is largely based on an interview with Chris Janse, a teacher from the *Gereformeerde Gemeenten* (Reformed Congregations) (September 21, 2006). Included in this 5 percent are some families who, while members of the large, generally theologically liberal Protestant Church in the Netherlands, are themselves Reformed in a traditional, orthodox sense and send their children to schools based on their beliefs.

62. Van Bijsterveld, "Church and State in the Netherlands," 373. Although we cite here the second, 2005 edition of this work, the same quotation can be found in the first edition, published in 1996.

63. Interview with Sophie C. van Bijsterveld (February 9,1996).

64. Bartho M. Janssen, "The Position of Umbrella Organizations, Advocacy and Commitment to the Central Policy," in Van der Ploeg and Sap, eds., *Rethinking the Balance*, 68.

65. Interview with Chris Janse (September 21, 2006).

66. Van Bijsterveld, "State and Church in the Netherlands in 2002," 91.

67. Interview with Kees Klop, Ministry of Justice, Strategy Development Department (September 19, 2006).

68. Interview with Veit Bader, University of Amsterdam (September 22, 2006).

69. Interview with Chris Janse (September 21, 2006).

70. M. L. Kreuzen, "Freedom Within Bounds—or the Regulated Autonomy," in Van der Ploeg and Sap, eds., *Rethinking the Balance*, 73.

71. Interview with Sophie C. van Bijsterveld (September 25, 2006).

72. Van Bijsterveld, "State and Church in the Netherlands," 379.

73. Based on 2006 student numbers given at http://en.wikipedia.org/wiki.Dutch universities.

74. Herman Aquina, "PGOs in the Netherlands," in Christopher Hood and Gunnar F. Schuppert, eds., *Delivering Public Services in Western Europe* (London: Sage, 1988), 94.

75. Lester M. Salamon, S. Wojciech Sokolowski, and Regina List, *Global Civil Society: An Overview* (Baltimore, Md.: Johns Hopkins University Institute for Policy Studies, 2003), 32.

76. Lester M. Salamon, S. Wojciech Sokolowski, et al., *Global Civil Society: Dimensions of the Nonprofit Sector*, vol. 2 (Bloomfield, Conn.: Kumarian Press, 2004), 301.

77. Vic Veldheer and Ary Burger, "History of the Nonprofit Sector in the Netherlands," *Working Paper of the Johns Hopkins Comparative Nonprofit Sector Project*, no. 35, Lester M. Salamon and Helmut K. Anheier, eds. (Baltimore, Md.: Johns Hopkins Institute for Policy Studies, 1999), 23.

78. Ibid., 26.

79. Marten J. Hoekstra, "The Division of Roles Between Government and Non-Governmental Organizations in Making Youth Drug Policy," in Van der Ploeg and Sap, eds., *Rethinking the Balance*, 98.

80. Veldheer and Burger, "History of the Nonprofit Sector in the Netherlands," 24. Also see Ralph M. Kramer, "Governmental-Voluntary Agency Relationships in the Netherlands," *Netherlands' Journal of Sociology* 25 (1979), 155.

81. Tymen J. van der Ploeg, "Changing Relationships between Private Organizations and Government in the Netherlands," in Kathleen D. McCarthy, Virginia A. Hodgkinson, and Russy D. Sumariwalla, eds., *The Nonprofit Sector in the Global Community* (San Francisco: Jossey-Bass, 1992), 194.

82. Interview with Stavros Zouridis, Ministry of Justice, Strategy Development Department (September 19, 2006).

83. Jaap E. Doek, "Relations in Child Protection: An Overview," in Van der Ploeg and Sap, eds., *Rethinking the Balance*, 86.

84. Interview with Stavros Zouridis (September 19, 2006). This control over the nonprofit service organizations by the government appears to be of recent origin. As recently as 1981 Ralph Kramer wrote: "Despite the belief that he who pays the piper usually calls the tune, CRM [the Ministry of Culture, Recreation, and Social Welfare] evidently exerts relatively little central control over the PIs [voluntary agencies]." Ralph M. Kramer, *Voluntary Agencies in the Welfare State* (Berkeley: University of California Press, 1981), 32.

85. Interview with Chris Janse (September 21, 2006).

86. Interview with Rabbi Raphael Evers (February 29, 1996).

87. Demant, Maussen, and Rath, *Muslims in the EU*, 35.

88. E-mail from Marianne Vorthoren to Marcel Maussen (May 30, 2007). Translated by Irene Konyndyk.

89. Interview with Frans Koopmans of De Hoop (February 5, 1996).

90. Interview with Frans Koopmans (February 5, 1996).

91. Interview with Martin J. de Jong (January 30, 1996).

92. Interview with Maria Martens of VKMO (February 5, 1996).

93. Interview with Sophie C. van Bijsterveld (February 9, 1996).

94. Interview with Frans Koopmans (February 5, 1996).

95. For example, George Harinck of the Free University of Amsterdam told us of a Protestant agency working with the blind that has requested one of his graduate students or him to do a study of the agency and its Protestant roots and rationale and their relevance for today. It hopes that with a more clearly articulated, religiously based vision it will be in a better position to resist governmental pressures. Interview with George Harinck (September 20, 2006).

96. Interview with Sophie C. van Bijsterveld (February 9, 1996).

97. Interview with Veit Bader (September 22, 2006).

98. Interview with Bob Goudzwaard of the Free University (February 7, 1996). Professor Goudzwaard is now retired.

99. Interview with Sophie C. van Bijsterveld (February 9, 1996).

∼

CHAPTER FOUR

Australia: Pragmatic Pluralism

The most important principles in church-state relations in Australia are pragmatism and tolerance. Pragmatic considerations have structured the state's resolution of church-state issues at every point in Australian history, and because the "practical" solution to church-state problems has changed over time, Australia has vacillated among four different church-state models in its two-hundred-year history: establishment, plural establishment, liberal separationism, and pragmatic pluralism. As with the Netherlands, Australian policy is consistent with governmental neutrality and religious pluralism, but it is rooted in pragmatic concerns, not in basic, theoretical principles as in the Netherlands. At the same time, there has been very little support in Australia for an American-style separationist model that would challenge public finance of religious schools and religious service organizations. Underlying this policy pragmatism is a socially tolerant political culture—a live-and-let-live attitude—that has led to a respect for and protection of the rights of religious minorities.

This chapter opens with a brief description of Australia's religious composition and the nation's political structures. It then considers the history of church-state relations in the Australian colonies, and in the Commonwealth of Australia after the colonies federated in 1901. The chapter follows with a consideration of the Australian approach to religious free exercise and establishment issues. The final section reviews the implications of Australia's pragmatic pluralism for public policy related to church-state issues.

The Nation

Australia has a population of more than twenty million people spread over a continent roughly the size of the United States. Australia has doubled in population over the past fifty years and is currently growing faster than any other country in our study. Because of harsh environmental conditions—much of Australia is virtually uninhabitable—three-quarters of the population live in urban areas, and most of them reside along a thousand-mile stretch of the southeastern seaboard between the cities of Adelaide and Brisbane. Roman Catholics and Anglicans are the two largest religious communities in Australia; according to the 2001 census, there are 5 million Catholics and 3.9 million Anglicans in the country. The next largest Christian groups are the Uniting Church (1.2 million), Presbyterians (638,000), Orthodox Christians (530,000), and Baptists (310,000). There are also 358,000 Buddhists, 282,000 Muslims, 95,000 Hindus, and 84,000 Jews.[1]

Over the past several decades, Australia has become more religiously pluralistic, less Christian, and more secular. The fastest-growing Christian groups have been Pentecostals, who have grown by 28 percent in the last decade and now account for nearly 300,000 members. The non-Christian population has experienced an even more dramatic increase in recent decades, growing from less than 1 percent of the total population in 1971, to 2.6 percent in 1991, and 4.8 percent in 2001. Specifically, from 1996 to 2001 the number of Buddhists in Australia grew from 200,000 to 358,000, while the number of Muslims increased from 200,000 to 282,000. Immigration is the primary reason for the dramatic growth in the Buddhist and Muslim populations. Nearly three-quarters of the Australian Buddhist population is foreign born, while more than 60 percent of Australian Muslims were born outside of the country.[2] There has also been a secularization trend in Australia. Between 1991 and 2001 those stating no religion in the census more than doubled, growing from 6.7 to 15.5 percent. Monthly church attendance has also dropped, falling from 36 percent in 1950, to 24 percent in 1989, and to less than 20 percent by 2001. The decline in church attendance has been particularly strong in the historically dominant Anglican, Presbyterian, Catholic, and Uniting churches, and less pronounced in evangelical congregations, Pentecostal churches, and among non-Christian groups. In comparative terms, the rate of monthly church attendance in Australia is roughly twice that of the European countries in our survey and half the rate in the United States.[3]

In terms of its political structures, Australia combines England's parliamentary form of government with America's institutional federalism.[4] The titular head of state of Australia is the British monarch, represented by a governor-general, who has very little real power. The prime minister is responsible to the House of Representatives and has effective executive power. The 150-member House of Representatives parallels the British House of Commons and is the Australian Parliament's more important chamber. There is also a seventy-six-member Senate. There are two major and several minor political parties in Australia. The largest parties are the center-right Liberal Party and the center-left Australian Labor Party (ALP). The National Party, which represents rural interests, is a coalition partner with the Liberal Party and, with ten House and two Senate seats, is Australia's most significant third party. John Howard led the Liberal Party government from 1996 to 2007. His cultivation of conservative Christians has led at least one analyst to draw a comparison between the American religious right's political activism and its supposed Australian counterpart.[5] There are Christian conservatives in Australia; they have mobilized on such issues as abortion, gay rights, and family values, and they are most likely to vote for Liberal Party candidates, but they are hardly comparable to the American religious right in terms of numbers or political significance. The Australian Labor Party, led by Kevin Rudd, defeated the Liberal Party and John Howard in the 2007 parliamentary elections.

As with most federal polities, Australia's federalism is a complex and dynamic relationship among the federal and six state governments and two self-governing territories. At the time of federation, the federal government's power was limited to its enumerated constitutional powers in interstate commerce, defense, foreign affairs, mass media, and immigration. States enjoyed "residual powers," which meant they could legislate in areas not specifically assigned to the federal government.[6] The balance of power, however, has shifted dramatically in the past fifty years toward the federal government. This is particularly clear in the Commonwealth's financial authority. The national government has sole access to personal and corporate income taxes, sales tax, and excise duties. State and local governments, however, continue to have jurisdiction over important policy areas such as education, health, welfare, criminal law, urban affairs, and the administration of justice.[7] What this has meant is that the Commonwealth government increasingly finances programs administered at the state and local levels. The Commonwealth spends roughly one-third of its total budget on outlays to state and local governments.[8] Australia's religious composition and political structures have had an important impact on the resolution of church-state practices. In order to appreciate how these factors have helped shape church-state policy, we turn now to an analysis of Australia's political history that has provided the framework for its model of pragmatic pluralism.

The Historical Background

Religion did not give birth to the first Australian settlements as it did in America, and church-state issues assumed a very different form in the emerging Australian state. The original purpose of the British settlement in New South Wales in 1788 was to imprison criminals from English cities. The British needed to find an alternative location for their prisoners after the American Revolution stopped them from being shipped to Georgia; convicted criminals made up half of the fifteen hundred people in the first fleet of ships to settle Australia. The church in Australia originated as a part of the British penal system. British authorities sent The Reverend Richard Johnson as the colony's first chaplain; he was joined shortly thereafter by Samuel Marsden, "the flogging pastor," so named because of his use of severe disciplinary measures on a population he believed to be morally and spiritually corrupt. As with many other early religious leaders, Marsden served both as chaplain and as a magistrate and superintendent of public affairs. Colonial elites assumed there would be an established Church of England in the Australian colonies, as there was in England, and for the first several decades the Anglican Church alone received state aid for education, clergy, and church buildings. The primary goal for colonial authorities, however, was control of the convict population, not religious conversion or liberty.[9]

While the institutions were closely united, an activist and powerful state dominated the church and other institutions of civil society. The Anglican Church was at the mercy of colonial authorities for financial aid and there were persistent disputes between chaplains and governors about the appropriate levels of state support. The state provided aid, but on utilitarian and pragmatic grounds. There was little or no religious motivation to the state's action; religion served the state's secular interests by providing moral order and social control among a penal population considered dangerous and morally corrupt. In return, colonial authorities expected the church to help foster political legitimacy in the new state.[10] Some Anglicans challenged the relationship on the grounds that it compromised the church's evangelistic message and independence, but Anglican clergy generally accepted their role as magistrates, moral policemen, and chaplains to the convict and settler population. Given the traditional dependence of the Church of England on the British crown, this is not surprising. The church had grown accustomed to looking to the state for support and providing political legitimacy in return. As one analyst has noted, "the Anglican church existed before 1820 as the arm of the government, which provided financial backing and practical support."[11]

The degree of state regulation of religion varied among the Australian colonies. In the earliest days of colonial settlement in New South Wales, the state appointed Anglican clergymen and did not allow clergy from other faiths to minister to the convict population. Despite the fact that Irish Roman Catholics made up fully one-third of the convict population by the early 1800s, for example, prison authorities initially barred Catholic priests from celebrating the mass and required attendance at Anglican chapel services. Not surprisingly, the convict population largely rejected the established Church of England, although the church had greater success attracting the growing number of free and freed colonists.[12] For the most part, however, the colonies did not regulate religious practices or place severe social and political disabilities on those who practiced other faiths. As a result, a more liberal policy of religious free exercise rights gradually developed in each of the colonies. The absence of a state-imposed religious monopoly allowed Australia to become a religiously diverse mix of Anglicans, Catholics, Presbyterians, and other religious nonconformists.

This diversity made it increasingly difficult for the colonies to maintain the English church-state model, however, as state support for the Anglican Church aroused hostility from the competing denominations. Because state elites did not have a strong theological attachment to an established church model, they could more easily contemplate a different political arrangement than their English counterparts, and they began to look for a more palatable church-state arrangement. The New South Wales Church Act of 1836 seemed to offer the ideal solution. The act revised the established church model by allocating colonial funds on a more equal basis to the largest denominations in the colony without discrimination. The state provided funds to recruit and deploy clergy, to defray the cost for the building of churches, and later to help finance schools run by the churches. Even the small Jewish community eventually received grants for religious personnel.[13] This plural or multiple establishment was a bold and innovative policy at the time, and the other Australian colonies followed with similar acts within a few decades.[14]

The Church Act was driven more by political pragmatism than by a specific religious or ideological commitment. This outlook led Australian colonial leaders to "invent their own solution to the problems of church-state relations," as Michael Hogan has noted, that borrowed from but also differed from England with its established church and the United States with its principle of church-state separation.[15] Colonial governors turned to religious neutrality to take religion out of the political arena and to enable the churches more effectively to promote a Christian moral order and political legitimacy in the Australian state. Since the initial impetus for Anglican ascendancy in New South Wales had been the promotion of moral order among the convict population, how much more effective could that process be if money flowed to all of the churches? If the "problem" with England's established church model was that it pitted religionists against each other, why not fund all of the churches and thereby depoliticize religious disputes? Contrary to the Dutch experience, however, Australian elites provided little philosophical justification for this kind of state neutrality. It was not a principled commitment to pluralism that drove the policy; few people argued that the Church Act could be defended on the ground that the policy was a nondiscriminatory way to protect and promote Australia's religious diversity. The intent of the policy was to make life easier for colonial authorities who had grown weary of denominational conflict and to empower churches to provide moral guidance to their members.[16]

At the same time, the Church Act established two important precedents that continue to shape public policy in contemporary Australia. First, when the government provides funds to a religious denomination, they are generally available to all denominations on some basis of equality.[17] There was and is a basic commitment to a nondiscrimination principle among the churches when the state provides aid. This will become even more apparent when we look at the current policy on state aid to religious schools and nonprofit organizations. Second, pragmatism has been the norm when political leaders deal with church-state issues. Policy makers viewed religious issues as a problem to be solved in the most expedient manner possible, which in the mid-nineteenth century led them to support what was, for the time, a remarkable policy of plural establishment. The policy exhibited a respect for the rights of religious minorities that was distinctive by the standards of the day. In England, by comparison, the state barred Catholics from admission to universities and had only just granted them political emancipation when New South Wales passed the Church Act.

Despite the intent of the Church Act, it did not dissipate sectarian rivalry among the denominations. Initially, many Anglican Church leaders opposed the system on the ground that aid should only go to the one true Church; most of the other churches, by contrast, contended that the policy advantaged the Church of England because of its size, organization, and the lingering prejudice of the Anglican governing class against Roman Catholics and nonconformists. While the act reduced the disparity in state aid among the denominations, because it was the denomination with the largest number of members, the Anglican Church was the principal beneficiary of the system.[18] Roman Catholics pressed for a reformation of the act, some nonconformists pushed for the voluntary principle of no state aid as a way to escape Anglican domination, and secularists—who were indifferent to Christianity— had gained a foothold in Australia by the end of the nineteenth century. Finally, as the Australian state became more stable, it no longer looked to social institutions like the church for political legitimacy. In the absence of secular justifications for state aid, political leaders had fewer grounds on which to defend the policy. Because there had never been an overriding commitment by the state to promote religious pluralism, governing officials quickly abandoned the act when it proved costly, difficult to administer, and politically contentious. By the turn of the century each of the Australian states adopted a new policy of church-state separation rooted in the principles of Enlightenment liberalism. This meant an end to direct state funding for clergy, church buildings, and church schools.

The major political challenge to the model of plural establishment occurred in the field of education. Religious schools, particularly Anglican schools, had a virtual monopoly on education in the Australian colonies in the early nineteenth century. Colonial governments, under the Church Act, funded denominational schools on a largely equal basis. Religious schools could not keep up with the demand for public education in the mid-nineteenth century, however, and pressure grew in all the Australian colonies for a free, compulsory, and "secular" education system.[19] Until the 1860s, Anglicans and Catholics formed a powerful political coalition that preserved the denominational system from religious dissenters and secular liberals who wanted to make education a state function and believed that religious control of education threatened to undermine the assimilationist purposes of a universal system of education.

Anglican Church leaders were not, however, as committed to the principle that education should be a religious function as were their Catholic counterparts, and their opposition to state control of education gradually dissipated. Many of the church's leaders joined forces with secular rationalists to end state aid to denominational schools. As in the United States, the Protestant objection to public finance of religious schools had much to do with Protestant hostility to Catholicism. Protestants became convinced that state funding of the denominational system advantaged Roman Catholics, and because they strongly opposed Catholicism they united to stop state aid for all religious schools.[20] In addition, Protestants did not generally believe that a secular educational system threatened their religious values because it allowed for instruction and worship of the general principles of Christianity. In contrast to the Netherlands and similar to the United States, there was no Protestant movement in Australia that saw public schools as a threat to their religious values. The New South Wales Public Instruction Act of 1880 typified this "secular" approach to teaching religion: "In all schools under this Act the teaching shall be strictly non-sectarian, but the words 'secular instruction' shall be held to include general religious teaching as distinguished from dogmatical or polemical theology."[21] To make clear that a secular education did not preclude religious instruction, the author of the act, Sir Henry Parker, noted: "it was never the intention of the framers of this Bill to exclude such knowledge of the Bible as all divisions of the Christian Church must possess, or a knowledge of the great truths of Revelation."[22]

Australia's secular educational system shared several of the liberal presuppositions of the American common school movement. First was the belief that a primary function of the public school was to assimilate persons of different religious, class, and ethnic backgrounds by introducing them to the key values of Australian society. In Australia, this primarily meant Roman Catholics, who had "alien" religious views and suspect political sympathies. It is not surprising, for example, that all schoolchildren were required to pledge their loyalty to God as well as to the King or Queen and the British Empire. Patriotism was among the key political virtues that the public schools would inculcate children with, particularly Irish Catholics who had a history of opposition to the British crown and who needed to be socialized with "proper" social and political values.

Second, the Enlightenment liberals leading the public school movement believed that a nonsectarian, moralistic religion had a place in the schools. While reformers viewed the particularistic elements of the various churches as divisive and dangerous, they thought that the core consensual features of the Christian faith could provide the basis for a common morality. They shared Horace Mann's optimism that common religious beliefs were discoverable by human reason. What this ignored was the incommensurability of religious and moral viewpoints and the political power structures that lay behind the rationalization that the established Protestant viewpoint was rational or consensual. Protestant church leaders did not challenge this liberal vision because they saw it as consistent with their understanding of the social role of Christianity. Nor did they appreciate that the rationalistic assumptions of the liberal educational model undermined a distinctively religious point of view in the schools.

The education acts passed by the various states allowed independent religious schools to operate, but they rescinded public finance of them. State officials expected that Catholic schools would collapse without state funding and that the public schools would become a vehicle for Irish Catholic assimilation. This did not happen. The Catholic hierarchy rejected the public schools as dangerously liberal and antireligious, defended their educational principles, and committed additional resources to the preservation of a Catholic school system. Catholic parents similarly viewed the public schools as unsympathetic to their cultural and religious sensibilities. Fueled in part by Protestant antipathy, the Catholic school system incorporated most Catholic children and the religious rivalry between Protestants and Catholics intensified in Australia for the next half-century.

Religion played only a small role as Australia moved toward federation at the end of the century. The six colonies that united to form the Australian Commonwealth in 1901 asked for the "blessings of Almighty God" in the preamble to the new national Constitution, and the drafters self-consciously modeled Section 116 on the First Amendment of the U.S. Constitution. Section 116 states:

> The Commonwealth shall not make any law for establishing any religion, or for imposing any religious observance, or for prohibiting the free exercise of any religion, and no religious test shall be required as a qualification for any office or public trust under the Constitution.

The purpose of Section 116 was to depoliticize religion as much as possible in order to keep the Commonwealth out of the religious field. As we have seen, sectarian strife was a political reality in each of the Australian colonies and political leaders did not want religious rivalries spilling over into federation politics. Australia's religious diversity made it difficult to defend an established church. At the time of federation, Anglicans represented a plurality of the nation's population at 40 percent, but Catholics were 23 percent, and Methodists and Presbyterians each had 12 percent.[23]

In addition, there were no practical reasons for the drafters of the new constitution to press for an established Anglican Church in the Australian Commonwealth. The Anglican Church lacked the political power to force this model on recalcitrant policy makers and, just as significantly, the state's interest in religion had always been pragmatic. Political elites in Australia did not assume, as they likely would have in England at the time, that the state had a positive obligation to defend an established church. Without this philosophical commitment to an establishment model, political leaders did all that they could to maximize support for the federation. This meant giving individual states effective power over religious matters. While the Constitution forbade the Commonwealth from formally establishing a church or restricting religious free exercise rights, states could do both. The importance of state governments in the resolution of church-state issues became particularly apparent in subsequent rulings of the Australian High Court dealing with free exercise rights.

The Free Exercise of Religion

As with the other countries in our study, Australia struggles with the question of how far to go to permit religious beliefs and practices that conflict with social welfare and societal norms. In balancing individual rights and state power, however, Australia has more closely followed the English model that trusts the democratic political process rather than the American system where the courts define and apply rights against state and federal actions. There are two important reasons for this. First, the Australian Constitution lacks a comprehensive bill of rights. As a consequence, the High Court has had few opportunities to play an aggressive role in defining and protecting rights. One of the few expressed constitutional rights is that of freedom of religion, found in Section 116, which was explicitly modeled on the First Amendment to the American Constitution. Even here, however, the Court has played a limited role. In two key free exercise clause cases, the Court has established the precedent that the Constitution provides very little protection for the religious beliefs and practices of Australian citizens. The Court has interpreted Section 116 narrowly, which has meant that religious liberty rights are at the mercy of the political process.[24]

A second reason for the Court's limited role in rights protection is that there is no Australian equivalent to the due process clause of the U.S. Constitution's Fourteenth Amendment and its provision that "no state shall make or enforce any law which shall abridge the privileges or immunities of the citizens of the United States." Absent such language, the Australian Supreme Court has been unable to incorporate the religious provisions of Section 116 of the Constitution and apply them to the states. In theory, state and territory governments could establish a state church or religion, oppress religious beliefs, or require a religious test as a qualification for public office. A proposal to amend Section 116 to include coverage to the states failed in referendums in 1944 and 1988.[25]

The first major Australian case that tested free exercise rights was *Adelaide Company of Jehovah's Witnesses Inc. v. Commonwealth* (1943). This case involved opposition by the Jehovah's Witnesses to Australian involvement in World War II. A number of Australian churches opposed the war on religious grounds, including the Quakers, but they were able to convince the government that they did not pose a security risk to the state. The Jehovah's Witnesses were not so fortunate and the Commonwealth government seized church property and declared the Adelaide branch of the church a proscribed organization. Since the proscription came from the Australian Commonwealth, rather than a state government, the church appealed on the ground that the law violated their free exercise rights guaranteed in Section 116 of the federal constitution.

In his decision, Chief Justice John Latham recognized that the purpose of Section 116 was to "protect the religion (or absence of religion) of minorities, and, in particular, of unpopular minorities." Nevertheless, he ruled that the state may infringe upon religious liberty when it is necessary to protect civil government or the continued existence of the community: "Section 116 of the Constitution does not prevent the Commonwealth from making laws prohibiting the advocacy of doctrines which, though advocated in pursuance of religious convictions, are prejudicial to the prosecution of a war in which the Commonwealth is engaged."[26]

Latham emphasized an important point in his decision: it is appropriate for the state to restrict religious freedom when the exercise of that right has the effect of endangering the entire political community. Australia faced the very real danger of being invaded by Japan, which had earlier bombed the city of Darwin, during World War II. The state had legitimate concerns about the prosecution of the war, and understandable reasons to worry about groups that actively opposed the Australian state. The problem with the decision, however, is that Latham did not examine in any detail the words and actions of the Witnesses to determine if they posed a genuine threat to the government or the community. Instead, he inferred that the church's teaching that the Commonwealth was an organ of Satan was necessarily prejudicial to the defense of the Commonwealth and that the government could legitimately proscribe the organization. The Court did not use the decision, therefore, to articulate a standard by which to judge when it was appropriate for the state to limit free exercise rights. In failing to do that, the Court effectively sent the message that it would not be a strong advocate for religious freedom. The contrast with the Netherlands is again instructive. Article 6 of the Dutch Constitution specifically articulates the conditions under which the state can limit religious liberty.

A second significant Australian free exercise case, *Grace Bible Church Inc. v. Reedman* (1984), demonstrated again the limited nature of free exercise protections under the Australian Constitution. The case involved the conviction of Grace Bible Church for running an unregistered private school contrary to South Australia's Education Act between 1972 and 1981. Under that act, the state could fine the governing authority of an unregistered school that enrolled students for instruction. The church claimed that registration would place the church school under the state's authority, which violated their religious belief that God controlled the school. South Australian authorities convicted Grace Bible Church and fined the school's governing authority $365.

The school appealed the conviction to the High Court and argued that South Australia's Education Act interfered with the freedom of religious worship and expression that is an inalienable right under the Australian Constitution. The Court rejected this argument with the terse statement that the rights guaranteed in Section 116 "cannot be of any relevance because it only imposes a prohibition upon the law-making powers of the Commonwealth Parliament."[27] The Court refused to interpret Section 116 as a restriction of a state's power in the field of religion. The issue of whether a state's action limits a person's free exercise right was moot, therefore, because the Court did not have the power to overturn such a state law. The Court further contended, following its decision in *Adelaide*, that there is no inalienable right of religious freedom under the Australian Constitution or common law, and that even if there were such a right, it could still be "invaded by an Act of the Parliament of this State."[28]

The Court sympathized with the plight of the school and recognized that the registration of a private school is dependent upon the satisfaction of the education board, which gives state officials wide discretion to determine the appropriate place for religious instruction. The Court concluded, however, that the political process is the only avenue for groups dissatisfied with a state's law: "the remedy for this state of affairs, if a remedy is required, is a political one and not a legal one."[29] Interestingly, the Court did not discuss if South Australia's law placed a burden on religion and, if it did, whether the state's interest in the law could justify such a restriction. The High Court simply asserted that it was bound by the rule of law and the Constitution, which, when narrowly read, does not give it the power to overturn acts of state parliaments in the field of religious free exercise.

A pair of 1992 cases, *Nationwide News v. Wills*[30] and *Australian Capital Television v. Australia*,[31] suggested that the Court might play a more active role in defining and protecting civil liberties. In those cases, the Court found that a right to freedom of political speech was implied by sections of the Constitution dealing with representative and responsible government.[32] Writing for the Court in *Australian Capital Television v. Australia*, Chief Justice Anthony Mason asserted that the freedom of communication, though not stated in the Constitution, is "so indispensable to the efficacy of the system of representative government for which the Constitution makes provision that it is necessarily implied in the making of that provision."[33] One possible implication of the decision was that the Constitution gave the Commonwealth—and the High Court—an implied power to safeguard the rights and freedoms associated with a liberal polity. Had the Court continued in this direction it might have led to the judicially enforced protection of religious rights. However, these cases proved to be the Court's high water mark for judicially enforced rights protection; the Court has since returned to its more traditionally conservative and cautious role in rights protection.

The High Court's decision in *Grace Bible Church* established the precedent that there are no constitutional grounds for the protection of religious liberties against the actions of state governments. In *Adelaide*, the Court failed to establish a clear standard by which to judge limits on religious rights and sent the message that it would not be an institutional advocate for religious freedom. The Court's approach to free exercise issues reflects the policy pragmatism that has marked the resolution of church-state issues throughout Australian history. The state has sought workable solutions to religious disputes, which in most cases has meant giving to colonies, or now individual states, the power to determine for themselves what is the best church-state policy.

The defense of religious rights in Australia comes from each of the state constitutions, Commonwealth and state legislation, and to a lesser extent the Human Rights and Equal Opportunity Commission, an independent statutory agency that reports to the Commonwealth government. Several states have made discrimination on the basis of religion unlawful and have established antidiscrimination boards to deal with individual cases of religious discrimination. By comparison, Australia's most populous state, New South Wales, prohibits discrimination on many grounds but not on the ground of religion. The federal government's Racial Discrimination Act provides limited protection for discrimination on the basis of religion, but only if a religious group can be also be classified as an "ethnic" group. There is no national legislation that specifically bars discrimination on the basis of religion. Tasmania is the only state that has a religious free exercise provision in its constitution, but this provides little protection because it can be overridden by an act of Tasmania's parliament.[34]

A recent report by the Human Rights and Equal Opportunity Commission on religious freedom concluded that current law does not adequately protect religious rights; new religious movements, indigenous beliefs, and minority faiths are the most susceptible to discriminatory treatment.[35] Borrowing language from the *International Covenant on Civil and Political Rights*, the Commission recommended that the Commonwealth Parliament should enact a Religious Freedom Act that would protect persons against religious discrimination and provide for the "freedom to hold a particular religion or belief" and to "manifest religion or belief in worship, observance, practice and teaching."[36] The recommendations were never implemented by the federal government.

Australia has made progress in the area of religious rights. A growing number of private businesses and government agencies make provisions for religious free exercise in such areas as dress codes, dietary restrictions, and recognition of religious holidays. Public opinion and cultural values have been the most significant determinants of this change. As Gary Bouma writes, Australia has developed "a notion of fair play, (the) equal worth of human dignity and live and let live."[37] The introduction to the Commission's report on religious freedom similarly noted that "we Australians pride ourselves on tolerance and easy-going acceptance of other cultures and beliefs."[38] These social values have contributed to an atmosphere that supports religious free exercise rights and has generally allowed new religious groups to negotiate their way into Australian society. The best example of this is Australia's current education policy that, as we shall detail below, provides public finance for schools from virtually every major and minor religious group in Australia.

While public opinion and cultural values can be a nebulous way to protect religious freedom, it is nevertheless significant that Australia has had less conflict around the rights of Muslims than have the European countries in our study. There was an increase in the number of reported incidences of discrimination and abuse directed toward Muslims after the September 2001 terrorist attacks on the United States and the Bali bombings in October 2002 that killed eighty-eight Australian tourists.[39] Ikebal Patel, president of the Australian Federation of Islamic Councils, the national umbrella organization representing Australian Muslims, commented to us that there is some Islamophobia in Australian society and it is particularly pronounced "around election times because some politicians believe it helps to win races."[40] However, Australia seems fully committed to a process of negotiation and compromise with Muslims and other religious minorities. Patel himself noted that state and federal government officials are "by and large very fair and equitable in their treatment of Muslims."[41] This compares quite favorably to Germany, where Muslims have failed to win evenhanded treatment from the state, and even England, which has struggled with how best to accommodate Muslims into its religious establishment model.

This openness has been evident since liberalization of the government's immigration policy in the past several decades. An open preference for white, western immigrants characterized Australia's immigration policy for much of the past century. From 1900 until 1945 the so-called White Australia Policy used racial characteristics to exclude nonwhites and thus most non-Christians from entering Australia. From 1947 to 1972, the state used public moneys to induce immigration among preferred migrant groups, which were the British and northern and southern Europeans. In 1957, for example, the state launched a "Bring out a Briton" campaign and worked closely with churches to implement the policy.[42] The purpose of the policy was to facilitate the migration of whites and of Roman Catholics and Protestants, groups that fit comfortably into the established cultural and religious molds. The few non-Christian Australians were expected to assimilate to those values. As late as 1947, the three largest denominations, Anglican, Roman Catholic, and Uniting Church, represented over 80 percent of Australia's total population.

The dissolution of the White Australia Policy in the early 1970s led to a dramatic increase in Australia's racial and religious diversity. By 2001, Anglicans, Catholics, and Uniting Church members represented just over half (57 percent) of the country's population. As we noted above, over the past fifty years there has been a rapid increase in the numbers of new Christian groups (Pentecostal, Orthodox Christians), non-Christian religious groups (Buddhist, Hindu, Muslim), and those with no religion. The immigration of new religious groups has helped to make Australia among the most ethnically diverse countries in the world. For the most part, Australia has not responded defensively to the immigration of non-Christian groups, as has occurred in other countries, but appears committed to a process of negotiation with them to minimize areas of religious conflict. For many years, the government has been committed to accommodating religious differences by adopting a policy of multiculturalism in the schools.[43]

The current status of religious rights in Australia is not ideal; there is no enshrined, constitutional protection of religious liberty and no Commonwealth law that specifically bars religious discrimination. The state has, nonetheless, made strides toward the pluralistic goal of equal treatment of all religious groups. As we will see in the next section, there is an equal commitment to this pluralistic model in religious establishment issues, particularly in public finance to religious schools and nonprofit organizations.

Church, State, and Education

The Australian educational system mixes features of the American and English systems. As in the United States, individual states and territories have the primary responsibility for funding government schools in Australia. Unlike the United States, however, the federal government has become the primary source of funding for private schools. Like England, as we will see in the next chapter, religious schools receive considerable funding from the state, but in contrast with England those schools are considered non-government schools that are not part of the state sector. Australia's history and politics help to explain its unique educational policy.

Catholics retained their independent school system at the end of the nineteenth century despite the fact that the state rescinded state aid to denominational schools. A smaller number of high-fee independent schools more loosely associated with Protestant denominations also continued to exist. With limited financial resources and rising school costs, however, Catholic schools increasingly found it difficult to compete with government schools. By the late 1950s the disparity between state-run and Catholic schools became apparent and the church concluded that the Catholic school system would cease to exist without state support. The bishops committed themselves to preserving Catholic schools and they intensified their political pressure for state aid.

The federal election of 1963 brought the issue of state aid back onto the political agenda for the first time since the previous century. The push for state aid coincided with a growing split between the Catholic right and the secular left within the Labor Party. Working-class Catholics, who traditionally voted Labor, pressed the party to abandon its longstanding opposition to state aid for religious schools. Hoping to capitalize on Catholic disaffection with the Labor Party, Liberal Prime Minister Robert Menzies committed his party to a policy that would have provided Commonwealth grants to public and private schools for the purpose of science education. Protestants had originally joined forces with secular liberals to oppose public finance of religious schools because of their hostility to Roman Catholics. By the early 1960s, however, Protestant opposition to Catholics had waned considerably, making it easier for the largely Protestant Liberal Party to support state aid to private religious schools. Support grew among Protestants for the right of parents to exercise a choice in schooling and for the government to fund students exercising that right. In response, Gough Whitlam, the Labor Party candidate for prime minister, successfully pressed his party to abandon its opposition to school funding.[44] Menzies's initiative was the first formal entry of the Commonwealth government into direct school funding, but it proved to be the tip of the iceberg. Both the Liberal and Labor parties had a political imperative to press for state aid, and in the 1972 federal election both parties pledged major increases in grants to all private schools in need of support. The Labor Party, led by Whitlam, won the election and created the Schools Commission to formalize Commonwealth educational policy. Under the policy instituted by the Commission in 1974 the Commonwealth provided direct grants to nongovernment schools.

Opponents of state aid challenged the policy on the grounds that the payment of government grants to denominational schools violated Section 116 of the Australian Constitution, which does not allow the Commonwealth to make any law "for establishing any religion." The vast majority of private schools had some religious affiliation, and opponents contended that aid to religious schools constituted a de facto establishment of religion. In *Attorney General for the State of Victoria v. The Commonwealth of Australia* (1981), the High Court affirmed the validity of the legislative action. Relying upon what he called the "plain" or "usual" meaning of the words "for establishing any religion" in Section 116, Justice Garfield Barwick, writing for the majority, argued that establishing a religion involves "the identification of the religion with the civil authority so as to involve the citizens in a duty to maintain it and the obligation of, in this case, the Commonwealth to patronize, protect and promote the established religion."[45] According to this reading of Section 116, Barwick could not rationally see how "the law for providing the funds for the forwarding of the education of Australians by non-government schools is a law for establishing Christian religion."[46] In a concurring opinion, Justice Harry Gibbs put the point even more strongly: "I consider the words in Section 116 to mean that the Commonwealth Parliament shall not make any law for conferring on a particular religion or religious body the position of a state (or national) religion or church."[47] The Court rejected the plaintiffs' attempts to use the U.S. Supreme Court's rendering of the First Amendment no establishment clause cases as a guide for this decision. Barwick contended that the American cases that barred aid to religious schools were irrelevant because of the "radically different language in our Constitution."[48] Barwick asserted that the wording of the Australian Constitution, "for establishing any religion" was narrower in meaning from the "respecting an establishment of religion" phrase of the American First Amendment. The Australian Constitution, Barwick argued, prohibits only those parliamentary laws that formally establish *a* religion (our emphasis), it does not involve "the prohibition of any law which may assist the practice of religion."[49] The decision removed the last serious obstacle to state aid for religious schools, but left unanswered the question of whether aid had to be nonpreferential, i.e., available to any religious groups that wanted to form a school, or if public money could go only to existing church schools.

For the most part, state and federal administrators have consistently pursued a neutral policy in which aid is available equally to religious and nonreligious schools alike. This is a stark contrast with England where, as we will see in the following chapter, funding for Islamic schools took decades to achieve. According to Aurora Andrushka, of the Department of Education, Employment, and Youth Affairs, "in terms of funding, we take a no favoritism approach; we look at a school regardless of its religious affiliation, its curriculum, or its philosophy."[50] In recent years, government policy has actually eased the process for approving new schools as the Howard government dropped requirements that made federal funding contingent on standards such as minimum enrollments. As a result, the number of religious schools has escalated.

There are two main categories of private schools in Australia: Catholic schools and independent schools (the vast majority of which are also religious). Both are eligible for Commonwealth funding under two main programs: The Capital Grants Programme and the General Recurrent Grants Programme. The former provides schools with money to help with infrastructure costs and for programs that serve the most educationally disadvantaged students. Of the $346 million spent by the Australian government under the Capital Grants Programme in 2004, 35 percent went to private schools. In 2004, for example, the Saint Francis of Assisi Primary School (Catholic) in Glendenning, New South Wales, received a capital grant of $207,514 for the construction of six general-purpose learning areas and student amenities; the Ipswich Adventist School (Seventh-day Adventist) in Brassall, Queensland, obtained $118,900 for building two general learning areas; and the Minaret College (Muslim) of Springvale, Victoria, acquired $600,000 for building an administration area and a car park, to name a few of the recipients.[51]

General recurrent funding is provided by the government on a per student basis and is the largest source of Commonwealth funding for private schools. In 2004, the federal government distributed more than $4.1 billion to private schools as per capita grants. Under the program, the government uses a needs-based model to determine the socioeconomic status of the school's community. The poorest schools receive the largest grants, but even the wealthiest independent schools receive some state aid. In 2004, the per student grants to private schools ranged from $902 to $4,606 for primary schools (751 to 3,835 US$) and from $1,178 to $6,017 for secondary schools (981 to 5,010 US$).[52] Catholic schools typically receive close to the maximum allowable. As a proportion of total resources, state and Commonwealth funding represents a significant source of revenue for most private schools, although it varies between the Catholic and independent school sectors. Commonwealth and state funding accounted for roughly two-thirds of the recurrent education costs in Catholic schools and one-third of the total cost in independent schools.[53] The primary reason for the difference is the fee structure in the two types of schools; the average annual fee for a Catholic school in 2002 was $2,500 (2,080 US$), compared to $6,000 (4,992 US$) for independent schools. The most elite private schools in Australia charge considerably more. While government aid to private schools is substantial, students attending government schools receive more funding when both Commonwealth and state funding is taken into account.[54]

State aid to private schools has had a profound impact on education in Australia. Enrollment in those schools had been gradually falling throughout the 1960s, reaching an historic low of 22 percent of all students in 1971, but with government funding the percentage of students in private schools rose to 28 percent in 1990, 30 percent in 2000, and 33 percent in 2005. In the decade from 1995 to 2005, the total number of students attending a private school increased by more than 22 percent.[55] In 2005, government funds went to a plethora of religious schools, including Roman Catholic (1,698 schools), Anglican (150), nondenominational Christian (175), Lutheran (82), Seventh-day Adventist (56), Baptist (42), Islamic (29), Jewish (19), Pentecostal (18), Assemblies of God (15), Greek Orthodox (8), Ananda Marga (3), and Hare Krishna (1), to name some. In addition, the state provides aid to nonreligious private schools such as Rudolph Steiner (45) and Montessori (35).[56]

The original purpose of state aid was to save the Catholic school system; an unintended consequence of the policy has been the proliferation of non-Catholic, but religiously based, private schools. In 1971, Catholic schools enrolled over 80 percent of nongovernment school students; this proportion fell to 68 percent in 1994 and to 61 percent in 2005. The growth in the private school sector has come primarily among evangelical Protestant and Muslim schools. According to one report, a new religious school opens in the state of New South Wales every six weeks, while the demand for Islamic education is so great that each of the thirteen Muslim schools in Sydney has plans to expand its campus.[57]

There are various reasons why state aid has fueled the rise of private schools. For one, such schools are now more affordable; lowering their cost has made them more attractive to middle-income parents. At the same time, however, the popularity of independent schools reflects a growing parental preference for an education infused with religious values. A 1993 survey conducted by the Immigration Bureau of the Jewish community in Australia noted that the more than 8,800 children attending Jewish day schools in Melbourne represented over 70 percent of the school-age population in the Jewish community. The report concluded: "There is a growing and widely shared belief that young people are more likely to develop a solid and lasting sense of Jewish ethnic identity if they spend at least some of their school years in a pedagogical and social environment that is strongly supportive of Jewish ideas and values."[58] The same parental interest in a religiously grounded education explains the dramatic increase in the number of Muslims attending Islamic schools, from 2,500 students in such schools in 1994 to 14,415 in 2005.[59] The website for the Al-Hidavah Islamic School in Perth describes its mission in this way: "Our aim is to provide education in religious studies and government curriculum to the highest possible standards in an Islamic environment suitable for any child."[60] At present, an estimated 10 percent of Muslims send their children to Islamic schools, but the demand for such schools is much, much higher.[61]

There have been some questions raised in Parliament about the curriculum in independent schools, particularly Islamic ones. Shortly after the London train bombings in 2005, Prime Minister Howard held a counterterrorism summit to discuss a coordinated Australian effort against terrorist attacks; one of the summit's recommendations was that Islamic schools should be encouraged to denounce terrorism and teach about Australian values and culture. Howard's education minister, Brendan Nelson, suggested that those Islamic schools that failed to do so should "clear off."[62] Muslim leaders countered that Islamic schools *are* teaching Australian values, and they also pointed out that a more serious concern might be that there was not a single Muslim parliamentarian in the Australian federal government, and only a handful at the state level. On the other hand, Ikebal Patel, president of the Australian Federation of Islamic Councils, acknowledged to us that government licensing for Islamic schools has been completely evenhanded: "Our new schools are approved exactly like any other new religious school. If they meet the criterion, it is not a problem [to get it approved]."[63]

What is even more instructive, however, is the degree to which other school organizations and leaders have come to the defense of their Muslim colleagues. The executive officers of the National Catholic Education Commission (NCEC) and the Australian Association of Christian Schools indicated to us, for example, that they have supported expanding government funding to Muslim schools. As Bob Johnson, executive director for the Australian Association of Christian Schools, pointed out to us: "an even playing field [in education] means that what is allowed for one religious group must be allowed for others."[64] The formation of dozens of independent school organizations, both denominational and peak bodies, has eased the application process for new schools and provided valuable political support for the sector as a whole. Organizations give advice to prospective new school applicants and represent their political interests before the various government agencies. Because state aid had foundered on the sectarian divide in the past, the major churches joined forces in the 1960s to present a united front for state aid and these school organizations advocate for government funding for all eligible schools. There are some groups in Australia that are implacably opposed to the current system of aid to private religious schools, but as Johnson pointed out to us, "when 33 percent of the student population is in nongovernment schools, and when 90 percent of those students are in religious schools, there is a critical mass that will protect the current policy."[65]

Catholic and independent schools have similarly joined forces to preserve the right of religious schools to hire persons who share the institution's values. Potential challenges to this practice have come from the Sex Discrimination Act in 1984, which prohibited discrimination in hiring on the grounds of sex, marital status, or pregnancy, and various state laws that ban discrimination against persons in a same-sex relationship. In its formal response to the Human Rights and Equal Opportunities Commission inquiry on discrimination against persons in same-sex relationships, the Association of Independent Schools (AISSA) presented its position in this way: "The AISSA calls on the Human Rights and Equal Opportunities Commission to recognize the importance of religion and religious beliefs and to recommend that exemptions which protect the right of faith based schools to operate in accordance with the religious tenets and beliefs upon which they have been founded remain protected."[66] In general, private schools are exempt from antidiscrimination legislation if they can demonstrate that the proposed policy violates a religious principle, and no Catholic school has lost a case brought against it on antidiscrimination grounds.[67]

Schools are also free to develop their own philosophies and curricula. Schools that are members of Christian Schools Australia, for example, are committed to seeing "Christian beliefs and values impact on all aspects of practice and community life in member schools,"[68] while the curriculum in Roman Catholic schools "must give a central place to education in faith and acknowledge the relevance to all areas of teaching of a Christian view of life as interpreted in the Catholic tradition."[69] Consistent with these practices is the right of schools to give preference in faculty hiring and student admission to people who share the school's governing philosophy and who are members of the founding church. Two-thirds of the students in Catholic schools are themselves Roman Catholic, a percentage of coreligionists that would be on par with most religious schools.

In order to receive recurrent grants, private schools have to be licensed with the Department of Education, Science, and Training and by each state's

Department of Education. There are accountability requirements for private schools in such areas as student assessment, providing data on student background, and even a Commonwealth requirement that all schools fly the Australian flag.[70] While there is no national curriculum, there are learning objectives and tests in English, math, science, and Australian history in years three, five, seven, and nine. Some private school advocates have suggested that the tests can function as a de facto national curriculum. Bob Johnson commented to us that the tests have led some state education officials to "become more prescriptive in making schools accountable for the content of their courses."[71] At present, there is a delicate balance between holding private religious schools accountable to national education goals while giving them the autonomy to educate in ways consistent with their worldviews. There are, for example, evangelical schools that teach creation science along with evolutionary biology. The pressure such schools face is not only from "secular" government officials, but from school parents and Christian school educators who want students to do well on examinations at the end of secondary education. Peter Crimmins, director of Policy and Research for Christian Schools Australia, articulated precisely this view: "A Christian educational perspective is essential, but it is very important for our schools to get acceptability. If Christian schools are not aspiring to be as good as the best public schools in the country they are shortchanging the kids and their parents."[72]

In the final analysis, what seems to matter most in regulating private religious schools is performance. There are numerous difficulties in drawing comparisons between private and public schools, but by virtually all measures private schools fare very well. Private school students, in both Catholic and independent schools, have higher retention rates than their counterparts in state-run schools, and a much higher percentage of private school graduates enter universities.[73] Faculty-to-student ratios are actually higher in Catholic schools than in state-run schools, but much lower in other private schools. At the same time, the selectivity of the nongovernment sector and its ability to expel "problem" students likely gives it a competitive advantage over the state-run sector. While most religious schools are committed to educating children regardless of socioeconomic circumstances, government schools still educate more students from lower socioeconomic backgrounds than do private schools.[74]

A common criticism of separate schools, particularly separate Islamic schools, is that they do not adequately assimilate students into the values of the culture at large; the assumption is that those schools often fail to promote the liberal, democratic, pluralistic norms that are essential for living in a multicultural context. When asked about this claim, Patel noted to us a unique advantage of the Australian arrangement: "I would much rather have Islamic schools operating under the auspices of a government that makes them go through a rigorous regulation process, instead of having independent Islamic schools that are under virtually no government control and oversight."[75] Patel's point seems to be that private Islamic schools are going to exist and that it is far better to have them within the state system—where they are accountable for their actions—than out of it—where they are not. Ironically, it might be that private school advocates have more to fear from government finance than do government school supporters. The paradox, as many have noted, is that equalizing school funding and moving toward corporatist political arrangements among the various educational sectors often blurs the differences between private and public schools.[76]

In our view, Australian policy is neutral in that it neither advantages nor disadvantages any particular religion, nor does it advantage or disadvantage religion or secularism generally. State aid to religious schools makes it possible for parents who want a religious education for their children to exercise that option, while parents who want a nonreligious secular education can opt for a state school or a nonreligious private school. Government officials justify the policy in precisely these terms. One educational official noted to us that "These [educational] priorities are aimed at ensuring that all students are allowed to realize their full potential and they include support for the principle of access, choice, equity and excellence in schooling by encouraging the provision of a strong, viable and diverse selection of schools from which parents may choose."[77] Australia also seems to have discovered a healthy balance between allowing religious schools to maintain a clear sense of their mission, on the one hand, with appropriate regulation of their practices, on the other.

Finally, there is the question of the role of religion in state-run schools.[78] Most states provide for nonsectarian secular instruction that includes general religious teaching (GRT). As we noted, liberal reformers opposed "sectarian" religious instruction in public schools, but they believed that secular instruction should include the consensual features of the Christian faith that would provide the basis for a common morality. The state justified religious observances as a method of reinforcing corporate identity and instilling essential social values. When states began to provide public education at the end of the nineteenth century, therefore, the legislation typically allowed for nondogmatic religious instruction. In practice, GRT focused almost exclusively on Christianity, even Protestant Christianity when antipathy to Roman Catholics remained high. GRT has become more generally Christian in recent decades, but questions have been raised about the appropriateness of religious instruction in the schools. The New South Wales State Supreme Court ruled in 1976 that prayers, Bible readings, hymns, and grace before school meals were consistent with the provisions of GRT. The opinion of the court stated that religious instruction, even Christian instruction, was appropriate, so long as the state did not promote the teachings of a particular church: "It is natural that where a common form of teaching Christian beliefs had been adopted for use in State schools, and was acceptable to the various Christian churches, the State, in promoting secular education, should be at pains to prevent the beliefs of any one church from being advanced over others, and to ensure a lowest common denominator for general religious teaching."[79]

As Australia has become more religiously pluralistic, the problems with this approach have become apparent. The presence of Christian and non-Christian traditions that are uncomfortable with a lowest common denominator Christianity in the public schools challenges the optimistic assumption of the nineteenth-century legislation that it is possible to discern consensual religious beliefs, incorporate them into the public schools, and make them the basis for a common social morality. While there is a need for some common values and beliefs to bind society together, attempts to root them in religion run the risk of violating governmental religious neutrality. States have made some effort to include the study of other religions in their GRT, but in practice the lessons are drawn overwhelmingly from the Christian tradition. The state, in pushing these particular "consensual" religious values, implicitly gives mainstream Christian practices its imprimatur and violates the basic ideal of governmental neutrality that we believe should govern church-state relations.

Despite these challenges, or possibly because of them, in 2006 the Howard government initiated the National School Chaplaincy Programme. Under the three-year, $90-million program, government and private schools can apply for a grant to supplement the cost of hiring a chaplain. The program is voluntary; schools do not have to apply for money for the chaplain and students are not obligated to participate in any of the services provided by the school's chaplain. According to the program's guidelines, chaplains will "be expected to provide general religious and personal advice, comfort and support to all students and staff, regardless of their religious denomination, irrespective of their religious beliefs."[80] In one sense, the program rather naively presumes that a chaplain from a particular religious tradition (Protestant, Catholic, Jewish, Muslim) can provide generic religious and moral instruction for an increasingly diverse student population. Predictably, the teacher unions universally rejected the proposal while church leaders generally supported it.[81] What is more surprising, at least by American standards, is that the opposition Labor Party supported the program. The only caveat that Labor spokeswoman Jenny Macklin offered was that the government's scheme must not favor people of any one faith.[82] She had little to fear; members of the National School Chaplaincy Reference Group appointed by the government to make recommendations on school applications included Catholic, Protestant, Jewish, and Islamic members. In recent years, funds have gone to government and to nongovernment schools, and to a wide variety of religious schools within the nongovernment sector. In 2006 and 2007, for example, money under the program went to, among others, a Jewish school (Adass Israel School), an Islamic school (Al Faisal College), a Greek Orthodox school (All Saints Greek Orthodox Grammar School), and a Lutheran school (Trinity Lutheran College), to name just a few.[83] There is no indication that the newly elected Labor government has any intention of ending the program.

An educational official pointed out to us what she considered to be a crucial point about the program: "it is important to note that the National School Chaplaincy Programme is voluntary and school communities decide if they want to apply for funding. School communities will also determine the role and the faith and/or denomination of the chaplain."[84] What this official assumes, and what is so different from American practices and legal precedents, is that so long as a program is voluntary and the government is evenhanded among religious traditions, there is nothing wrong with funding a religious program.

More in keeping with Australia's commitment to pluralism and neutrality are the Special Religious Instruction (SRI) programs instituted by each of the six states at the turn of the century and still in use today. Under SRI— what Americans term released time programs—religious leaders or accredited representatives of a faith group can provide religious teaching at the school for those children whose parents want them to receive it. Parents have the right to withdraw their children from SRI. This is a type of program that the U.S. Supreme Court has rejected under strict separation reasoning and, as we will see later, is widespread in Germany. As Australia has become more religiously pluralistic, the number of different religions providing SRI has increased. According to one estimate, there are, for example, 6,000 primary schoolchildren in Australia who attend Bahá'í classes.[85]

Church, State, and Nonprofit Community
Service Organization

Australia's nonprofit sector is complex, expanding, and diverse. The broadest definition of the sector is that it "encompasses all those organizations that are not part of the public or business sectors"[86] and includes churches, nursing homes, sports and recreation clubs, private schools, and arts and culture associations, to name a few. Our principal interest in this section, however, is with community service organizations, those groups that provide various health and social welfare services.

Christian groups have dominated the community service field for much of Australia's history, but, as with education, the state has more recently adopted a "neutral" policy that has led to public finance for non-Christian welfare agencies. Churches took the lead in providing social welfare in colonial Australia. Evangelical Protestants, in particular, gave a religious impetus for the formation of charitable organizations that addressed the problems of poverty, child neglect, and homelessness.[87] There was little direct government provision of services in the early nineteenth century, so these organizations were the only means of aid for the unemployed and economically destitute. Most of the finance for these charities came initially from the churches and wealthy philanthropists, but the state gradually expanded its role as a source of funding for these church-based organizations. Agencies that worked toward the religious reformation of the "deserving" poor fit comfortably with the state's interest in the social control of a growing population of poor people.[88]

Reformist ideas that emerged at the turn of the century questioned the value of church-based charitable organizations by promoting the notion of a universal right to services and support based on need, and not the selective idea of moral worth. At the same time, church agencies could not meet the growing demand for services brought on by the economic depressions of the 1890s and 1930s. Gradually, the state began to take over more of the functions it previously had subsidized and adopted some reforming ideas with policies of basic income support, child care, and old age pensions. The Constitutional Amendment of 1946 overcame doubts about the Commonwealth government's power with regard to social welfare by establishing its sovereignty to legislate in eleven key areas of social welfare, including maternity and family allowances, widow pensions, child endowment, and unemployment and sickness benefits.[89]

The federal government also emerged from World War II fiscally dominant over the states and a pattern emerged whereby the Commonwealth collected most of the tax revenues and established national welfare priorities, but state governments or nonprofit agencies actually provided most of the human services.[90] The government expanded its welfare role in the 1960s and 1970s as public support grew for health insurance, income redistribution, and Aboriginal rights. Nonprofit organizations continued to be an important part of the social welfare network, but they became more dependent on state finance and they gradually adopted the norms of the emerging social welfare profession. A large number of secular nonprofits emerged in the postwar years that utilized a professional social work model in service provision. The conservative critique of welfare systems in Britain and the United States in the 1970s and 1980s also affected Australian policy. Nonprofit organizations benefited, at least in the short run, from new right attacks on the welfare state because they were seen to be more flexible, efficient, and cost-effective than services provided directly by the government. Policy makers began to favor the devolution of some services to nonprofit groups and in the decade between 1976–1977 and 1986–1987 direct support for nonprofit organizations by all levels of government in Australia more than doubled in real terms.[91]

A 2000 report by the Australian Bureau of Statistics indicated that there were 9,278 employing organizations providing community services (child care, accommodation for the aged, residential care, employment services) in Australia.[92] Nonprofit organizations represented more than two-thirds of these groups and they accounted for a majority of the direct expenditures for community services. The combined total expenditure for community services organizations in 1999–2000 was $12.8 billion; the government funded nearly 60 percent of the recurrent expenditures for nonprofit organizations, though larger agencies tended to be less reliant on government finance than smaller ones.

While the Christian values base and the link between agencies and the local church of many existing religious agencies eroded throughout the twentieth century, a large percentage of nonprofit community service organizations retain a religious identification of some kind. According to a 1995 survey of the nonprofit sector conducted by the Industry Commission, twenty-one of the top fifty nongovernment agencies in terms of total income had a religious affiliation, including the Salvation Army, World Vision, Wesley Mission Sydney, Anglican Homes for the Elderly, and Baptist Community Services, to name a few.[93] There are thousands of smaller Christian, Jewish, and Muslim agencies as well. The degree to which a religious ethos permeates the activities of these agencies varies a great deal. The Wesley Mission Sydney, Australia's fifth-largest nonprofit organization, describes itself in this way: "Wesley Mission is committed to the proclamation of the Gospel, to sharing God's love with multicultural Australians, to assimilating previously unchurched people into the life of the church and to nurturing the faith of God's children."[94] The Salvation Army mission statement affirms that, "The Salvation Army is an evangelical part of the universal Christian Church. Its message is based on the Bible. Its ministry is motivated by the love of God. Its mission is to preach the gospel of Jesus Christ and to meet human needs in His name without discrimination."[95]

The government finances religious and nonreligious community service agencies almost equally; the largest religious agencies received, on average, 48.4 percent of their total income from government funding, while the largest nonreligious agencies received 51.6 percent.[96] In 2006, 64 percent of Baptist Community Services' $139 million budget came from the government, as did 45 percent of the $325 million dollar budget for the Salvation Army Eastern Territory. The other of the three largest community service agencies, the Wesley Mission Sydney, made up 35 percent of its budget from government grants and subsidies.[97]

Australian welfare policy reflects an overriding pragmatism, which comes out most clearly in the government's commitment to economic efficiency and cost-effectiveness in service provision. The most common type of government payment to a community service organization is a fee for service. Organizations contract with the government to provide specified services, such as residential aged care, for a fixed fee. In terms of program monitoring, this model focuses on the outputs delivered by a community service organization. Religious agencies, like their secular counterparts, have questioned the appropriateness of applying free market economic principles to social welfare provision. According to Community Services Australia, the peak body for Uniting Church welfare agencies, "quality of service is more about people's lives, well being and acceptance in the community than it is about economic efficiency."[98]

Debate is inevitable about what constitutes a positive client outcome in areas such as mental health, disability, or employment services. The government's focus on efficient and cost-effective services will not settle the difficult question of how to assess the quality of services an agency provides, but a virtue of policy pragmatism is that the government remains neutral in terms of how services are delivered and who provides them. David Pollard, executive director of the Industry Commission, an agency set up by the government to analyze and make recommendations about social services, describes funding arrangements in this way: "Funding is generally conceived as a contract for the supply of services to a target group from a range of suppliers some of which happen to be church auspiced."[99] Pollard's attitude is indicative of the government's pragmatic interest in the number of services an agency provides, and its relative indifference to who provides them and how they do it.

In addition to pragmatism, the principles of pluralism, tolerance, and governmental neutrality are well established in Australian social welfare policy. In addition to providing funding to religious agencies, the government gives them considerable autonomy in how they deliver services. In contrast to the United States, religious agencies have generally been granted exemption from equal opportunities legislation with no great controversy. They are free to hire whomever they want for key positions within the agency. While not all agencies give preference to coreligionists in hiring, a majority of the ones we interviewed do, either explicitly or implicitly. Marilyn Webster of the Catholic Social Welfare Commission noted that "service agreements do not specify staff qualifications and the standard practice in most Catholic agencies is, whenever possible, to hire within the Catholic social welfare network."[100] World Vision, the Salvation Army, and the Wesley Mission Sydney also give a preference in hiring to coreligionists. Philip Hunt, executive director of World Vision Australia, justifies the agency's hiring policy in this way: "We believe that the only way for World Vision to maintain its religious mission is to select employees who are going to be consistent with our organization's values." World Vision also has religious services and Bible studies for employees, and while they are not mandatory Hunt said that most people choose to attend them.[101]

Agencies are generally allowed to offer religious services as a part of their program. Ed Dawkins, the community services secretary for the Salvation Army Eastern Command, noted that "we have drug and rehabilitation programs that have a strong spiritual dimension, including chapel services. We believe that the spiritual dimension is crucial to rehabilitation."[102] The Salvation Army makes clients aware of the religious elements of their various programs, but it does not discriminate against non-Christians who choose to sign up for one of them. Dawkins concluded that in his twenty-five years in social work the government had not once prevented him from "providing the spiritual ministry that I see as my mandate."[103] Overseas aid and development agencies are not allowed to use government money for religious purposes in their projects, but religious values and practices are still an important part of the work of many of these organizations. The initial point of contact for most church-based development agencies is a local church, and a number of these agencies, including the largest, World Vision, emphasize the connection between development and evangelism in their literature.[104]

Some government programs require religious organizations to provide equal access and equity in the services they provide. There is often a self-selection bias, however, on the part of clients who want a religiously oriented social service. Paul Tyrell, executive director of Centacare, the national body of Catholic welfare agencies, indicated to us that Centacare agencies do not discriminate among clients on the basis of religion, but that the government understands that "as a Catholic agency a majority of our clients are going to be Catholic."[105] According to Tyrell, half of all Centacare clients are Roman Catholics, many of them having been referred to the agency by a local priest. When we pointed these data out to David Pollard, he simply stated that "the fact that religious agencies may draw most of their customers from the ranks of their religious supporters is not of great concern."[106]

The devolution of services to nongovernment agencies in the 1970s coincided with the immigration of new religious and ethnic groups into Australia. This multiculturalism challenged the government's commitment to pluralism as immigrant groups often preferred services provided by their own community organizations rather than the existing government and nongovernment agencies. According to a recent survey of the Australian Jewish population, 53 percent of Jewish parents would prefer Jewish child care services for their children and 82 percent of the elderly would prefer accommodation in a specifically Jewish hostel or nursing home.[107] The same is often true for Muslims and Buddhists, and the government has responded by turning to religious and ethnic organizations as the primary service providers for those communities. A growing number of community organizations offer "ethno-specific services," a trend supported by the Industry Commission in its recent report: "cultural differences may necessitate a completely different approach to meeting community need."[108] Government policy recognizes that ethnic and religious agencies are popular among immigrants and are likely to have the best access to those targeted groups. As Pollard pointed out to us, "Islamic organizations have been funded because they have the best access to certain target groups."[109] This comment reflects once again the pragmatism that is the norm with aid to nonprofit organizations that has allowed for a diversity of religious organizations to receive public aid.

Concluding Observations

In slightly more than two hundred years, Australia's church-state policy has vacillated among four distinct models: religious establishment, plural establishment, liberal separationism, and pragmatic pluralism. Because Australian policy makers have never committed themselves to a single church-state model, they have had the freedom to adopt the most politically favorable model at a given time. Political and pragmatic considerations, in other words, have been far more important in Australian church-state issues than theoretical considerations. This is in contrast to the Netherlands, where self-consciously held principles such as a positive right to governmental neutrality have always shaped church-state practices, or the United States with its ideological commitment to church-state separation. Australia's church-state practices, though they are pragmatically based, come closest to those of the Dutch. Both countries seek to accommodate and support a wide diversity of religious and secular systems of belief. Australian policy, therefore, fits most closely with the third of our church-state models: pluralism. The state recognizes that religious life is not limited to the private sphere, but has an important public component, and accommodates a wide variety of religious groups with funding for such diverse societal activities as education, mental health, and welfare services, to name a few. This is most evident in state funding for private religious schools, and it provides the ideological justification for the chaplaincy program. In addition, the government generally does not favor any one religious group over another, nor does it advantage religious over secular perspectives.

Australia's pragmatic pluralism has gradually increased the free exercise rights of religious groups. Australian practice in this area is not much different from that of the other countries in our study. Like these countries, Australia struggles with how far to extend religious rights, but there is a cultural commitment to the values of accommodation, tolerance, compromise, and neutrality that makes possible the free expression of religious ideas. A problem with the Australian approach, however, is that the state has not solidified its guarantee of religious liberty through judicial decisions or legislation. The Australian High Court has narrowly interpreted the free exercise right of Section 116 of the Constitution and there is no federal law that specifically bars religious discrimination. This is a significant deficiency, in our view, not because there is widespread religious discrimination in Australia, because there is not, but because there are no established guidelines as to how far groups can go to exercise their religious liberty. This seems to be a particular issue for Muslims, who have been the targets of abuse in the aftermath of 9/11 and the Bali bombings.

Pragmatism has also driven the state's commitment to providing aid to religious schools and nonprofit organizations, and to the state's policy of religion in the public schools. The impetus for state aid to schools in the 1960s and 1970s was political and pragmatic; both major political parties hoped to secure Catholic support with schemes of direct aid to parochial schools. Similarly, a pragmatic concern about cost-effectiveness drove the government's decision to devolve service delivery to nongovernment organizations in the 1970s and 1980s. As the state became multicultural and the desire for religiously grounded education and services intensified, Australia successfully integrated new religious groups, such as Muslims, and allowed them to express their differences in publicly financed organizations. This demonstrates a practical commitment by the state to encourage both religious pluralism and diversity. To its credit, Australia has adopted these policies without the level of political conflict that has occurred around identical issues in many of the other countries in our study. There is agreement between Australia's two largest parties— the left-leaning Labor Party and the right-leaning Liberal Party—on these policies. That is an impressive achievement.

Australian policy makers have rarely given much thought to the normative implications of Australia's church-state policy. There is little explicit reference to religious freedom as a positive right that the state has an obligation to accommodate. Nevertheless, Australia's pragmatic pluralism implicitly reaches the goal of governmental neutrality that we established as the basic ideal for church-state relations on this question. In practice, if not always in theory, Australian policy discriminates neither among religious groups nor between religious and nonreligious belief systems.

Notes

1. Population data are available from the Australian Bureau of Statistics at http://www.abs.gov.au.

2. Desmond Cahill, Gary Bouma, Hass Dellal, and Michael Leahy, "Religion, Cultural Diversity, and Safeguarding Australia" (Canberra: Department of Immigration and Multicultural and Indigenous Affairs and the Australian Multicultural Foundation, 2004), 48.

3. Gary D. Bouma and Michael Mason, "Baby Boomers Downunder: The Case of Australia," in Wade Clark Roof, Jackson W. Carroll, and David A. Roozen, eds., *The Post-War Generation and Establishment Religion* (Boulder, Colo.: Westview Press, 1995), 27–58; and the National Church Life Survey, available at www.ncls.org.au.

4. Jeremy Moon and Campbell Sharman, eds., *Australian Politics and Government: The Commonwealth, the States, and the Territories* (New York: Cambridge University Press, 2003); and David Solomon, *Australia's Government and Parliament* (Melbourne: Longman Cheshire, 1988).

5. Marion Maddox, *God Under Howard: The Rise of the Religious Right in Australian Politics* (Sydney: Allen and Unwin, 2005).

6. Graham Maddox, *Australia's Democracy: In Theory and Practice* (Melbourne: Longman Cheshire, 1985), chap. 5.

7. Campbell Sharman, "The Commonwealth, the States, and Federalism," in Dennis Woodward, Andrew Parkin, and John Summers, eds., *Government, Politics, and Power in Australia* (Melbourne: Longman Cheshire, 1985), 108–20.

8. Solomon, *Australia's Government and Parliament*, chap. 2.

9. Ian Breward, *A History of the Australian Churches* (Sydney: Allen and Unwin, 1993), chap. 2; Cahill, Bouma, Dellal, and Leahy, "Religion, Cultural Diversity, and Safeguarding Australia," chap. 2; and Richard Kaye, ed., *Anglicanism in Australia: A History* (Melbourne: Melbourne University Press, 2002).

10. Michael Hogan, *The Sectarian Strand* (New York: Penguin Books, 1987), chap. 1; Bryan S. Turner, "Religion, State, and Civil Society: Nation Building in Australia," in Thomas Robbins and Roland Robertson, eds., *Church-State Relations: Tensions and Transitions* (New Brunswick, N.J.: Transaction Books, 1987), 233–51.

11. Brian Fletcher, "The Anglican Ascendancy," in Bruce Kay, ed., *Anglicanism in Australia: A History* (Melbourne: Melbourne University Press, 2002), 9.

12. Fletcher, "The Anglican Ascendancy," 30; and Roger C. Thompson, *Religion in Australia: A History* (Melbourne: Oxford University Press, 1994), chap. 1.

13. Suzanne Rutland, "Early Jewish Settlement, 1788–1800," in James Jupp, ed., *The Australian People: An Encyclopedia of the Australian Nation, Its People and Their Origins* (Cambridge: Cambridge University Press, 2002), 525–28.

14. Gary D. Bouma, "The Emergence of Religious Plurality in Australia: A Multicultural Society," *Sociology of Religion* 56 (1995), 285–302; and Hans Mol, *The Faith of Australians* (Sydney: Allen and Unwin, 1985), chap. 9.

15. Michael Hogan, "Worrying About Religion," *Australian Review of Public Affairs* 7, 1 (2006), 102–5.

16. Patricia Curthoys, "State Support for Churches: 1836–1860," in Bruce Kay, ed., *Anglicanism in Australia: A History* (Melbourne: Melbourne University Press, 2002), 31–51.

17. Hogan, *The Sectarian Strand*, chap. 2.

18. Breward, *A History of the Australian Churches*, chap. 4; and Curthoys, "State Support for Churches: 1836–1860," 50.

19. Thompson, *Religion in Australia*, chap. 2.

20. Hogan, *The Sectarian Strand*, chap. 4.

21. Quoted in *Discrimination and Religious Conviction* (Sydney: New South Wales Anti-Discrimination Board, 1984), 319.

22. Quoted in *Discrimination and Religious Conviction*, 321.

23. Mol, *The Faith of Australians*, chap. 1.

24. Tom Campbell, Jeffrey Goldsworthy, and Adrienne Stone, eds., *Protecting Rights Without a Bill of Rights: Institutional Performance and Reform in Australia* (Aldershot, England: Ashgate, 2006).

25. Pervaiz Ahmad Buttar and Lynette Joy Mattingley, *Religious Conviction and the "New Magna Charta"* (Brisbane: James Cook University, Centre for Southeast Asia Studies, 1986); and Jeffrey Goldsworthy, "Introduction," in Campbell, Goldsworthy, and Stone, eds., *Protecting Rights Without a Bill of Rights: Institutional Performance and Reform in Australia*, 1–13.

26. Quoted in Hogan, *The Sectarian Strand*, 228.

27. *Grace Bible Church Inc. v. Reedman*, 54 ALR 571 (1984).

28. *Grace Bible Church Inc. v. Reedman*, 54 ALR (1984), p. 16.

29. *Grace Bible Church Inc. v. Reedman*, 54 ALR (1984), p. 21.

30. *Nationwide News v. Wills*, 177 CLR 1 (1992).

31. *Australian Capital Television Pty Ltd and Others v. The Commonwealth of Australia*, 108 ALR 577 (1992).

32. Brian Galligan and F. L. (Ted) Morton, "Australian Exceptionalism: Rights Protections Without a Bill of Rights," in Campbell, Goldsworthy, and Stone, eds., *Protecting Rights Without a Bill of Rights: Institutional Performance and Reform in Australia*, 17–39.

33. *Australian Capital Television Pty Ltd and Others v. The Commonwealth of Australia* at 596.

34. *Article 18: Freedom of Religion and Belief* (Sydney: Human Rights and Equal Opportunity Commission, 1998).

35. *Article 18: Freedom of Religion and Belief.*

36. *Article 18: Freedom of Religion and Belief*, 3–4.

37. Gary D. Bouma, *Mosques and Muslim Settlements in Australia* (Canberra: Australian Government Publishing Service, 1994), 90.

38. *Article 18: Freedom of Religion and Belief*, 7.

39. Scott Poynting, "Living with Racism: The Experience and Reporting by Arab and Muslims Australians of Discrimination, Abuse and Violence Since 11 September 2001" (A Report to the Human Rights and Equal Opportunity Commission, April 2004).

40. Telephone interview with Ikebal Patel, President, Australian Federation of Islamic Councils (June 5, 2007).

41. Telephone interview with Ikebal Patel, President, Australian Federation of Islamic Councils (June 5, 2007).

42. John Chesterman, "Natural Born Subjects? Race and British Subjecthood in Australia," *Australian Journal of Politics and History* 51, 1 (2005), 30–39; Lois Foster and David Stockley, *Australian Multiculturalism: A Documentary History and Critique* (Philadelphia: Multilingual Matters, 1988); and Anthony Moran, "White Australia, Settler Nationalism and Aboriginal Assimilation," *Australian Journal of Politics and History* 51, 2 (2005), 168–93.

43. Abdullah Saeed and Shahram Akbarzadeh, eds., *Muslim Communities in Australia* (Sydney: UNSW Press, 2001); and Abdullah Saeed, *Muslim Australians: Their Beliefs, Practices, and Institutions* (Canberra: Commonwealth of Australia, 2004).

44. Hogan, *The Sectarian Strand*, chap. 9.

45. *Attorney General for the State of Victoria (at the relation of Black) v. The Commonwealth of Australia*, 146 CLR 559 at 328 (1981).

46. *Attorney General for the State of Victoria (at the relation of Black) v. The Commonwealth of Australia*, at 330.

47. *Attorney General for the State of Victoria (at the relation of Black) v. The Commonwealth of Australia*, at 345.

48. *Attorney General for the State of Victoria (at the relation of Black) v. The Common-wealth of Australia*, at 326.

49. *Attorney General for the State of Victoria (at the relation of Black) v. The Common-wealth of Australia*, at 330.

50. Personal interview with Aurora Andrushka, Department of Education, Employment, and Youth Affairs (July 26, 1995).

51. "Financial Assistance Granted to Each State in Respect of 2004 States Grants Primary and Secondary Assistance Act 2000" (Canberra: The Australian Government Department of Education, Science, and Training, 2005).

52. "Australian Government Programmes for Schools: Quadrennial Administrative Guidelines 2005–2008 (Canberra: The Australian Government Department of Education, Science, and Training, 2006).

53. Chris Ryan and Louise Watson, "The Drift to Private Schools in Australia: Understanding Its Features" (Discussion Paper No. 479, The Australian National University for Economic Policy Research, September 2004), 17.

54. Data are available from the Independent Schools Council of Australia at http://www.isca.edu.au.

55. "Schools: 2005" (Canberra: Australian Bureau of Statistics, 2005).

56. "Schools: 2005" (Canberra: Australian Bureau of Statistics, 2005); "Independent Schools in Australia: 2006–2008" (Canberra: Independent Schools Council of Australia, 2006).

57. "God in the Classroom," *Sydney Morning Herald,* June 23, 2003; Linda Morris, "Islam Leads in Rush to Faith Education," *Sydney Morning Herald,* June 23, 2003. Both articles are available at www.smh.com.au.

58. John Goldlust, *The Melbourne Jewish Community: A Needs Assessment* (Canberra: Australian Government Publishing Service, 1993), 15.

59. *Discussion Paper: Review of the New Schools Policy* (Canberra: Australian Government Publishing Service, 1995), 15; "Independent Schools in Australia: 2006–2008," 65.

60. Available at http://www.islamicschool.com.au/mission.html.

61. Irene Donohue Clyne, "Educating Muslim Children in Australia," in Abdullah Saeed and Shahram Akbarzadeh, eds., *Muslim Communities in Australia* (Sydney: UNSW Press, 2001), 116–37.

62. "Minister Tells Muslims: Accept Aussie Values or 'Clear Off'," *ABA Online.* Available at http://www.abc.net.au/news/newsitems/200508/s1445181.htm.

63. Telephone interview with Ikebal Patel, President, Australian Federation of Islamic Councils (June 5, 2007).

64. Telephone interview with Bob Johnson, Executive Officer, Australian Association of Christian Schools (June 4, 2007).

65. Telephone interview with Bob Johnson, Executive Officer, Australian Association of Christian Schools (June 4, 2007).

66. "National Inquiry into Discrimination Against People in Same-Sex Relationships: Financial and Work-Related Entitlements and Benefits" (Undated publication of the Association of Independent Schools of South Australia).

67. Personal interview with Kevin Vassarotti, Executive Officer, National Catholic Education Commission (July 28, 1995).

68. Available at http://www.csa.edu.au/index.php.

69. *National Catholic Education Commission: School Funding Policy*, 3.

70. "Information for Independent Schools on Educational Accountability Requirements for 2007 and 2008" (Undated publication of the Independent Schools Council of Australia). Report is available at: www.isa.edu.au.

71. Telephone interview with Bob Johnson, Executive Officer, Australian Association of Christian Schools (June 4, 2007).

72. Personal interview with Peter Crimmins, Director of Policy and Research, Christian Schools Australia, and former Executive Director, Australian Association of Christian Schools (July 27, 1995).

73. "Schools: 2005" (Canberra: Australian Bureau of Statistics, 2005).

74. Ryan and Watson, "The Drift to Private Schools in Australia."

75. Telephone interview with Ikebal Patel, President, Australian Federation of Islamic Councils (June 5, 2007).

76. William Lowe Boyd, "Balancing Public and Private Schools: The Australian Experience and American Implications," in William Lowe Boyd and James G. Cibulka, eds., *Private Schools and Public Policy: International Perspectives* (London: Falmer Press, 1989), 162.

77. Personal correspondence from Suzanne Northcutt, Branch Manager for Schools Funding and Coordination and the Schools Resource Group, Department of Education, Science and Training (July 2, 2007).

78. For an excellent overview of religion in state-run schools, see *Discrimination and Religious Conviction*, chap. 6.

79. Quoted in *Discrimination and Religious Conviction*, 325.

80. "National School Chaplaincy Programme: Guidelines" (Canberra: Australian Government Department of Education, Science and Training, 2006).

81. Jill Rowbotham, "Teachers Baulk at Howard's Chaplains," *The Australian*, October 30, 2006, 4.

82. Allison Rehn, "Religious Rancor Over Schools," *Daily Telegraph*, October 30, 2006, 3.

83. For general information about the chaplaincy program and for a list of schools that have received government grants, see www.dest.gov.au/sectors/school_education/policy_initiatives_reviews/key_issues/school_chaplaincy_programme/default.htm.

84. Personal correspondence from Suzanne Northcutt, Branch Manager for Schools Funding and Coordination and the Schools Resource Group, Department of Education, Science and Training (July 2, 2007).

85. "In Australia, Bahá'í Religious Classes in State Schools Find Wide Appeal," *One Country: The Online Newsletter of the Bahá'í International Community*. Available at: www.onecountry.org.

86. Mark Lyons, *Third Sector: The Contribution of Nonprofit and Cooperative Enterprise in Australia* (Sydney: Allen and Unwin, 2001), 5.

87. Brian Dickey, *No Charity There* (Sydney: Allen and Unwin, 1989).

88. Elizabeth Windschuttle, "Women and the Origins of Colonial Philanthropy," in Richard Kennedy, ed., *Australian Welfare History: Critical Essays* (Melbourne: Macmillan, 1982), 10–31.

89. *Australia's Welfare 1993: Services and Assistance* (Canberra: Australian Government Publishing Service, 1993), chap. 1.

90. Adam Graycar and Adam Jamrozik, *How Australians Live: Social Policy in Theory and Practice* (Melbourne: Macmillan, 1989), 115.

91. *Charitable Organizations in Australia* (Melbourne: Australian Government Publishing Service, 1995), chapter 5.

92. Australian Bureau of Statistics, *Community Services, Australia, 1999–2000.* Catalogue No. 8696.0 (Canberra: Australian Bureau of Statistics, 2000).

93. *Charitable Organizations in Australia* (Melbourne: Australian Government Publishing Service, 1995), chap. 12.

94. Available at http://www.wesleymission.org.au/About/.

95. Available at http://www.salvos.org.au/about-us/overview/our-mission.php.

96. *Charitable Organizations in Australia*, Appendix C.

97. Financial data available for the three organizations available at: http://www.salvos.org.au/about-us/annual-report-and-funding/; http://www.wesleymission.org.au/publications/annrpt/2006/financial.asp; and http://www.bca.org.au.

98. "Response to the Draft Report: Charitable Organizations in Australia" (Undated publication of Community Services Australia).

99. Personal interview with David Pollard, Industry Commission (July 19, 1995).

100. Personal interview with Marilyn Webster, Catholic Social Welfare Commission (July 18, 1995).

101. Personal interview with Philip Hunt, Executive Director of World Vision Australia (July 21, 1995).

102. Personal interview with Ed Dawkins, Community Service Secretary for the Salvation Army Eastern Command (July 31, 1995).

103. Personal interview with Ed Dawkins, Community Service Secretary for the Salvation Army Eastern Command (July 31, 1995).

104. Laurie Zivitz and Anne Ryan, "World Vision in Australia," in Laurie Zivitz, ed., *Doing Good in Australia* (Sydney: Allen and Unwin, 1991), 267–80.

105. Personal interview with Paul Tyrell, Executive Director of Centacare (July 26, 1995).

106. Personal interview with David Pollard, Industry Commission (July 19, 1995).

107. Goldlust, *The Melbourne Jewish Community*, xv–xvii.

108. *Charitable Organizations in Australia*, 48.

109. Personal interview with David Pollard, Industry Commission (July 19, 1995).

~

CHAPTER FIVE

England: Partial Establishment

England is the only country in our study with a formally established church, the Church of England, which has been the recognized church since the middle of the sixteenth century. There has been a progressive dilution in the Church's political powers and privileges since that time, but the fact that England has an established church remains an important factor in the resolution of church-state issues in contemporary politics. This church-state model, what we term a partial establishment, has done much to frame church-state questions. What is even more significant, the established church helps to sustain a cultural assumption that religion has a public function to perform, that it is appropriate for the state and church to cooperate in achieving common goals, and that political and religious authorities can and should negotiate on key policy issues of interest to both of them.

This chapter begins with a very brief description of British political institutions and religious life. It then gives a historical survey of England's religious establishment, followed by a consideration of the formal and informal powers associated with the Church of England. The chapter then reviews how this church-state model structures the English approach to free exercise issues and questions, and establishment issues related to education and nonprofit organizations. Finally, the last section makes some concluding observations.

The Nation

Great Britain comprises the three countries of England, Scotland, and Wales. The United Kingdom includes these three countries plus Northern Ireland.

In 2006, the United Kingdom had a population of just over sixty million; fifty million (or 83 percent) of the total population lived in England. Pragmatism characterizes English political culture, with a greater orientation toward what works than abstract theorizing. In this way, England is much like Australia. As a result of this practical orientation, change in English history has been incremental, not revolutionary. Politically, England has gradually evolved from a limited representative democracy in the thirteenth century, with the signing of the Magna Charta, to a full and participatory democracy by the end of the nineteenth century. Today, Britain has a parliamentary form of government with a bicameral legislative branch. The 646 members in the House of Commons are popularly elected and politically powerful. The Commons makes primary legislation—other than for matters devolved to the Scottish Parliament and the Northern Ireland Assembly—and selects the prime minister, who serves as the head of the government and is the highest political authority in the land. The nearly 750 members in House of Lords are not elected, but serve by virtue of birth, appointment by the Crown, or position. Although the prime minister and both houses of Parliament must formally pass legislation, by convention and law the Lords does not overturn a government bill and limits its role to discussion and debate.[1]

Unlike the other countries in our study, England does not have a written constitution, which has some effect on church-state issues. There is an uncodified British constitution that embodies the principle of a higher law, the most significant provisions of which are the rule of law, parliamentary government under a limited monarch, a unitary political system, and parliamentary sovereignty. Fundamental freedoms, including religious rights, however, do not lie in any constitutional mandate or bill of rights but in legislative statutes and in the capacity of the democratic society and Parliament to preserve shared values, which for the most part has been done.

According to the 2001 Census, 71 percent of the population of England and Wales is Christian, 2.7 percent is Muslim, and 1 percent is Hindu. Those with no religion were actually the second-largest group of respondents (15.5 percent), which is almost certainly lower than the actual percentage of nonreligious persons. The religion question was the only voluntary question on the 2001 Census and 7 percent chose not to state their religion. The largest Christian denominations are Anglican, Roman Catholic, Presbyterian, and Methodist, but the only Christian churches that are experiencing sustained growth are those that serve the burgeoning African and Caribbean communities. From 2002 to 2007, black churches grew by 18 percent, and blacks accounted for more than two-thirds of the churchgoers in London.[2] In terms of active church membership and attendance (once a week or more), England

is the most secular country in our study. The rate of active church membership in England fell from 22 percent of the population in 1970, to 9.6 percent in 1990, and 8.2 percent in 2000.[3]

For the vast majority of the English population, however, the situation is
one aptly described by Grace Davie as one of "believing without belonging."
Belief in God remains relatively high (71 percent), but over half of the respondents in a 1990 survey (56 percent) claim never to attend church.[4]
While formal membership in the Church of England is low, it is concentrated
in the middle class. In addition, many of the nation's elite private schools,
called "public" schools in Britain, are affiliated with the Anglican Church.
Both of these facts help to explain how the Anglican Church has come to
have significant representation in the upper echelons of the nation's political, legal, and cultural institutions.[5]

At the same time that a secular ethos has become more prominent, the
number of British Muslims has grown from an estimated 369,000 in 1971, to
690,000 in 1981, and 1.6 million in the 2001 National Census.[6] In terms of
active religious involvement Muslims have actually outstripped the number
of regular worshippers in the Church of England. An estimated 930,000 Muslims attend a place of worship once a week, compared to 916,000 Anglicans.[7]
Most of this growth has come as a consequence of the immigration of Muslims from India and Pakistan after the Second World War. In the midst of
postwar labor shortages, England actively recruited low-wage labor from its
former colonies to help rebuild cities devastated by the war. For various reasons, a good percentage of those economic migrants eventually settled in
England, the result of which has been a dramatic growth in the number of
British Muslims.[8] There has been a similar increase in England's nonwhite
population, from 5.5 percent of the total population in the 1991 Census to
7.9 percent in the 2001 Census. This diversity has spawned ethnic and racial
tensions, particularly in urban areas where the nonwhite community is concentrated.

The Church of England was once famously described as the Conservative
Party at prayer, indicating the close political alliance between the two powerful institutions. Historically, the Conservatives generally represented the political interests of the established church, while dissenting Protestants and
Catholics identified with the Liberal Party. To some extent, those historical
connections survived into the modern era. According to a 1992 survey of Conservative Party members, there was a strong link between party and church involvement, with 70 percent of party members claiming regular church worship.[9] However, the ties that bound the Conservative Party with the Church
of England have clearly weakened. Political support for the Conservative Party

among bishops, clergy, and active lay members of the Anglican Church has been declining for decades. A 1992 survey of more than five hundred members of the Church of England indicated that only a quarter of the bishops or clergy voted Conservative in that year's election, and that was a good election for the Tory Party as it won its fourth consecutive election.[10]

A further challenge to the established religious-political alliances in British politics was Tony Blair's tenure as Labour Party prime minister from 1997 to 2007. While not initially publicly expressive of his Christian faith, at least by American standards, Blair was arguably the most deeply religious prime minister in postwar British history and his faith was a driving force in his political life.[11] In an increasingly secular political environment, Blair was quite sympathetic to religious groups in public policy and over time he became slightly more open about his faith. Most notably, and most controversially, Blair said that his decision to go to war in Iraq would ultimately be judged by God, a conviction that led to considerable criticism by the British press and political elites. Religion remains a factor in British politics, but the tidy assumptions about church membership and party support are not as relevant as they once were. With the exception of Northern Ireland, the political salience of religion has fallen throughout the twentieth century as social class, rather than religion, has become the most important point of political cleavage throughout Britain. None of the major parties make overt appeals to religious groups, as do their American counterparts. England's religious diversity and secularism are themes that we will return to later in this chapter. For now, it is important to understand the historical forces that have shaped contemporary church-state issues in England.

The Historical Background

When Pope Clement VII famously refused to grant Henry VIII an annulment from Catherine of Aragon, Henry broke from the Roman Catholic Church, married Anne Boleyn, and took political control of the English church. While Henry's divorce was the occasion for the religious split, the causes of the rift lay much deeper and they led eventually to the establishment of the broadly Protestant Church of England during Elizabeth I's reign. From the earliest days of the establishment, the Church of England enjoyed an unusual degree of autonomy in the power of appointments and in managing its own funds, but a close relationship nevertheless developed between the state and the Anglican Church in which the institutions worked in concert for shared political and religious goals. The ideal envisioned by Richard Hooker, the sixteenth-century apologist for the Anglican establishment, was to unify church membership with membership in the political community so that there would be no division between the secular goals of the state and the sacred purposes of the church. Hooker provided a theological justification for this political arrangement; he believed that the church had a positive obligation to be involved in civil society and in the value of the state to the church. In terms of the law, this came to mean a state-supported and state-enforced religion with the imposition of various restrictions on religious dissenters. The Corporation Act of 1661 and the Test Act of 1673, for example, effectively excluded Roman Catholics and Protestant nonconformists from participation in political affairs.[12]

Religious pluralism and intense conflict among Anglicans, Roman Catholics, and Protestant nonconformists made it difficult to sustain Hooker's organic vision. The Treaty of Union with Scotland in 1707, for example, allowed for the establishment of the Presbyterian Church of Scotland. Driven by this division in the rest of Great Britain, the state grudgingly conceded freedom of worship to Protestant religious dissenters with the passage of the Toleration Act of 1689. The Toleration Act repealed some of the restrictions on Protestant nonconformists, such as those affecting their meeting and conducting acts of worship, but the Test and Corporation Acts were retained. It was not until the nineteenth century that the state finally lifted most of the disabilities attached to religious nonconformity. Protestant nonconformists and Roman Catholics won political emancipation in 1824 and 1829 respectively, in 1858 Jews were able to become members of Parliament, and in 1871 Parliament abolished religious tests for admission to universities. The Church of Wales was disestablished in 1920.[13]

The impetus for reform did not come from the Church of England, which opposed much of the legislation and used its power in the House of Lords to delay passage of various bills removing religious disabilities. The Church feared that the reforms would de-Christianize the legislature and imperil the country's religion. The reforms also did not signal the supremacy of a liberal political philosophy with its commitment to church-state separation. Social and religious pluralism forced a more liberal policy on a state that had become weary of dealing with politicized religious conflict. State officials eventually came to the realization that they could not effectively force religious conformity on a recalcitrant nation; this fact eventually led them by degrees to a more liberal church-state policy. As Steve Bruce and Chris Wright note, "only when the fragmentation of the religious culture had gone so far as to be obviously irreversible and the price of trying to enforce religious orthodoxy became too great did the establishment accept that there could no longer be an effective state religion."[14]

There were also efforts to disestablish the Church of England. The Anti-State Church Association, founded in 1844, and the Liberation Society, 1853, led the disestablishment movement, but there was insufficient political and elite support for this effort. Ironically, the most earnest challenge to the status of the Church of England came not from religious dissenters, but from Catholic (Anglo-Catholics) and evangelical wings *within* the Anglican Church. Some dissenters eventually seceded from the Church of England into the ranks of Roman Catholicism or evangelical nonconformity, but most stayed within the Church of England. Neither side strongly opposed the religious establishment; both factions wanted the state to use its coercive powers to further the one "true" religion. Only when evangelicals and Anglo-Catholics realized by the end of the nineteenth century that they would be unable to take over the state Church did they begin to question the wisdom of having a church so closely united with the state.[15]

The strong rivalry between the Church of England and nonconformist churches spilled over into party politics in the nineteenth century. The Liberal Party committed itself to state neutrality among religious groups and consolidated most nonconformist political support. The Conservative Party, on the other hand, defended the established Church and attracted most Anglican votes.[16] The education issue crystallized the religious division in British politics at this time. All the major churches founded schools in the early nineteenth century to propagate the faith and educate the children of church members, although Anglican schools were by far the most numerous. The state had very little role in providing public education until the passage of the Education Act of 1870 that created tax-supported schools under the control of local boards. The legislation assumed that religious schools would, with state financial aid, continue to provide education for members; the state's role was to fill the gaps where voluntary action by the churches could not meet the growing demand for education. State schools provided nonsectarian religious instruction, but there was less Christian content in the curriculum than in church schools.[17]

Protestant nonconformists and the Liberal Party opposed the bill on two grounds. First, some Liberals were religious voluntarists who opposed state aid to religious organizations because they felt it would compromise church autonomy. They also contended that public education should be free of church, i.e., Anglican, control. More radical elements of the Liberal Party, in the mold of Enlightenment liberalism, wanted a purely secular state educational system free of any religious influence whatsoever. Second, most Protestants opposed the Roman Catholic Church and did not want public money to aid what they termed an unorthodox religion. Anglicans and the Conservative Party, on the other hand, supported the bill and believed that it would achieve the best possible results for society and the church. The act would enable more children to receive a basic education, but would still allow the state to fund existing church schools, a majority of which were Anglican. In addition, Anglicans believed that religious instruction in state-supported schools benefited the nation as a whole. According to this establishment mind-set, religious education would provide the basis for a common Christian morality for the nation's schoolchildren. The bill passed, but the education issue continued to divide religionists for the next three decades.[18]

The relaxation of restrictions on religious dissenters in the nineteenth century, coupled with the growing secularity of British society, helped to depoliticize religious disputes in the early twentieth century. The emerging Labour Party had roots in the nonconformist chapels, but it gradually became more closely associated with a socialist ideology as the twentieth century progressed. When the Labour Party displaced the Liberal Party as one of the two main parties in the 1920s, social class, rather than religious issues, became politically salient.[19] Unlike many of its European counterparts, British politics never experienced a strong anticlerical movement, or a direct threat from sectarian liberalism, either of which might have driven the church from politics.[20] However, it was not so much the power of the churches that explains the absence of this political challenge, but the fact that religion had become politically less important. Even the socialist Labour Party was more indifferent than hostile to religion. As a consequence, the churches did not feel compelled to defend and preserve their role in society; it is noteworthy that a Christian Democratic movement and political party never emerged in England as it did in Germany and the Netherlands.

In practice, if not always in law, the Anglican Church that emerged from the sectarian rivalries of the late nineteenth and early twentieth centuries was far different from the one envisioned by Hooker two centuries earlier. The Church of England retained its establishment status, in contrast to the religious establishments in two former British colonies, America and Australia, but the nature of that establishment had radically shifted. The formal ties between church and state loosened as Parliament ceded greater control over the church's spiritual direction to ecclesiastical bodies, and the church's social and political role became more diffuse and ceremonial. In contrast to Hooker's model, the Church of England came to see itself as a comprehensive national institution that would guard and preserve the nation's shared cultural norms and serve as a religious counterpart to civil society. As religion became less socially significant, the Anglican Church became more ecumenical and accepting of pluralism. As a result, both church and state supported other denominations seeking the state's public recognition, and politicized religious disputes largely disappeared from British politics in the twentieth century. The Church continued to press for a political role, but it began to advocate an ecumenical Christian view of the nation's affairs, rather than a denominational one.

The debate around the Education Act of 1944 demonstrates the changing role of religion in England. The established Church of England and other Christian denominations fought one another on the education issue in the late nineteenth century, but religious animosities had been reduced by 1944 and the churches formed a powerful political coalition to protect the privileged position of their schools. Anglicans and Catholics, who had the largest stake in private religious schools, argued together that denominational schools deserved public funding because church schools provided a public good and gave parents the opportunity to exercise their right to direct the education of their children. Policy makers, who recognized the political power of these religious bodies and generally shared their view that religious education provided a public good, financed almost all the costs of existing church schools. The Education Act created a dual system with state-run and religious schools sharing the responsibility for the education of English children.[21]

The act further stipulated that religious education be provided in all state-run schools and that each school day begin with an act of collective worship. It created a Standing Advisory Council for Religious Education (SACRE) to advise local educational authorities on the methods of teaching religious education. SACRE consisted of representatives from the Church of England, other religious denominations, the teachers unions, and the local council. All the existing churches, in short, could have a decisive influence on the content of religious education in state schools. The act forbade narrowly denominational teaching in state schools, but the clear intention was to make the religious dimension broadly Christian. Parents and teachers retained the right to opt out of religious instruction and worship, but the act did not allow for religious instruction in other faiths. Because England contained so little religious diversity at the time, the 1944 act simply assumed that nondenominational Christianity would prevail.

Policy makers self-consciously designed religious education as a way to further the goals of the state, and not simply as a way to placate church leaders. There was great optimism in the early years after the act passed that religious education could provide some unity of purpose for English schoolchildren. The hope was that it would nurture children in the dominant values and beliefs of English society, which were broadly Christian. Religious education became a part of the civic culture and national heritage. Religious education in state-supported schools was consistent with a cultural consensus about the role of the established Church of England. In both instances, political elites viewed religion, the Christian religion specifically, as a significant influence on English culture, society, and history that could continue to play a useful role in shaping citizens' moral values.

Of the five countries in our study, England's establishment model lent itself most easily to a state promotion of "consensual" religious values. The established Church had historically seen its role as working in concert with the state to promote common values, which it increasingly viewed in ecumenical and pluralistic terms. Religious education seemed ideally suited to this task as it could provide the moral framework necessary to inculcate English schoolchildren with norms that would bind society together. There was little appreciation, at this point, that religious diversity and secularization might introduce conflict and thereby challenge this civil religious model, or that religionists might oppose so utilitarian an understanding of the place of faith in public life. Developments in the latter half of the twentieth century challenged these assumptions and led, as we will show in our review of current educational policy, to questions about the place of religion in state-supported schools. For now, however, we want to turn to a review of the Church of England's legal status that continues to influence the resolution of church-state issues in England.

England's Partial Establishment

The Church of England lost most of its privileges by the end of the nineteenth century, but legal and cultural ramifications associated with England's religious establishment remained. Unlike some churches in the European community, the Church of England does not receive a direct state subsidy, but in many other respects the links between church and state are much closer. The Church of England is the established church in England, but not in the rest of Great Britain. The Presbyterian Church of Scotland has been the established church in Scotland since 1707, and the Church of Wales and Northern Ireland were disestablished in the twentieth century. The monarch is the head of the Church and may not be nor marry a Roman Catholic. The Church carries out the coronation and all other state functions where prayer or religious exercises may be required.[22]

From a historical standpoint, the formal ties between Parliament and the Church of England have diminished, but from a comparative perspective the role of the government in church life is still remarkable. As an established church, the canon law of the Church of England is a part of English law, and until the early twentieth century Parliament passed much legislation affecting the Church. Under the Enabling Act of 1919, the Church's General Synod gained the authority to make changes in church liturgy and doctrine, although Parliament remains technically responsible for some matters of church law and can (but seldom does) reject a measure passed by the General Synod. In addition, the monarch, advised by the prime minister, has the power to appoint the archbishops and the diocesan bishops of the Church of England, although the choice is made from a field of candidates nominated by the Church. In no other country in our study are the formal, legal ties between church and state as strong as in England and it is impossible even to imagine the state having this kind of authority over a church in them.

The Church of England continues to have a formal political role by virtue of the automatic membership in the House of Lords for the archbishops of Canterbury and York and the twenty-four senior diocesan bishops of the Church. The Church of England is the only religious body with reserved seats. While the House of Lords occupies a subordinate position to the House of Commons and for the most part is limited to offering advise to the elected government and amendments to bills, it does provide a forum for discussion and debate about government bills and important public issues. In 1999, the Blair government appointed a royal commission to make recommendations about the future of the House of Lords. The resulting report, A House for the Future, proposed that twenty-six places be reserved for members of the British faith community. In contrast with historical precedent, however, those places would not automatically go to bishops of the Church of England, but would be selected to "be broadly representative of the different non-Christian faith communities."[23] While those recommendations were never enacted by the Blair government, there has been an expansion in the representation of other religious communities in the House of Lords. There are, at present, Jewish, Sikh, and Muslim members of the Upper House.

A 2007 legislative debate on the Equality Act (Sexual Orientations) highlights the role played by religious members of the House of Lords. The regulations prohibited discrimination in the provision of goods, services, and education on the grounds of sexual orientation.[24] While religious organizations could discriminate on the grounds of sexual orientation in their membership and activities (a church would not be obligated to marry a gay couple), if churches, religious agencies, or religious schools were providing goods on behalf of a public authority they would have to comply with the regulations. Prime Minister Blair specifically rejected a proposal from the Catholic Church to exempt faith-based adoption and foster agencies from the law's reach. In the placement of foster children, in short, such agencies could not refuse to place children with a gay couple. The law did not, however, apply to hiring practices. The law passed easily in the House of Commons by a vote of 310 to 100.

In the aftermath of the Commons' vote, religious organizations and leaders mobilized opposition for the upcoming vote in the House of Lords. Dr. Rowan Williams, the Archbishop of Canterbury, and Cardinal Cormac Murphy-O'Connor, the Roman Catholic Archbishop of Westminster, each wrote to the prime minister objecting to the regulations as an infringement of religious freedom. Jewish and Muslim leaders followed suit. Opponents of the bill organized a demonstration to coincide with the debate and vote in the House of Lords.[25] The religious groups claimed that the law might restrict their right to religious freedom. In the Lords' debate, the Archbishop of York argued that the government was seeking to have "consciences surgically removed" and to introduce a "new hierarchy of rights" where people of faith had become a "new sub-category."[26] The Bishop of Southwell and Nottingham affirmed that there was much in the legislation that "is both sensible and uncontentious," and suggested that the Church of England "will certainly support the use of law to tackle discrimination and basic injustice." However, he warned that the regulations went too far and forced religious persons to "choose between acting in a way that conflicts with their religious convictions and closing down work that is manifestly for the common good," and thereby reflected "a new kind of secular dogmatism."[27] The bill's fate, however, was foreordained. Tory peers were allowed a free vote, but Labour and Liberal Democratic peers were told to support the regulations, and the bill passed the Upper House by a vote of 168 to 122.

This debate underscored both the opportunities and limitations afforded to the Church of England through its formal membership in the House of Lords. On the one hand, the presence of Anglican clergy in the Upper House supports the idea that the Church of England and its bishops, along with other religious leaders, will have a voice in major pieces of moral legislation and when legislation touches on the work of the churches. On the other hand, the bill succeeded despite widespread religious opposition, which simply reinforces the secularizing trend within England. Religious leaders had the opportunity formally to voice their concerns, but it hardly assured them that they would be able to dictate the outcome of the legislation.

The Church also receives considerable press coverage, particularly when leaders take positions that are at odds with government policy. In 1982, the press reported extensively on a working paper for the Church's Board for Social Responsibility, *The Church and the Bomb*, which advocated unilateral nuclear disarmament. The publication of a report in 1985 by the Archbishop of Canterbury's Commission on Urban Priority Areas, *Faith in the City*, also attracted much discussion in the press. The press rightly interpreted the report as the Church's repudiation of Prime Minister Margaret Thatcher's economic policies. More recently, the press has focused intently on the opposition of the Bishops of the Church of England to the war in Iraq. The Bishops resisted Britain's involvement in the 2003 invasion of Iraq and called at one point for the nation's Christian leaders to make a public act of repentance for Britain's involvement in the war and its aftermath.[28] The point is that the media, in looking for the "religious" response to government policy, often focus on the views expressed by representatives of the Church of England. This partly reflects the fact that Anglican bishops have a platform in the House of Lords to make political pronouncements, and it suggests that the Church of England is considered the nation's leading Christian religious voice.

The Church of England also has what Paul Weller describes as a "structurally privileged position" on such policy issues as education, state provision of hospital and military chaplaincies, and religious broadcasting on the publicly supported British Broadcasting Corporation (BBC).[29] To the extent that the Church does enjoy such a position, however, it has largely used it to make it easier for other religious groups to gain access to state benefits. Anglican bishops have consistently supported an expansion of the Upper House to include Jewish, Sikh, and Muslim members. An exhaustive study of prison chaplaincies demonstrated the creative efforts of Anglican clergy to make chaplain positions available to religious leaders outside the Christian tradition.[30] There was a time in the history of the BBC when all of its religious shows would have been Christian, and most of those would have been Anglican. That is not so true now. The BBC continues to offer hundreds of hours for religious broadcasting each week, and while nearly all of the actual religious services that are broadcast are Christian, there are myriad religious programs that cover Britain's diverse traditions.[31] In contrast with the Netherlands, however, time is not specifically given to Muslims to broadcast their religious services.

Finally, until very recently, Christian, or more specifically, Anglican, doctrines were protected against blasphemy.[32] Non-Christian religions received no specific legal protections. There were some noteworthy blasphemy cases over the years, but most people considered the law an ancient relic. Ironically, what brought the law to the forefront was the publication of Salman Rushdie's 1988 novel, *The Satanic Verses*. Rushdie's portrayal of the prophet Muhammad deeply offended many British Muslims. The book was burned in public demonstrations; the Supreme Leader of Iran, the Ayatollah Ruhollah

Khomeini, issued a fatwa calling on all good Muslims to kill Rushdie and his publishers; and many Muslim leaders argued that the blasphemy law should be expanded to protect Islamic doctrines. The ensuing debate brought an un-precedented amount of coverage—much of it negative—to the British Mus-lim community, but there was no expansion of the blasphemy law.[33] Instead, in 2008 the government voted to abolish the blasphemy law, but only after it had consulted with leaders of the Church of England. For the most part, Church leaders were not committed to salvaging the blasphemy law. How-ever, Archbishop Williams and others wanted to make it clear that this de-cision did not indicate a "secularizing move" or a generalized attack on the nation's religious foundation.[34]

More important than the Church's legal status is the cultural assumption that sustains a public, political role for the Church of England, specifically, and for religious groups more generally. This model affirms the idea that re-ligious groups have an important cultural and social function to play, which the state should both recognize and support. The state pursues policies that accommodate organized religion as a whole because of a conviction shared by most political elites and the public that religion is morally and socially beneficial. Citizens perceive the religious establishment as, at best, a source of social cohesion and consensus and, at worst, as harmless.

As we will document in the pages below, the accommodation of religious minorities has posed a challenge to this establishment mind-set, and it has led some political figures to question the very idea of state aid to religion. However, religious minorities, particularly British Muslims, do not so much oppose the current system as they wish that it would be expanded to include more religious groups. Muslim leaders consistently argue that a virtue of the religious establishment is that it preserves the idea that religion has a public political role to play. Dr. Fatma Amer, director of Education and Interfaith Relations at the London Central Mosque, put it succinctly when she noted to us: "there is much good in keeping the religious establishment intact. It makes possible a recognition of a person's right to put into action what he most sincerely believes in."[35]

A recent controversy about the acceptance of Islamic law in Britain high-lights the unique role of the Anglican establishment and the degree to which it is customarily an institutional ally for religious minorities. In 2008, Rowan Williams, the Archbishop of Canterbury and spiritual leader of the Church of England, suggested that it was "unavoidable" that certain elements of Is-lamic law or Sharia will have to be accepted in Britain. His suggestion set off a wave of criticism that was covered extensively in the elite and popular press. Prime Minister Gordon Brown distanced the government from the proposal, although he did not rule it out, and some political and religious leaders called for Williams to resign his position.[36] Williams later clarified his stance by saying that he believed that Sharia should only apply in limited areas such as family law, as it does for Orthodox Jews in certain cases, and only when all parties agreed to submit to the alternative legal forum.

There are two instructive points about this controversy. First, it highlights the important role played by leaders of the established Church of England. The press coverage of Williams's proposal would simply not have been as extensive had he not been the most prominent spokesperson of the established Church of England. Second, the controversy highlights the degree to which Williams has been, as have most Anglican religious leaders, an ally for the rights of religious minorities. In the midst of the debate, the Islamic Human Rights Commission strongly defended Williams, saying that it was "shocked by what seems to be a systematic and malicious misunderstanding of what the Archbishop of Canterbury said in his speech about accommodating religious minorities in Britain."[37]

For many religious minorities, English secularization poses a much more serious challenge to religion than does the established Church. Based on empirical research he conducted for the Policy Studies Institute, political scientist Tariq Modood contends that "the real division of opinion is not between a conservative element of the Church of England versus the rest of the country, but between those who think that religion has a place in secular public culture, that religious communities are part of the state, and those that do not."[38] In contrast to state secularism, the religious establishment preserves the idea that religion should be actively involved in social and political affairs, and facilitates a space for religious minorities who believe that the public sphere should take their values seriously. The point of contention for most religious minorities is not the religious establishment per se; what they argue instead is that the system should officially expand to include them in the benefits that come with state recognition.

There is almost no formal political opposition to the religious establishment. The Liberal Democratic Party periodically advocates against it, as do politically marginal interest groups such as the National Secular Society and the British Humanist Association, but these efforts have gone nowhere.[39] Nor does there appear to be widespread opposition from religious groups that are not formally part of the establishment. The research organization New Politics Network interviewed religious leaders outside the Church of England and found that one-third opposed the current system, one-third supported it, and one-third had reservations about the system, but mostly they wished to expand the system to include additional faith traditions. One way of interpreting the results, in short, is that two-thirds of religious leaders *outside* of the Church of England support the current system or advocate an enhancement of that arrangement.[40]

This establishment mind-set might also explain why a majority of people in England consider themselves to be religious despite the fact that very few people actually go to church. Because the state offers a "free" religion—Anglican churches cannot easily turn away even inactive members of their parish if they want to be married in the church or have their children baptized by their local priest—people have less incentive formally to join and participate in church life. It is also possible, as Rodney Stark and others argue, that state support for an established church, however minimal, impedes the development of competition from other churches and decreases the overall levels of religious participation.[41]

The Free Exercise of Religion

As stated earlier, England, unlike the other countries in our study, does not have a codified constitution or a bill of rights and so there are no constitutional guarantees for religious freedom. There is no equivalent in England to the First Amendment to the United States Constitution. The absence of constitutional protections for religious rights has meant that the English courts have not historically been a forum where religious groups have been able to protest their treatment. England also lacks the theoretical commitment to religious freedom as a positive right that is so strong in both Germany and the Netherlands. Instead, religious rights in England are ensured by domestic legal provisions and international law, both of which have at times been wanting. However, in the past decade there have been significant legal changes in both arenas that have moved England more in the direction of its continental counterparts.

Historically, the most important legal assurances for religious liberty were the acts passed at the end of the nineteenth century that gave religious dissenters various rights. These law, however, were never interpreted as guaranteeing people a fundamental right of religious free exercise. More recently, the Employment Protection (Consolidation) Act of 1978 protects employees from losing their jobs because of religious practice, unless the dismissal can be justified in law. English courts have consistently upheld dismissals, however, when the religious obligations of employees led them to violate the terms of their contract. The Court of Appeal sustained the firing of a member of the Seventh-day Adventist Church who refused on religious grounds to work on Saturdays, as was required under his contract, and the dismissal of a Sikh who lost his job at an ice cream factory when he decided, in violation of hygiene rules, to grow a beard because of his religious beliefs. Similarly, in a case involving a Muslim who excused himself for part of Friday to attend prayers in the mosque, the court ruled that the employer's right to have him present at all times in the work day took precedence over his religious free exercise right.[42] Other laws that might have touched on religious discrimination were often narrowly interpreted to the disadvantage of religious groups. The Race Relations Act of 1976 provided a legal framework for fighting against racial discrimination, and the courts deemed Sikhs and Jews to be racial groups that deserved legal protection under that legislation. Christians and Muslims, however, were considered to be religious groups and were not covered under the provisions of the act.[43]

At other times, laws have been passed that advanced the claims of religious liberty. Parents, for example, are allowed to withdraw their children from religious education and worship in state-run schools, Sikhs are exempt from the requirements to wear a safety hat on a construction site, and Jews and Muslims have been given the right to slaughter animals in keeping with their religious requirements.[44]

Recent years have witnessed even more significant legal developments dealing with religious freedom. Until recently, British law disqualified clergy of the Churches of England, Scotland, and Ireland; and the Roman Catholic Church from sitting in the House of Commons, in clear violation of basic religious free exercise rights. The House of Commons (Removal of Clergy Disqualifications) Act of 2001 removed those restrictions. The Employment Equality (Religion or Belief) Regulations of 2003 provide additional protection for people on the grounds of religion or belief in the workplace. The regulations specifically ban direct and indirect discrimination in all aspects of employment on the basis of a person's religion or lack of a religion. The Racial and Religious Hatred Act of 2006 (RRHA) similarly touched on issues of equal treatment. As we noted above, under the Race Relations Act, Jews and Sikhs were deemed by the courts to be racial groups and were protected from racial discrimination, but Muslims and Christians were considered religious groups and did not receive the same legal protection. For years, Muslim leaders pressed the government to amend the law.[45] Initially introduced in 2001, the bill received considerable opposition, particularly in the House of Lords, on the ground that the proposed legislation would restrict free speech rights. Nonetheless, the Labour government pressed the issue and after a five-year effort the bill was passed into law in 2006. The law defines religious hatred as "hatred against a group of persons defined by reference to religious belief or lack of religious belief." A person who "uses threatening words or behaviors" is guilty of an offense "if he intends thereby to stir up religious hatred."[46]

By far the most important legal development in the area of religious freedom, however, was the passage of the Human Rights Act (HRA) in 1998. The HRA incorporated the European Convention on Human Rights (ECHR) and granted, in theory at least, the idea that there might be a British Bill of Rights that would include the right of religious freedom. Article 9 of the ECHR provides that "everyone has a right to freedom of thought, conscience and religion . . . either alone or in community with others and . . . to manifest his religion or belief in worship, teaching, practice, and observance." Section 13(1) of the HRA suggested that Parliament wished the courts to be particularly sensitive to limitations on religious freedom: "If a court's determination of any question arising under this Act might affect the exercise by a religious organisation (itself or its members collectively) of the Convention right to freedom of thought, conscience and religion, it must have particular regard to the importance of that right."[47] In theory, it is possible that the passage of the act will lead the British to become more like the United States and the Netherlands in formally recognizing a right of religious free exercise. In practice, however, it is too early to tell if this kind of policy convergence will emerge as a consequence of this act alone. There is vigorous debate if the HRA does or should constitute a de facto British bill of rights, and court action on the act has thus far been limited.[48]

This is not to suggest that religious discrimination is widespread in England, because it is not. One concrete issue demonstrates the vaunted British pragmatism at work: the wearing by Muslim schoolgirls and teachers of the *hijab*. This issue has caused considerable controversy in both France and Germany but, with little fanfare or debate, British policy makers reached a compromise that allows Muslim girls to wear the *hijab* so long as it conforms with the color requirements of the school uniform.[49] Not one Muslim interviewed for this project suggested that there is any problem associated with the right of Muslim schoolgirls or teachers to wear the *hijab*. There are, however, limits to pragmatism when it comes to religious free exercise rights. In 2007, the government gave school authorities the right to forbid the wearing of the *niqaab*, a veil that covers all of the face except the eyes, if they believe that their wearing one would affect safety, security, or a child's ability to learn. At least one teacher was dismissed from her position as a teaching aide in a Church of England school for her refusal to take off the face veil, and a handful of children have been ordered to remove the *niqaab*. During the debate on the proposed regulation, former prime minister Blair described the *niqaab* as a "mark of separation" that made "other people from outside the community feel uncomfortable."[50]

Our point is not so much that the British are terribly misguided in allowing schools to ban the *niqaab*; there are reasonable disagreements on where to draw the line between the state's interest in educating children and its protection of religious rights. The more salient point is that when religious discrimination exists, the groups that have the most to fear from the absence of legal or constitutional protections are new religious movements whose practices are not as socially accepted as the older, more traditional religions. As Eileen Barker notes, "the longer a religious movement has been around, the greater the chance it has of being protected by the law."[51] Formerly excluded religious groups, such as Roman Catholics and Jews, have become integrated and respected members of the English community and they do not face religious discrimination. The public has come to accept and appreciate both of these religious traditions, and the increasingly generic, partial religious establishment has been able to incorporate their views.

The same is true for public acceptance of those without a religious belief. In contrast with the United States, there is no informal disability associated with persons running for political office who have no religious faith. Only 8 percent of respondents in a 1991 British survey agreed that politicians who do not believe in God are unfit for public office. By contrast, 53 percent of Americans in a 2008 poll indicated that they would not vote for an atheist for president, even if that person were nominated by their party and were well qualified for the position.[52] This difference helps to explain why in 2007 the leader of the British Liberal Democratic Party, Nick Clegg, affirmed, without any apparent controversy, that he did not believe in God. No American presidential candidate for a major American party has ever made that claim.

An obvious and important difference between England and the United States is that members of minority faiths in England that suffer because of their beliefs do not have the same recourse to the legal system to protect their religious rights, as they do in the United States, although, as seen earlier, the U.S. legal system is no sure guarantee of minority religious freedoms. The fact that there is no constitutional guarantee of religious freedom in England does affect the resolution of free exercise issues. The state generally protects religious rights, for the religious and the nonreligious, but until recently this has been more a function of elite and public opinion than legal principles. Well-established churches have less to fear from public opinion and the political process precisely because they have socially accepted values; religious minorities cannot always comfortably rely upon the political process to protect their rights. Discrimination against minority religious groups has historically been even more apparent in the area of public aid to private religious schools.

Church, State, and Education

England's educational system differs from those of every other country in our study, both in terms of actual policy and even in the use of terms to describe that policy. As an example, the term "public schools" in England usually refers to what Americans would call "private" or independent schools, while the vast majority of "religious" schools in England are considered to be a part of the state system. The distinguishing mark of the English educational system is that religious schools (schools that are owned by a religious body and that have religious exercises and teachings) are public (in the sense of being financed by the government). The vast majority of religious schools get state funding under virtually the same conditions that apply to community schools, i.e., schools that are publicly funded but have no religious character. When applied to education, the English model promotes equality between religious and nonreligious educational perspectives, although it raises controversial issues about which schools should receive state funding and under what conditions.

The genesis for this dual educational system dates back to the middle of the nineteenth century, when churches began offering basic education to poor children at a time that the state did not. State provision of universal elementary education came with the passage of the Education Act of 1870. The act led to the creation of thousands of state schools, but they supplemented rather than replaced the existing Church schools. Gradually the state developed a pattern of working with the churches in providing education. The 1944 Education Act solidified this partnership and is more or less in effect today.[53]

The act created county (later renamed "community") schools that are wholly owned and maintained by the Local Education Authorities (LEAs) and two broad categories of Church schools that are also part of the state or maintained system, voluntary aided and voluntary controlled. In voluntary-aided schools, the Church appoints a majority of the school governors and the governors determine the school admission policy and hire the teaching and support staff. In voluntary-controlled schools, by contrast, the Church appoints a minority of the school governors, and the governors share with their LEA the responsibility for the school admission policy and employment decisions. The state covers all capital costs for voluntary-controlled schools and 90 percent of those costs in voluntary-aided schools. A majority of Church schools are voluntary aided. All maintained schools (community, aided, controlled) receive a tuition grant from their LEA for each pupil who attends, they must follow the national curriculum, and they are all subject to state inspection. The central government provides all the funding for LEAs. Faith schools make up nearly one-third of all publicly financed English schools, and they educate about one-quarter of all English schoolchildren.[54] There are a small number of independent schools, religious and nonreligious, that charge fees for admission, but they receive no state funding.

Church schools are popular in England, both because they generally outperform state schools on standardized tests and because there is a strong desire on the part of parents, who may or may not be religiously active, for their children to have a religious education. Church schools, particularly voluntary-aided ones, have greater control over admissions procedures than do community schools, and in many cases preference is given to coreligionists, particularly when the school is oversubscribed. A recent survey conducted by the Church of England's Board of Education found that more than three-quarters of voluntary-aided schools had a religious affiliation in their admissions criteria.[55] While this might on paper seem to promote a sectarian viewpoint, both the state and Church school advocates understand their role as offering a valuable public service. David Lankshear, former executive director of the Board of Education for the Church of England, articulated this perspective to us in an interview: "In Church of England schools there is a clear understanding that the churches are in partnership with the state. Very many of our schools operate on the basis of a commitment to Christian service to the public."[56] To explain the idea of Christian service to the public, Lankshear described a Church of England primary school with a majority of Islamic students. He claimed that these schools serve the public by teaching Islamic students the values necessary to help them assimilate into English society. A document from the government's Department of Children, Schools and Families similarly affirms the contribution "these [faith] schools make to the wider school system and to society in England."[57]

Anglicans and Roman Catholics had the largest stake in education in 1944 and they quickly became partners with the state in terms of policy formation and planning for education. Both churches have powerful education boards that negotiate with government officials on issues of funding, curriculum, and school governance.[58] At present, they represent nearly 95 percent of pupils in religious schools. There were also a small number of Methodist, Baptist, and Jewish schools included in the provisions of the 1944 act. Because the state determines which new church schools to finance, however, there has been considerable controversy in recent decades on whether to expand the existing system to include other religious groups, particularly Muslims.

For many years, Muslims pressed for their own publicly funded religious schools. On three separate occasions, the government turned down applications from Muslim schools. In each case, the secretary of state for Education claimed that the refusal had nothing to do with the school being Islamic. Muslims, however, were understandably frustrated with a system where Christian and Jewish schools were fully financed by the government but their own schools were not. As one British Muslim leader noted to us, "the fact that there were no government-funded Muslim schools was a ridiculous anomaly that had to go."[59] In 1997 the Blair Labour government finally approved the first Muslim state primary schools. He reinforced this decision with a Green Paper on education that proposed expanding both the number of religious schools and their diversity: ". . . we welcome more schools provided by the churches and other major faith groups."[60] Since 1997, Muslim, Sikh, Seventh-day Adventist, Greek Orthodox, and Hindu schools have joined the maintained sector. The overall number of Christian schools (7,000) dwarfs the seven publicly financed Islamic schools, thirty-six Jewish schools, and a handful of others, but the Blair government certainly moved the system in a more pluralistic direction. The government also provides information and personnel to help new schools negotiate the complicated process of securing state aid.[61]

Public funding for Islamic schools has occasioned a good deal of political controversy. As far back as 1985, a government report on education and ethnic communities concluded "separate schools would not be in the long term interest of ethnic minority communities."[62] The report recognized the need for a multicultural education that would expose students to the religious pluralism in Britain, but implied that state schools would better serve ethnic and religious minorities because they would more effectively integrate minorities into mainstream British culture. Opponents of state aid perceive religious schools to be socially divisive because they segregate children along religious lines, a process that militates against the development of the common bonds and values necessary in a liberal, pluralistic culture. These concerns intensified in the aftermath of racial riots in the cities of Oldham and Bradford in the summer of 2001. A Home Office–commissioned study of the riots highlighted the problem of racial and religious segregation and recommended that all religious schools offer 25 percent of all places to students of other faiths or no faith. Such a practice would be "more inclusive and create better representation of all cultures and ethnicities."[63] The government briefly considered making this recommendation on admission policy mandatory, but quickly backed down in the face of united opposition from faith school providers.

Public anxiety about separate schools also rose in the aftermath of the London train bombings by Muslim extremists in July 2005. A poll conducted shortly after those bombings found that nearly two-thirds of the British public opposed the government's plan to increase the number of religious schools, a finding that was almost certainly more a function of the publicity surrounding the attacks than any deeply grounded public opposition to faith schools.[64] British Muslims understandably perceive attacks on faith schools as an implicit criticism of their schools. Ibrahim Hewitt, deputy chairperson of the Association of British Schools, wryly noted that "recent criticism of faith schools is not a new phenomenon, but neither is it historically based. Education for centuries had a religious foundation. Until Muslim schools came on the scene, though, faith schools weren't described as 'separate' schools nor were they criticized as they are today."[65] Muslim leaders also pointed out that none of the British Muslims convicted in the Bradford and Oldham riots or any of those linked to the London bombings had been to an Islamic secondary school.

Like their Christian school counterparts, Islamic schools incorporate religious elements into the curriculum and they give preference to Muslim applicants in the admission process. There is plenty of demand for those few spots. According to a 2005 survey commissioned by the Islamic Human Rights Commission, of the 1,125 British Muslims surveyed, 47.5 percent indicated that they would prefer to send their children to an Islamic school rather than a state school. Interestingly, however, the survey also found that respondents placed academic success and religious affiliation as equal considerations in choosing a school.[66] While there is little empirical research on the success of Islamic schools, data based on one of those schools, Leicester Islamic Academy, demonstrate that students are achieving twice the national average grades in the examinations taken around the age of 16.[67]

Despite the concern expressed by some, the government has moved forward with plans to expand the faith school system. A joint document signed by the Department for Children, Schools and Families and leaders of Britain's main faith communities committed the government to opening more faith schools where there was parental demand, while religious groups pledged themselves to promote social cohesion in their schools.[68] There is plenty of parental demand for faith schools in the Muslim community. As we noted above, there are seven Islamic schools currently in the maintained sector, but there are more than one hundred independent Islamic schools educating an estimated 15,000 Muslim children that are not at present a part of the state system.

Independent schools are not required to follow the national curriculum and they face far less governmental oversight than do religious schools that are in the maintained sector. There are good reasons to believe that bringing more of those independent schools into the state system is a better way to ensure the successful integration of Muslims and other religious minorities into the liberal values of British culture than leaving them outside of the current dual system. This point was reinforced in the statement signed by the government and faith school providers: "[faith schools] have a particular role to play in helping to meet the needs of those people in their faith communities who would otherwise be hard to reach, thus enabling them to integrate into society."[69] Finally, there is also a growing body of evidence that suggests that, like their Anglican and Catholic counterparts before them, Muslim, Sikh, Hindu, and Greek Orthodox schools are perfectly capable of preserving their group's religious identity while preparing their children for life in the broader British community.[70]

The British educational policy demonstrates a healthy neutrality on the part of the state between a religious and nonreligious perspective, and stands in stark contrast to policy in the United States that disadvantages parents who desire an education for their children in the context of their religious beliefs. State aid to religious schools in Britain, as is the case in the Netherlands, makes possible a more robust form of pluralism and allows religious groups to teach their children their distinctive religious and cultural beliefs and practices in the schools. The Church of England affirms that "the justification for Church schools lies in offering children and young people an opportunity to experience the meaning of the Christian faith,"[71] while the website for the Islamia primary school, the first publicly financed Islamic school in Britain, proclaims that the school "strives to provide the best education, in a secure Islamic environment, through the knowledge and application of the Qur'an & Sunnah."[72] The current system is balanced between secular and religious viewpoints and is increasingly equitable among religious groups.

Religious education and worship have also been a part of the formal curriculum in all maintained schools since the 1944 Education Act. Under the law, the LEA works with the SACRE to draft a syllabus for religious education and a policy on religious worship. Voluntary-aided schools have the right to teach religious education in accordance with the tenets of their faith and can include worship in one of their own religious buildings. Community and voluntary-controlled schools, whether they are religious or not, must teach religious education and have acts of collective worship. The Education Reform Act of 1988 reaffirmed those requirements and strengthened the specifically Christian aspects of the policy. The law now requires that religious instruction "reflect the fact that the religious traditions in Great Britain are in the main Christian whilst taking account of the teaching and practice of the other principal religions represented in Great Britain," and mandates that the daily act of worship be of a "broadly Christian character." Parents have the right to withdraw their children from religious instruction and worship, and schools may petition their SACRE to allow the daily act of worship to reflect the predominant faith found in the school, or the range of faiths in the school.[73] Because of its establishment model, however, Britain has not chosen the route of released time programs either for religious instruction or collective worship, as is the case with other countries in our study.

While on its surface the law clearly preferences Christianity, in practice most religious education curricula take a multicultural and multifaith approach to the topic. The Durham agreed syllabus on religious education, as an example, includes a consideration of Christianity, Judaism, Buddhism, Hinduism, Sikhism, and Islam.[74] For the most part, religious minorities have not opposed the religious requirements of the act, but have instead sought to work with the government to ensure that their tradition is adequately presented. Dr. Fatma Amer, former head of education and interfaith relations at the London Central Mosque, noted to us that "we [Muslims] have a good relationship with the government's Department for Children, Schools and Families . . . and we have good relations with SACREs in most boroughs."[75] The data on the collective worship aspect of the act are more mixed. A government evaluation on this issue discovered that many schools fail to comply with the requirements for collective worship and that SACREs are not particularly successful at making compliance a high priority.[76]

The fact that there is religious education and worship reflects the continued significance of England's established church-state model. However minimal its formal powers might be, the fact that there is an established church sustains a view that religion has a role to play in public institutions. Public support for religious education is high and no government, Labour or Conservative, has argued that the existing arrangements should be fundamentally changed. As we have seen, the religious establishment is not aggressively Christian. The rationale for the policy is that religious education and worship can be the basis for cultural cohesion and moral development. Religious education, one government document asserts, can "develop a respect for and sensitivity to others, in particular those whose faith and beliefs are different from their own . . . [and] enable pupils to combat prejudice and contribute to community cohesion."[77] According to a statement by the Church of England's Education Policy Committee, collective worship "contributes toward students' spiritual and moral development."[78]

There are, of course, a number of philosophical and practical difficulties inherent in the English arrangement. The policy implies that religious education and worship, of a very general character and guided by an establishment, nonsectarian perspective, can provide moral absolutes for schoolchildren. But that begs the question if religion can be the basis for the definition of consensual values in a society increasingly divided by religion. Britain's religious diversity challenges this assumption. The difficulty that many local education authorities have had in following the policy's guidelines on collective worship suggests that religion, by itself, cannot perform this cultural function. The current policy is also a problem for those persons—religious or nonreligious—who do not accept that there are such things as "consensual" religious beliefs.

England is involved with religion in ways that are not possible in the United States. As we have noted, English educational policy encourages pluralism and is ever more evenhanded among religious traditions. However, one can argue that the policy violates the principle of government neutrality because—on paper, if not always in practice—the policy prefers Christian instruction and worship.

Church, State, and Nonprofit Service Organizations

As with education, British churches led the way in forming social service agencies in the late nineteenth century.[79] Religious values motivated the work of these early reform efforts in child care, poor relief, prison reform, and public health. Religious charities could not generate adequate resources to meet the growing demand for human services in the twentieth century, nor did they provide their services evenly. They practiced what Lester Salamon calls philanthropic particularism.[80] Religious philanthropy focused on specific subgroups of the population but often ignored others. Evangelical groups, who led the way in welfare reform in Britain, frequently made a distinction between the "deserving" and "undeserving" poor. As popular support for public welfare grew, government involvement increased to correct for inherent shortcomings of the voluntary sector.

Following World War II, legislation on health, housing, education, and income support formed the basis for a comprehensive British welfare state. Social welfare provision in Britain differed from that of Germany and the Netherlands in that it was never pillarized on the basis of religious differences. Religious philanthropy survived in the postwar period, but in the new statutory system the role of religious nonprofit agencies gradually diminished as the state assumed primary responsibility for the delivery, regulation, and funding of public welfare.[81] Religious agencies also faced increasing secularizing pressures from the emerging social work and health care professions that dominated public welfare. Social work professionals stressed "objective" and "scientific" criteria that they often believed excluded or made irrelevant a religiously informed point of view. Christian agencies, which in many cases shared the ideological presuppositions of the profession, fueled the secularization process by redefining their work in more "acceptable," i.e., nonreligious, terms. As one expert on the history of voluntary organizations has noted, the state expanded its social welfare provision often at the expense of efforts by Christian agencies.[82]

Conservative Party prime minister Margaret Thatcher introduced considerable change to the voluntary sector, particularly in her third term of office at the end of the 1980s. In keeping with her commitment to privatization, public choice, and reducing the government's role, Thatcher stressed the benefits of using voluntary organizations and for-profit companies rather than the state to provide public services. She argued that voluntary agencies could expand consumer choice, reduce costs, and promote efficiency by introducing competition to public services. Contrary to popular imagination and her rhetoric, Thatcher did not reduce public spending on welfare; spending and public support for the welfare state remained high throughout her time in office.[83] Thatcher did, however, alter how the state provided public goods; her policies shifted the responsibility for social services from the national government to local communities' social welfare departments, and those agencies increasingly turned to the voluntary and for-profit sectors to deliver social services. In 1990–1991, direct grants paid by government departments to voluntary organizations stood at £2.6 billion—a rise of more than 100 percent in real terms since 1980–1981.[84]

The push to change how the state was involved in social welfare policy continued with the election of Tony Blair, who institutionalized the devolution of social welfare provision to voluntary agencies and for-profit companies.[85] In a 2006 speech, Blair outlined an arrangement where the state would finance most social services, but it would turn to the voluntary sector to deliver them: "government as a whole is necessary in terms of funding, it is necessary in terms of setting clear objectives, it is not always necessary in terms of delivering the actual service. . . . Those organisations that are doing the most ground-breaking work, most innovative work are to be found in the voluntary sector today."[86] He also created a cabinet-level Office of the Third Sector to coordinate and strengthen the bonds between government and the voluntary sector.

If funding is any indication, the bonds between the government and the voluntary sector are quite strong. A survey of more than 3,800 charities found more than 80 percent of the income—in the form of grants and contracts for services—for the largest charities that receive public funds comes from the government. The study also found that smaller charities receive less of their annual income from government sources.[87]

Religious agencies remain an important part of the voluntary sector. With an annual budget of £236 million, the Salvation Army is England's sixth-largest charity and reasonably claims that it is the most diverse provider of social welfare in England after the government. It employs 4,000 workers, serves two million meals per year to people in need, provides addiction services to 1,000 people at any one time, and helps more than 1,300 people per year move from homelessness to independent living. In 2006, a majority of its budget came from the government.[88] One of England's oldest voluntary organizations, the Shaftesbury Society, founded in 1844 by the Christian philanthropist Lord Shaftesbury, receives more than 90 percent of its £28 million budget for working with disabled people from the government.[89]

Christian agencies have historically dominated the social welfare scene, although there were no political debates around the issue of state aid to diverse Christian organizations as there had been with the issue of public funding of denominational schools. Notably, the Church of England did not dominate the charity field in the late nineteenth century as many of the initial organizations were nondenominational. Of the nearly one hundred social welfare and children's care and adoption agencies listed in the most comprehensive guide to Christian agencies in the United Kingdom, 60 percent are nondenominational, 20 percent are Roman Catholic, 10 percent are Anglican, and the rest are from various Christian churches.[90] Jewish organizations have also received extensive government aid; Muslim and Sikh agencies are in their infancy, but some of them have received government money as well. In 2005, for example, the Department for Business Enterprise and Regulatory Reform awarded a £250,000 contract to the Muslim Council of Britain to raise awareness in the Muslim community about the Employment Equality (Religion or Belief) Regulations.

With increased funding have come questions about the independence of voluntary organizations. The national survey of charities highlighted above indicated that only a quarter of the agencies that receive government money agreed with the statement that they are free to make decisions without pressure to conform to the wishes of the funders.[91] Most of the struggles between government and agencies seem to focus on issues related to a cutback of government funds and to matters related to professional standards. However, government funding can be an additional burden for religious agencies where, as Peter Dobkin Hall notes, "quality of service has tended to be defined in less than calculable ways."[92] What is less clear is whether or not those religious agencies that wish to retain a distinctive set of values on questions related to hiring and offering services in ways consistent with their religious mission may do so. The recent experience of the Yeldall Christian Centres is instructive of this tension. Yeldall is a nonprofit agency that runs residential drug and alcohol rehabilitation homes in Britain. For Yeldall, there is a very close link between its religious and social work. The organization describes its mission in this way: "Yeldall is a Christian centre. This means that all of the members of the staff are Christian and that we use the bible as the basis for much of the teaching and groups in the programme."[93] Clients do not have to be Christian, or even religious, to participate but they are asked to respect the Christian aspects of the program. Since its founding in 1977, Yeldall has received a sizeable percentage of its annual budget from the government. In their most recent application for government funds, however, Ken Wiltshire, the director of one of Yeldall's residential centers, noted that "they [government officials] kept asking questions about why our staff were exclusively Christian and why there had to be a Christian component to our regime."[94] Despite the questions raised by government officials about their hiring policies, in the end Yeldall received its funding.

In many respects, English policy is bifurcated. On the one hand, Labour and Conservative governments are equally committed to giving voluntary organizations greater responsibility and flexibility in delivering social services. Somewhat in tension with this principle, however, has been a push by the government to ensure that any organization that receives government funds comply with equal opportunities legislation. The passage of the Equality Act (Sexual Orientations) Bill has raised alarm among some religious agencies about the kinds of services that they provide, and whether this portends an increased effort by the government to limit religious agencies' autonomy. As England becomes ever more secular, and possibly less sympathetic to deeply religious viewpoints, it is possible that religious voluntary organizations will increasingly face pressures by the government to secularize their programs, or will at least be asked questions to justify a link between their provision of social services and their religious mission.

Our interviews with agency heads suggest that agencies can, and in many cases do, retain a distinctive religious orientation if they are clear and consistent with government officials about why those values are important to them. David Tribble, divisional director for Social Services of the Yorkshire Division of the Salvation Army, noted to us both the challenges of the current policy, but also the freedom that the Salvation Army has to pursue its distinct mission:

We have a commitment to Equal Opportunities Employment, i.e., we do not discriminate on the basis of race, faith, or sexual orientation. However, if in the job description there is a specific need for a faith element then we can employ a person with that qualification. So, as part of a social project we need the managers to lead (as a part of their work) Christian worship. As this is an explicit part of their work it is not considered, legally, an issue to recruit for this. This is not always appreciated by some funders . . . who are not always happy about us employing only Christian managers.[95]

It is common for Salvation Army service centers to have religious symbols on the walls, spoken prayers at meals, voluntary religious services, and Bible studies. In short, while the policies of religious agencies receiving government funds have been an issue, they have not risen to the level of contentiousness that we saw they have in the United States.

Policy makers seem mostly concerned about the quality of the services nonprofit groups provide; few have questioned the legal system that allows religious agencies to receive state funding. Rab Rabindran, an official with the Department of Health, stated this view succinctly in an interview: "The government concern is that nonprofit agencies provide a service in the health and human social services field. We don't care who provides it, or really how they provide it, so long as they are providing what we think is the best service."[96]

Nor does the religious establishment serve as a deterrent for voluntary groups outside of the Church of England. As another person from the Salvation Army said to us, "it [the religious establishment] helps the Salvation Army because it creates a certain viewpoint that is accepting of state support for the religious activities of social service agencies."[97] We believe that there is much to this argument; the fact that there is an established church in Britain makes it easier for religious groups and the state to work in a cooperative relationship. The state accommodates religious social service organizations because the state perceives them to be for the public good. Church-based agencies have worked in partnership with the state, and, because virtually all religious agencies are eligible for public funds, there has not been the conflict that has occurred with state funding of religious schools.

Concluding Observations

England is the only country in our study that has retained a formal religious establishment, the second of our two church-state models. At first glance, this religious establishment might seem little more than a cultural relic of a bygone era that has little or no practical meaning today. It is certainly true that the partnership between church and state is not as strong as it once was, when the relationship between these two powerful institutions was seen as crucial for the nation's political stability and religious prosperity. We contend, however, that England's religious establishment continues to provide an alternative church-state model for pluralistic democracies, particularly in terms of the cultural assumptions and values it represents. The most important of these assumptions is that religion and religious organizations have an important public role to perform and that it therefore is appropriate for the state to take positive measures to recognize, accommodate, and support religion. The religious establishment serves as an acknowledgment by the state that faith has a public character to it, and that public policy can accommodate faith in a way that is equitable among religious groups and between religious and nonreligious perspectives.

To some degree the English church-state model does undermine, however, the basic goal of governmental neutrality on matters of religion. The key limitations of the current system are that it does not provide religious freedom for all or equal treatment among religions, specifically on the issue of religious instruction and worship in state-run schools. The rights of religious minorities have gradually expanded since the formal establishment of the Church of England in the sixteenth century. There are, however, no constitutional provisions protecting religious rights and not the same kind of theoretical commitment by the state to religious free exercise that is so robust in the Netherlands and in Germany. The passage of the Human Rights Act indicates a statutory movement in that direction, but it remains to be seen how far the British courts will go in applying it. At present, when religionists suffer because of their faith, they have less access to the legal system to secure their rights than is the case in the United States or Germany.

Historically, England's refusal to finance separate Islamic schools under the same conditions that applied to Catholic and Anglican schools also violated the equal treatment principle, but the government's decision in 1997 to fund two Islamic schools addressed that major problem. Even more significant has been the expansion of state aid to more Islamic schools, and to the schools of other religious minorities, over the past decade. In practice, on the issue of state aid to religious schools, English educational policy has moved much closer to that of the Netherlands and Australia.

More problematic, from the standpoint of equal treatment, is the place of religion in state-run schools. Under the current policy, religious instruction and acts of collective worship are intended to be primarily Christian. The current practice is oftentimes justified as a natural and necessary by-product of England's establishment model, but the policy raises any number of concerns. Historically, the religion provided in the schools was generically Christian, a recognition on the part of policy makers that it would be unacceptable for the schools to teach the particularistic doctrines of the Church of England. This accommodation worked particularly well in a culture where most people shared similar values and few took religion seriously. However, in a more religiously diverse and a more secular England, there are an increasing number of people who reject the "consensual" religion taught in the schools. Seen in this light, the current policy disadvantages secularists, fundamentalist Christians, Pentecostals, Muslims, and any others who do not consider themselves "generically" Christian. To be sure, many local education authorities have drafted curricula and instituted worship practices that introduce students to diverse religious traditions, and students can excuse themselves from the collective worship if they wish, but the law clearly preferences one religious viewpoint over others.

The paradox of England's partial religious establishment is that while it hinders the realization of governmental neutrality that we established as the basic standard by which to evaluate church-state practices in some cases, the system helps the state to achieve neutrality in even more respects. In terms of public funding for religious schools, the current system expands choice for Jewish, Christian, and Islamic parents who want a school permeated by religious ideas. In this way, the system is more neutral between a religious and nonreligious educational perspective than in the United States. This is also true for nonprofit social service organizations where the state provides funds for a wide variety of religious agencies to serve particular groups in the population. These nonprofit agencies achieve a diversity of service that would simply not be possible if the state provided the services by itself.

In some respects, religious pluralism in England has made it difficult to sustain this establishment model. One way to meet the goal of pluralism might be to stop funding religious schools and remove religious instruction and worship from state-run schools. Justice is best served, it could be argued, when state neutrality among the various religious traditions is gained by a strict separationist, no-aid-to-religion approach. This is the argument American strict separationists have made. Neutrality, in this view, means no state financial support or involvement with religious schools. In this way the state avoids favoring any particular faith, as it currently does with its partial support for church schools. The problem with this separationist approach, however, is that it is not truly neutral, but favors a nonreligious ethos over religious ones.

An alternative option that we believe is more genuinely neutral, and that has been increasingly practiced in England, has been the expansion of the current system to recognize more religious traditions, along the lines of the Dutch or Australian models. Religious minorities have looked to the state to recognize their rights, finance their schools, and make possible the public manifestation of their faith. In many respects, the religious establishment does make this possible. Not one of the Muslims that we interviewed for this project expressed opposition to the religious establishment; instead most of them see it as an ally in their quest for public recognition. Much as the state pragmatically accommodated Roman Catholics, Jews, and Protestant non-conformists in the past, England is increasingly accommodating Muslims, Sikhs, Buddhists, and other religious minorities in the present. In our view, this policy is consistent with the goal of neutrality among religious groups and between religious and nonreligious perspectives.

The limits to this expansion will come from secular voices that want to get rid of the religious establishment and from those who wish to defend a specifically Christian establishment. Neither group is particularly large in number and they obviously have divergent political goals, but they can and have joined forces on some matters, particularly on the issue of public funding for Islamic schools. In the aftermath of the terrorist attacks in Britain, secular and some conservative Christian voices questioned the wisdom of aiding "separate" Islamic schools. However, the government, the politically powerful churches, and the general public support both the establishment and an expansion of the current system. There is every reason to believe that England's religious establishment will continue to move toward the goal of recognizing and accommodating the diversity of religious voices in England.

Notes

1. For a good account of the British political system, see Philip Norton, *The British Polity*, 4th ed. (New York: Longman, 2001); and Philip Norton, *Parliament in British Politics* (New York: Palgrave Macmillan, 2005).

2. Cindi John, "Black Worshippers Keep the Faith," *BBC News*, January 8, 2005. Available at http://news.bbc.co.uk/.

3. Data on religion are available from the Office for National Statistics at http://www.statistics.gov.uk/census; the National Centre for Social Research at http://www.britsocat.com; and Peter Brierley, ed., *United Kingdom Christian Handbook: Religious Trends* (London: Christian Research, 2001).

4. Grace Davie, *Religion in Modern Europe: A Memory Mutates* (Oxford: Oxford University Press, 2000).

5. George Moyser, ed., *Church and Politics Today* (Edinburgh: T&T Clark, 1985).

6. For data on the number of Muslims in Britain, see Jørgen Nielsen, *Muslims in Western Europe*, 3rd ed. (Edinburgh: Edinburgh University Press, 2005); and Office for National Statistics at http://www.statistics.gov.uk/census.

7. Nicholas Hellen and Christopher Morgan, "Muslims Outpace Anglicans in UK," *Times Online*, January 25, 2004.

8. For a broad overview of this process, see Joel S. Fetzer and J. Christopher Soper, *Muslims and the State in Britain, France, and Germany* (Cambridge: Cambridge University Press, 2005).

9. Paul Whiteley, Patrick Seyd, and Jeremy Richardson, *True Blues: The Politics of the Conservative Party* (Oxford: Clarendon Press, 1994).

10. Ruth Gledhill, "Church Turns into Liberal Democrats at Prayer," *The Times (London)*, February 14, 1996.

11. Philip Stephens, *Tony Blair: The Price of Leadership* (London: Politico's Publishing, 2004); and Anthony Seldon, *Blair* (London: The Free Press, 2005).

12. For a good review of Hooker's influence, see Peter Cornwell, *Church and Nation* (Oxford: Basil Blackwell, 1983), chap. 1. For an overview of the Church of England, see W. L. Sachs, *The Transformation of Anglicanism from State Church to Global Communion* (Cambridge: Cambridge University Press, 1993).

13. For a good review of this period, see John Marshall, "Some Intellectual Consequences of the English Revolution," *The European Legacy* 5, no. 4 (2000), 515–30; and John Madeley, "Politics and the Pulpit: The Case of Protestant Europe," *West European Politics* (April 1982), 149–71.

14. Steve Bruce and Chris Wright, "Law, Social Change, and Religious Toleration," *Journal of Church and State* 37 (Winter 1995), 110.

15. Grayson Carter, *Anglican Evangelicals: Protestant Secessions from the Via Media, c. 1800–1850* (Oxford: Oxford University Press, 2001); and Kenneth Hylson-Smith, *Evangelicals in the Church of England* (Edinburgh: T&T Clark, 1988).

16. Laurence A. Kotler-Berkowitz, "Religion and Voting Behavior in Great Britain: A Reassessment," *British Journal of Political Science* 31 (2001), 523–54; Kenneth D. Wald, *Crosses on the Ballot* (Princeton, N.J.: Princeton University Press, 1983).

17. George Skinner, "Religious Pluralism and School Provision in Britain," *Intercultural Education* 13, no. 2 (2002), 171–81.

18. D. W. Bebbington, *Evangelicalism in Modern Britain* (London: Unwin Hyman, 1989), chap. 4.

19. Samuel Beer, *Modern British Politics* (London: Faber and Faber, 1969), chap. 2.

20. Michael Fogerty, "The Churches and Public Policy in Britain," *Political Quarterly* 63 (July–September 1992), 300–17.

21. Bernadette O'Keeffe, *Faith, Culture and the Dual System* (London: Falmer Press, 1986).

22. For a review of the legal status of the Church of England, see David McClean, "State and Church in the United Kingdom," in Gerhard Robbers, ed., *State and*

Church in the European Union, 2nd ed. (Baden-Baden, Germany: Nomos, 2005), 553–75; Kenneth Medhurst and George Moyser, *Church and Politics in a Secular Age* (Oxford: Clarendon Press, 1988).

23. *A House for the Future* (London: Stationery Office, 2000).

24. Russell Sandberg and Norman Doe, "Religious Exemptions in Discrimination Law," *Cambridge Law Journal* 66 (2007), 302–12.

25. Greg Hurst and Ruth Gledhill, "Peers Seek to Block Gay Rights Rules," *The Times* (March 21, 2007).

26. For a text of the debate, see http://www.publications.parliament.uk/pa/ld200607/ldhansrd/text/70321-0011.htm.

27. Ibid.

28. Ruth Gledhill, "Bishops Want to Apologize for Iraq War," *The Times* (September 19, 2005).

29. Paul Weller, "Equity, Inclusivity and Participation in a Plural Society: Challenging the Establishment of the Church of England," in Peter W. Edge and Graham Harvey, eds., *Law and Religion in Contemporary Society: Communities, Individualism, and the State* (Aldershot: Ashgate, 2000), 53–67.

30. James A. Beckford and Sophie Gilliat, *Religion in Prison: Equal Rites in a Multi-Faith Society* (Cambridge: Cambridge University Press, 1998).

31. Paul Donovan, "Faithful Service: Radio Waves," *The Times* (December 30, 2007).

32. Eileen Barker, "The British Right to Discriminate," in Thomas Robbins and Roland Robertson, eds., *Church-State Relations: Tensions and Transitions* (New Brunswick, N.J.: Transaction Books, 1987), 270–84.

33. Tariq Modood, "British Asians and the Rushdie Affair," *Political Quarterly* 61 (April–June, 1990), 143–60; and Philip Lewis, *Islamic Britain: Religion, Politics and Identity Among British Muslims* (London: I. B. Tauris, 1994).

34. Kim Murphy, "A British Law Is No Longer Sacred," *Los Angeles Times* (March 6, 2008), A3.

35. Personal interview with Dr. Fatma Amer, director of Education and Interfaith Relations at the London Central Mosque (April 11, 2001).

36. Kim Murphy, "Britain's Diversity Debate," *Los Angeles Times* (February 9, 2008), 1.

37. "Islamic Human Rights Commission Press Release: UK—Shock at Backlash Against Archbishop of Canterbury" (February 8, 2008). Available at http://www.ihrc.org/.

38. Tariq Modood, "Establishment, Multiculturalism and British Citizenship," *Political Quarterly* 65 (January–March 1994), 59.

39. David McClean, "Church and State in England, 1993," *European Journal of Church and State Research* 1 (1994), 19–22.

40. Iain McLean and Benjamin Linsley, *The Church of England and the State: Reforming Establishment for a Multi-Faith Britain* (London: The New Politics Network, 2004).

41. Rodney Stark and Laurence R. Iannaccone, "A Supply Side Reinterpretation of the 'Secularization' of Europe," *Journal for the Scientific Study of Religion* 33 (1994), 230–52; Rodney Stark and Roger Finke, *Acts of Faith: Explaining the Human Side of Religion* (Berkeley: University of California Press, 2000); Anthony Gill, *The Political Origins of Religious Liberty* (Cambridge: Cambridge University Press, 2008).

42. David McClean, "State and Church in the United Kingdom," 570.

43. Muhammad Anwar, *Race Relations Policies in Britain* (Warwick: Centre for Research in Ethnic Relations, 1991).

44. Sandberg and Doe, "Religious Exemptions in Discrimination Law."

45. *Anti-Muslim Hostility and Discrimination in the United Kingdom* (London: Islamic Human Rights Commission, 2000).

46. For the full text of the act, see the Office of Public Sector Information at http://www.opsi.gov.uk/ACTS/acts2006/ukpga_20060001_en_1.

47. David Leckie and David Pickersgill, *The 1998 Human Rights Act Explained* (London: Stationery Office, 1999).

48. For discussions of the reach of the Human Rights Act, see Peter Crumper, "Religious Organizations and the Human Rights Act 1998," in Peter W. Edge and Graham Harvey, eds., *Law and Religion in Contemporary Society: Communities, Individualism, and the State* (Aldershot: Ashgate, 2000), 53–68; and Peter W. Edge, *Legal Response to Religious Difference* (The Hague: Kluwer Law International, 2002), chap. 3.

49. Lina Molokotus-Liederman, "Pluralism in Education: The Display of Islamic Affiliation in French and British Schools," *Islam and Christian Muslim Relations* 11, 1 (2000), 105–17.

50. Alan Cowell, "Britain Proposes Allowing Schools to Forbid Full-Face Muslim Veils," *New York Times* (March 21, 2007), 5.

51. Barker, "The British Right to Discriminate," 279.

52. For British poll results, see British Social Attitudes at: http://www.britsocat.com/BodySecure.aspx?control=BritsocatMarginals&var=POLTNGOD&SurveyID=229; for American poll results, see the Gallup Organization at: http://www.gallup.com/poll/26611/Some-Americans-Reluctant-Vote-Mormon-72YearOld-Presidential-Candidates.aspx.

53. For good reviews of the history of British educational policy, see O'Keeffe, *Faith, Culture and the Dual System*; Skinner, "Religious Pluralism and School Provision in Britain"; and *Faith in the System: The Role of Schools with a Religious Character in English Education and Society* (London: Department for Children, Schools and Families, 2007).

54. Robert Burgess, "Five Items for the Policy Agenda in Church Schools," in Bernadette O'Keeffe, ed., *Schools for Tomorrow: Building Walls or Building Bridges* (London: Falmer Press, 1988), 162–81; David W. Lankshear, *A Shared Vision: Education in Church Schools* (London: Church House, 1992); *The Way Ahead: Church of England Schools in the New Millennium* (London: Church House Publishing, 2001).

55. *The Way Ahead*, 27.

56. Personal interview with David Lankshear, executive director of the Board of Education for the Church of England (May 13, 1994).

57. *Faith in the System*, 1.

58. Robert Waddington, "The Church and Educational Policy," in Moyser, ed., *Church and Politics Today*, 221–55.

59. Personal interview with Dr. Hesham El-Essawy, executive director of the Islamic Society for the Promotion of Religious Tolerance (April 10, 2001).

60. *Schools: Building on Success* (London: Crown Copyright, 2001).

61. "Guidance on the Establishment and Government of New Schools" (London: Department for Education and Skills, 2003).

62. Bernadette O'Keeffe, *Schools for Tomorrow*, chap. 1.

63. *Community Cohesion: A Report of the Independent Review Team Chaired by Ted Cantle* (London: Home Office, 2001).

64. Matthew Taylor, "Two-Thirds Oppose State Aided Faith Schools," *The Guardian* (August 23, 2005), 4.

65. Ibrahim Hewitt, "Schools of Good Faith," *Q News* 339–400 (January–February 2002),14.

66. Saied R. Ameli, Aliya Azam, and Arzu Merali, *Secular or Islamic? What Schools Do British Muslims Want for Their Children?* (London: Islamic Human Rights Commission, 2005).

67. Alan Cowell, "Islamic Schools Test Ideal of Integration in Britain," *New York Times* (October 15, 2006), 12.

68. *Faith in the System*.

69. *Faith in the System*, 1.

70. "Muslim Schools: Better Than Billed," *The Economist* (September 7, 2006).

71. *The Way Ahead*, 11.

72. Available at http://www.islamia-pri.brent.sch.uk/.

73. Richard Gold, *The Education Act Explained* (London: Stationery Office, 1999).

74. See http://www.coxhoe.durham.sch.uk/Curriculum/RE.htm.

75. Personal interview with Dr. Fatma Amer, head of Education and Interfaith Relations, London Central Mosque (April 11, 2001).

76. "An Evaluation of the Work of Standing Advisory Councils for Religious Education" (London: Crown Copyright, 2004).

77. *Faith in the System*, 10.

78. "The Churches and Collective Worship in Schools: A Position Paper." Available at: www.cofe.anglican.org.

79. For a review of this activism, see D. W. Bebbington, *Evangelicals in Modern Britain*, and June Rose, *For the Sake of the Children: Inside Dr. Barnardo's* (London: Hodder and Stoughton, 1987).

80. Lester Salamon, "Partners in Public Service: The Scope and Theory of Government-Nonprofit Relations," in Walter M. Powell, ed., *The Nonprofit Sector: A Research Handbook* (New Haven, Conn.: Yale University Press, 1987), 99–117.

81. James A. Beckford, "Great Britain: Voluntarism and Sectional Interests," in Robert Wuthnow, ed., *Between States and Markets* (Princeton, N.J.: Princeton University Press, 1991), 30–63.

82. Frank Prochaska, *Christianity and Social Service in Modern Britain: The Disinherited Spirit* (New York, Oxford: Oxford University Press, 2006).

83. Ivor Crewe, "The Thatcher Legacy," in Anthony King, ed., *Britain at the Polls: 1992* (Chatham, N.J.: Chatham House, 1993), 1–28.

84. Perri 6 and Penny Fieldgrass, *Britain's Voluntary Organizations: Snapshots of the Voluntary Sector* (London: NCVO Publications, 1992).

85. Margaret Harris and Colin Rochester, eds., *Voluntary Organizations and Social Policy in Britain: Perspectives on Change and Choice* (New York: Palgrave, 2001); and Thomas Bahle, "The Changing Institutionalization of Social Services in England and Wales, France and Germany: Is the Welfare State on the Retreat?" *Journal of European Social Policy* 13, 1 (2003), 1–20.

86. Full text of the speech is available at http://www.number10.gov.uk.

87. *Stand and Deliver: The Future for Charities Providing Public Services* (London: Crown Copyright, 2007).

88. *Salvation Army Annual Review 2006.* Available at www.salvationarmy.org.uk.

89. *Shaftesbury Annual Review 2005–2006.* Available at http://www.shaftesbury society.org/.

90. Heather Wraight, Peter Brierley, and David Longley, eds., *United Kingdom Christian Handbook: 2007/2008* (London: Christian Research, 2006).

91. *Stand and Deliver.*

92. Peter Dobkin Hall, "The History of Religious Philanthropy in America," in Robert Wuthnow and Virginia A. Hodgkinson, eds., *Faith and Philanthropy in America* (San Francisco: Jossey-Bass, 1990), 56.

93. "Information Packet for Applicants" (Undated Publication of Yeldall Christian Centre). Available at at www.yeldall.org.uk.

94. Quoted from Jonathan Oliver, "One Third of All Christians Say We've Suffered Discrimination," *Daily Mail* (March 17, 2007).

95. Personal correspondence with Major David J. Tribble, divisional director for Social Services of the Salvation Army, Yorkshire Division (February 14, 2008).

96. Personal interview with Rab Rabindran, Department of Health (May 16, 1994).

97. Personal interview with Christine McMillan, associate director, London Homeless Shelters for the Salvation Army (May 13, 1994).

~

CHAPTER SIX

Germany: Partnership and Autonomy

Discussions of church-state relations in Germany frequently invoke two basic principles: partnership and autonomy. Germans typically see church and state not as mutually exclusive, separate spheres of human endeavor, but as cooperative partners, both of which have a role to play in contributing to a prosperous, stable German society. Somewhat in tension with this principle—or at the least serving as a balance to it—is the principle of autonomy or self-determination.[1] The German mind-set sees churches and other religious organizations as possessing a basic right to an independence that leaves them in control of their own destiny and nature; they possess an autonomy on which the state is not to infringe.

Two additional values supplement these two principles: neutrality and freedom of religion as a positive freedom. Neutrality, as one German authority on church-state relations has noted, means "the State [is] not to identify with a Church; there is to be no Established Church. The State is not allowed to have any special inclination to a particular religious congregation. . . . On the other hand, religious institutions must not be placed in a more disadvantageous position than societal groups; this forbids a decision for State atheism."[2] Among all religious groups and between the religious and the nonreligious the state is to be neutral, not favoring one over another. Freedom of religion as a positive freedom insists that freedom of religion is more than a negative freedom; it extends beyond freedom from government restrictions on one's religious beliefs or practices to include positive efforts by the government to ensure that religious persons are in a position actually to exercise the freedoms assured them. Donald Kommers has put it well: "Freedom of religion in the positive sense implies an obligation on the part of the state to create a social order in which it is possible for the religious personality to develop and flourish conveniently and easily."[3]

These four principles work together to create an approach to church-state relations that to most Americans appears puzzling. The German Constitution clearly commands that "There shall be no state church," and Germans often speak of church-state separation and state neutrality on matters of religion. Yet Germany's equal emphasis on a church-state partnership and religious freedom as a positive freedom has led to practices many Americans would find in violation of church-state separation and neutrality. Germany's church-state thinking and practices have some parallels with both the principled pluralism of the Netherlands and the partial establishment of England.

In seeking to understand German church-state principles and practices, we first consider a few salient facts concerning Germany. The next section considers the historical background to contemporary church-state practices, paying special attention to how it has shaped the four principles already mentioned. The next four sections consider how in practice these principles and other forces have worked to mold the German approach to free exercise issues, to various forms of direct government cooperation with the churches, to religion and education, and to government policies toward religiously based social service programs. The final section presents some concluding observations.

The Nation

Germany is a country of a little more than eighty-two million people and 137,000 square miles, making it second to Russia as the most populous country of Europe. It has risen from the ashes of World War II to become a European and even a world economic and political powerhouse. Some have argued that the "economic miracle" of the 1950s, as it was often called, has been exceeded by the political miracle that has transformed a nation that had been marked by authoritarian government and political instability into a model of stability and liberal democracy for sixty years.

Ninety-one percent of the population is ethnically German, with the remaining 9 percent consisting of immigrants from Turkey, the countries of the former Yugoslavia, Italy, and a scattering of other countries. Religiously, 26.2 million (32 percent) are members of the Evangelical, or Protestant, Church; 26.5 million (32 percent) are members of the Catholic Church; 3.2 million (4 percent) are Muslims; 1.2 million are Orthodox Christians (1.4 percent);

100,000 are Jewish (.1 percent); and 22 million (27 percent) are without a religious affiliation.[4] There is also a scattering of Protestant churches, called free churches, which are not a part of the Evangelical Church in Germany (EKD). The latter is a federation of twenty-three regional Protestant churches, which are mostly Lutheran in background, while some come out of the Reformed (that is, Calvinist) tradition and some are products of a union between Lutheran and Reformed churches.[5]

The churches were one of the few German social structures that offered any significant opposition to the Nazi regime, and provided a certain moral strength in the immediate post–World War II period. The churches and the closely related Christian Democratic movement played major roles in the rise of Germany from the devastation of the war during the 1945–1960 period. However, already by 1973 one commentator wrote that "the church [has] lost a controlling influence over popular attitudes and with that its commanding position in society."[6] Less than 15 percent of the German population attends church at all regularly, and recent studies have shown that only 30 percent of German youths believe in a personal God.[7] But this low level of religious involvement can be misleading. There continues to be broad support and respect for both the Evangelical and Catholic churches. A 2005 survey found that 52 percent of the German population believes the Christian faith is not losing its significance, and 67 percent report they believe religion will either maintain or gain in significance in society.[8] The Christian Democrats have been the dominant party throughout most of the postwar era. A 1995 Constitutional Court decision ruling that crucifixes may not be displayed in public school classrooms if any student objects on religious grounds was greeted by a storm of denunciation and protest throughout Germany. Also, the person who is the foremost scholar of church-state relations in Germany reports: "Europe to many seems to be secular, agnostic, almost atheist—it is not. There is a strong underlying—and growing—religious spirit."[9]

Politically, Germany has a federal system with sixteen states (Länder). More power is centralized in the national government than is the case in the United States, but significant powers are assigned to the states. Germany has a parliamentary system of government, with a lower house, the Bundestag, directly elected by the people, and an upper house, the Bundesrat, composed of representatives of the states. The Bundesrat's approval is generally needed for legislation affecting the states, but on other legislation the Bundestag can override a negative vote by the Bundesrat by a simple majority. The chancellor is elected by the Bundestag. Germany has two major parties, the Christian Democratic Union (CDU) (the Christian Social Union [CSU] in

Bavaria) and the Social Democratic Party (SPD). Following the very close 2005 elections the Christian Democrats had 225 of the 613 seats in the Bundestag and the Social Democrats had 222 seats. The most important smaller parties are the Free Democratic Party with sixty-one seats (a liberal business-oriented party), the Alliance 90/Greens with fifty-three seats (a reform-minded environmental party), and the Left Party with fifty-two seats (a union of the recast Communist Party and several other left-wing parties). The current government is headed by Chancellor Angela Merkel, a Christian Democrat, who heads a Christian Democrat–Social Democrat coalition.

It is also important to note the role of the Federal Constitutional Court, since it has the power of judicial review. This is a court created by the 1949 Constitution to decide questions of constitutional interpretation.[10] It is divided into two Senates, as they are called, each composed of eight justices, and cases considered by the Constitutional Court are considered by one Senate or the other (referred to simply as the First Senate or the Second Senate). Half the justices are elected by the Bundestag and half by the Bundesrat. All serve twelve-year terms and are not allowed to serve more than one term. As we shall shortly see, the Constitutional Court has dealt with a number of crucial church-state issues.

Historical Background

There are five historical periods that are important in giving insight into German church-state practices and the origins of the four principles relevant to church-state relations mentioned in the introduction to the chapter. The first period is that of the Middle Ages and the Protestant Reformation. Throughout this era what is Germany today was a host of kingdoms and principalities very loosely tied together in the Holy Roman Empire; Germany as a nation-state did not exist. During the Middle Ages the concept of the "two-swords" or two authorities—church and civil rulers—took deep root in the German territories, as it did through most of Christendom. Under this concept the people were under two rulers, the prince and the church, and both worked for the stability and prosperity of society. This concept left undefined exactly which authority was responsible for what and led to many conflicts between the papacy and the Holy Roman Emperors, such as that between Pope Gregory VII and King Henry IV.

The Reformation shattered the unity of European Christendom. Most of the German territories followed the practice of *cuius regio, eius religio* ("the religion of the ruler is the religion of the state"). The 1648 Peace of Westphalia, which ended the devastating Thirty Years' War, reaffirmed the right of rulers to determine the religion to be followed in their territories, but also provided for the rights of dissenters. In each region, the prince determined whether his people were to be Catholic, Lutheran, or Calvinist. Given the relatively small size of many of the German principalities, this practice created areas almost totally committed to one of these religious traditions within Christianity. Up until the post–World War II era with its increasing prosperity and greater mobility, many areas of Germany remained overwhelmingly Catholic or Protestant. Even today this is still the case to a significant degree in some areas. The practice of *cuius regio, eius religio* also perpetuated the "two swords" concept, although in practice the secular authority came to dominate the spiritual authority. With the church (Protestant or Catholic) usually dependent on the civil rulers for its existence, this is not surprising.

It was from out of this time period that the tradition of a church-state partnership emerged. The well-being of society rested on the two pillars of church and state, or throne and altar, as it is often put. They were seen as united in a common cause. Thus cooperation and mutual support came to be the norm. The religious uniformity within the separate principalities made church-state cooperation and mutual support possible, for the most part, without raising charges of religious discrimination and favoritism. Paradoxically, the German tradition of church autonomy can also be traced to this same time period. The "two swords" doctrine held in theory—even if it was often not followed in practice—that the church and the state, the two swords, were coequal institutions, each with rights and responsibilities. In theory at least, the church was not an arm of or subservient to the state.

The second time period of importance for understanding the development of church-state relations in Germany is the era stretching from the Congress of Vienna in 1815 through World War I. At the close of the Napoleonic era the degree of unity that Napoleon had imposed dissipated. Germany was composed of nearly fifty principalities united into a very weak confederation and with conservative, nondemocratic forces dominant. From 1815 to 1871 weak, usually outmaneuvered liberal movements failed to gain ascendancy. Prussia gradually arose as a dominant force, and by 1871—with the help of military victories over Denmark, Austria, and France—had united Germany in a modern nation-state. Prussia thereby established the second German empire, which lasted until the end of World War I. It was a conservative regime, with a monarch (first William I, then Frederick III for a few months, followed by William I's grandson William II in 1888) and a parliament that was often overshadowed by a powerful chancellor responsible to the monarch.

Otto von Bismarck engineered the unification of Germany and served as its chancellor until 1890.[11]

Three marks of this period are important to note for understanding subsequent church-state developments and patterns. One is the nature and relative weakness of the liberal movement. Enlightenment liberalism never became the powerful, independent force it did in the other countries considered in this book. Instead, while present and influential, it cooperated with and in many ways came to be integrated with the still-powerful conservative landowning and titled classes. It never developed the same antireligious character it did in other European countries. This meant that the Catholics and Protestants did not face an independent, anticlerical liberal movement that might have forced them into cooperative efforts, as had occurred in the neighboring Netherlands; instead the Catholics were overshadowed by the Protestant leadership of the empire, who made common cause with the conservative forces.

The second point to be noted is that the second empire was marked by a very strong alliance between the Protestant Church and the newly formed German state. The various regional governments provided direct financial subsidies to the church, and "the church and its liturgical ceremonies became an important unifying force, binding the nation to the ruling dynasty and securing it through a providential interpretation of German history."[12] The close alliance between church and state that had existed from the Medieval and Reformation eras was maintained during the second empire.

A third important point is that it was during this era that the Catholics developed a significant political movement. At the time of German unification the new nation was clearly a Protestant nation. Its moving force was Prussia, which was strongly Protestant. For a period of time in the 1870s Bismarck launched what came to be called *Kulturkampf* (culture war), a series of oppressive and discriminatory measures against the Catholics. Doing so had the opposite effect of what was intended, as Catholics rallied behind their leaders and the Catholic Center Party developed into a political force that had to be reckoned with. Most of the discriminatory measures were repealed in the early 1880s, but the Center Party remained a political force.

Following the defeat of Germany in World War I the second empire came to an end and was replaced by the Weimar Republic, named after the city of Weimar where the new constitution was written. This is the third historical period to be noted here. Given the crisis created by the German defeat, the spirit of revolution that was in the air, and the generally liberal nature of the new constitution, one might suppose that the Weimar Constitution would have made a larger break with past church-state practices than what it did.

Historian Paul Means has noted that "the revolution was not as complete with respect to the church as its enemies had hoped and its friends had feared."[13] A variety of subsidies and privileges were kept by the Catholic and Evangelical churches. Nevertheless, the Weimar Constitution for the first time formally adopted the principle of church-state separation, declared there was to be no state church, and provided that "civil and political rights and duties shall be neither dependent on nor restricted by the exercise of religious freedom."[14] It thereby recognized the basic principle of governmental neutrality on matters of religion, as well as the earlier principle of autonomy. The significance of the Weimar Constitution for religious freedom can be seen in the fact that the current Constitution, when it was adopted after World War II, incorporated by reference the basic articles establishing religious freedom found in the Weimar Constitution.

The Nazi era is the fourth era of significance for present-day German church-state relations to be noted here. Most of the Evangelical and Catholic church leadership had remained largely negative toward the Weimar Constitution, attitudes that seemed to be vindicated when Germany experienced a series of severe economic reversals and political difficulties. Thus when Adolf Hitler and his National Socialists promised stability, prosperity, freedom to the churches, and greatness for the Fatherland, the churches, for the most part, initially rallied in support. The Catholic Center Party unanimously supported the Enabling Act in 1933 that gave Hitler dictatorial powers. In the same year the Vatican signed the famous Reichskonkordat with the Nazi regime, which assured the Catholic Church certain rights but also helped the Nazis consolidate their power. Within the Evangelical Church, a "German Christian" movement emerged that enthusiastically supported Hitler's rise to power and thoroughly wedded German discipline and greatness with Christianity.

On the other hand, the Catholic Church never truly supported the Nazi regime. It was more concerned with protecting its own institutional autonomy and maintaining a semblance of normal church life in the midst of political upheaval and war than either supporting or opposing Nazism. Also, many individual Catholic leaders, such as Cardinal Graf Galen of Munich, courageously opposed the Nazi regime. Within the more culturally powerful Evangelical Church—after an initial enthusiasm—opposition to Hitler quickly arose as the true nature of Nazism became evident. Frederic Spotts reports that by May 1934 already "anti-Nazi resistance had sufficiently crystallized for a Reich Synod of the opponents to be held in the Rhineland town of Barmen. Here, largely under the influence of Karl Barth, a 'Confessing Church' . . . was organized, based upon a confession of faith in the supremacy

of Scripture which might not be changed to suit prevailing ideological or political convictions."[15] This Confessing Church gained wide support and successfully opposed the pro-Nazi "German Evangelical Church." During the
Hitler regime, 3,000 pastors were arrested, at least 125 were sent to concentration camps, and 22 were executed, including the famous pastor and theologian Dietrich Bonhoeffer.[16] After the war the newly constituted Evangelical Church—under the leadership, among others, of Martin Niemoller, who
had recently been released from seven years in a concentration camp—
adopted the Stuttgart Declaration, which acknowledged the churches' and
the nation's guilt:

> We know ourselves to be with our nation not only in a great community of suf-
> fering but also in a solidarity of guilt. With great pain we say: because of us, in-
> finite suffering has been brought to many peoples and countries. . . . We con-
> demn ourselves because we did not believe more courageously, did not pray
> more devotedly, did not believe more joyously, and did not love more deeply.
> Now a fresh start is to be made in our churches.[17]

As a result of this highly traumatic era two lessons with lasting implications for church-state relations have been burned into German thinking.
One is that the church courts enormous danger when it is too subservient to
the state. The church up to that point in German history was suddenly seen
as being too subservient to the state, too ready to make common cause with
the state, and too quick to advance whatever policies the state was supporting. The principle of church autonomy, already present in the German tradition, received a new and urgent emphasis. A second lesson was that the
church must play a role in the political and social life of the nation. The big
error of the church was not seen as being its active support of Hitler—which
had been brief and limited—but its silence and acquiescence. Both the
Catholic and Evangelical churches emerged from the era of National Social-
ism with a greatly strengthened resolve to be active, positive forces in society. The concept of strict church-state separation even today is seen as a dangerous doctrine, one that implies the political realm is to be secularized, with
religion's influence muted or nonexistent.

The postwar era is the fifth of the historical time periods to be noted. It
saw the rise of the Christian Democratic movement, the most powerful political force in the postwar era.

> Christian Democracy was created by a few men—many of whom, being under
> death sentence for anti-Nazi activities, had no right to be alive in 1945—who

confounded some of the elementary rules of society and politics. This small group of persons . . . succeeded in establishing an inter-confessional political party in Berlin within a month of the collapse of the Third Reich and in most other parts of Germany within six months after that.[18]

This new party was interconfessional—including both Catholics and Protestants—and was firmly committed to liberal democracy and to learning from the bitter experiences under the Weimar Republic and the Third Reich. By firmly linking Christianity—both Protestant and Catholic—to the powerful democratic impulses sweeping postwar Germany, it made possible the continued cooperation or partnership of the state with religion. Religion and Christianity came to be seen as positive, democratizing forces and as bulwarks against the reemergence of Nazism. Church-state cooperation was thereby seen not as a danger to be avoided, but as an asset to be used in the search for democracy.

In 1948 the Western allies decided it was time to move ahead with a constitution for the three zones of Germany under their jurisdiction. The parliaments of the eleven German states that had been previously set up elected a Parliamentary Council to write the constitution. Working from a draft that a conference of experts had put together, the council wrote a new constitution.[19] It was approved by the Allies and the state parliaments, and went into effect in May 1949. Its preamble begins with a recognition of God: "Conscious of their responsibility before God and Humankind. . . ."[20] The first nineteen articles constitute a bill of rights, with Article 4 assuring that "(1) Freedom of faith and conscience as well as freedom of creed, religious or ideological, are inviolable," and "(2) The undisturbed practice of religion shall be guaranteed." Its third section provides for conscientious objectors to be relieved from military service. It is helpful to note that ideological as well as religious freedom and the practice as well as the freedom of conscience are safeguarded. Article 3 is also relevant to church-state issues. It provides that "All people are equal before the law" and "Nobody shall be prejudiced or favoured because of their sex, birth, race, language, national or social origin, faith, religion or political opinions." The basic principle of neutrality is seen in these provisions. Article 7 of the Constitution deals with education and, as will be seen later, contains several provisions crucial for church-state relations. The provisions of Articles 3 and 4 are supplemented by Article 140, which incorporates the basic religious freedom provisions of the old Weimar Constitution into the current Basic Law. Among the provisions thereby included in the Basic Law are a ban on the existence of a state church and, as we will see later, several provisions with implications for religious establishment issues.

In the German Democratic Republic (GDR) the churches faced enormous pressures for over forty years.[21] Although the outright opposition of the communist authorities waxed and waned over the forty years of their rule, even in the best of times parents were pressured not to baptize their children, church-going young people were often unable to obtain a college education, and active Christians were often denied government and business promotions. The church suffered as a result of such pressures. Just before the fall of the Berlin Wall in 1989, John Burgess reported that "by all measures of participation in traditional religious life, East Germany today is one of the world's most secularized societies."[22] From 1961 to 1989 the West German Evangelical Church lost 15 percent of its membership, but the East German Evangelical Church lost over 50 percent.[23] By several measures the population of the former GDR exhibits significantly more secularist attitudes than does the population of the old West Germany.[24]

Thus the unification of Germany in 1990 meant that German society as a whole became more secular than it had been when West Germany existed as a separate state. Also, the church leadership from the old GDR has a more cautious, suspicious outlook toward the government than does the West German church leadership. For the East Germans, over forty years under communist rule reinforced the lessons learned from Hitler's subversion and persecution of the churches.

Free Exercise Issues

In Germany, the free exercise of religion is seen as a basic, fundamental right that has been interpreted broadly by the courts. The free exercise of religion trumps, so to speak, concerns over the establishment of religion. This is a point explicitly made by Axel von Campenhausen, an Evangelical Church expert on church-state relations: "This is the main question. Is there religious liberty for everyone or not? The old democracies in Europe say this is the main purpose [of religious freedom]. Whether the church as an institution is independent from the state or not, whether the Queen of England is head of the church or of the Church of Scotland . . . is not so important if people are free to worship as they wish."[25]

The fact that Germany's Constitutional Court has interpreted free exercise rights more broadly than has the U.S. Supreme Court can be seen in the Constitutional Court's unambiguous holding that the free exercise of religion includes not only the right to believe, but also the right to act on one's beliefs. In a case dealing with a pastor who refused to take an oath when called to testify as a witness in a criminal trial, the Constitutional Court stated:

"Religious freedom under Article 4(1) of the Basic Law . . . encompasses not only the (internal) freedom to believe or not to believe but also the individual's right to align his behavior with the precepts of his faith and to act in accordance with his internal convictions."[26]

The strong emphasis on the free exercise of religion can also be seen in the tendency of the German courts to decide cases on free exercise grounds that in the United States would be seen as establishment of religion cases. This is due to the German courts' seeing religious freedom as having a positive as well as a negative aspect to it. In a 1979 decision finding the use of general prayers in the public schools constitutional, for example, the Constitutional Court based its decision on the concept of positive religious freedom: "To be sure, the state must balance this affirmative freedom to worship as expressed by permitting school prayer with the negative freedom of confession of other parents and pupils opposed to school prayer. Basically, [schools] may achieve this balance by guaranteeing that participation be voluntary for pupils and teachers."[27] The Constitutional Court saw allowing prayers in schools as making room for children who wanted to pray and disallowing such prayers as being a violation of their freedom to pray.

The expansive nature of religious freedom rights in Germany can also be seen in the commitment to including the charitable activities of churches and the organizations they sponsor within the scope of the religious freedom language of the Basic Law.[28] In contrast, the U.S. Supreme Court has tended to see organizations such as this engaged in both religious and secular activities and to extend free exercise rights only to their religious activities.

The strong emphasis on the free exercise of religion is rooted in the twin emphases on religious liberty as a positive right and the principle of neutrality. The Constitutional Court has frequently referred to neutrality as an important component of its free exercise decisions. Free exercise rights extend to people of all religious faiths and of none. In one of its decisions the Court declared: "The right to free exercise extends not only to Christian Churches but also to other religious creeds and ideological associations. This is a consequence of the ideological-religious neutrality to which the state is bound and the principle of equality with respect to churches and denominations."[29] In the case dealing with the pastor who had refused to take an oath in a criminal proceeding, the Court referred to "the command of ideological-religious neutrality that binds the state"[30] and gave a ringing endorsement of basic religious liberty: "The state may neither favor certain creeds nor evaluate the beliefs or lack of faith of its citizens. . . . The state may not evaluate its citizens' religious convictions or characterize these beliefs as right or wrong."[31] It upheld the right of the clergyman to refuse to take the oath.

Religious freedom as a positive right is also important in free exercise protections since freedom is seen as including the opportunity to exercise that freedom. In an interview Gerhard Robbers of Trier University's law faculty made clear that positive religious freedom is fully in keeping with religious neutrality: "Positive religious freedom means that government actively creates room for religious behavior, for religious life. . . . This is not promoting religion. That would be against neutrality. Atheists would object if government would promote religion. . . . It is making room for religion. It is just that there needs to be a basis, if people are religious, for them to practice their religion."[32]

The expansive and strong concept of free exercise does not mean it is unlimited. The Constitutional Court and German commentators have frequently stressed that when the free exercise of religion infringes on human dignity or public health and safety a certain balancing or weighing process must take place. In one decision the Court wrote that the church-state provisions of the Constitution require the courts "to balance and weigh the different interests and values at stake in the relationship between the freedom of the churches and the limits imposed on this freedom."[33] In an interview von Campenhausen stressed that in protecting public health or safety religious liberty can be infringed. He gave as an example the inappropriateness of a church cemetery being located near a town's water supply. "In the name of the sanitation of the water the state is able to reduce self-determination of the churches, even when the state is not antireligious, but friendly, neutral. Living together makes it necessary."[34] Then he cited a second example, "Of course, it is possible to have a demonstration or procession on the streets—a religious procession—but the traffic has its rights too. . . . You must compromise. So it is a balance."[35]

Some of the principles discussed thus far can be illustrated by reference to a particularly dramatic free exercise case that came before the Constitutional Court. A married couple, both of whom were members of the Association of Evangelical Brotherhood, held to a religious faith that believed it was inappropriate to make use of blood transfusions to solve medical problems. The wife suffered complications in the birth of the couple's fourth child, and the doctors thought a blood transfusion was essential. The wife, with the support of her husband, refused the blood transfusion and died. The husband was subsequently prosecuted and convicted for failure to provide his wife with necessary assistance. On appeal, the Court overturned the decisions of the lower courts on the basis of the free exercise provision of Article 4 of the Basic Law.

Three aspects of the Constitutional Court's decision in this case are instructive. First, the Court made a clear affirmation of religious liberty: "In a state in which human dignity is the highest value, and in which the free self-determination of the individual is also recognized as an important community value, freedom of belief affords the individual a legal realm free of state interference in which a person may live his life according to his convictions."[36]

Second, the Court went on to note that in this case personal religious freedom was clashing with a person's obligation to obey the law, but in this case the law must yield.

> The duty of all public authority to respect serious religious convictions, [as] contained in Article 4(1) of the Basic Law, must lead to a relaxation of criminal laws when an actual conflict between a generally accepted legal duty and a dictate of faith results in a spiritual crisis for the offender that, in view of the punishment labeling him a criminal, would represent an excessive social reaction violative of his human dignity.[37]

Thus the Court decided that even a law that was not aimed at constricting certain religious practices, but was a law of general applicability that met certain legitimate, appropriate public purposes, was overruled by the free exercise protections of Article 4. This is a position that the U.S. Supreme Court, as seen in chapter 2, has for the most part refused to adopt.

Third—and perhaps most importantly—there runs through the Court's decision a basic respect for the sincerity and importance of the religious beliefs of the husband whom most would judge helped cause his wife's death.

> The duties which the complainant owed to his children would lead to a different conclusion if, under the pretext of his own convictions, the complainant had allowed his wife to die, thus depriving his children of their mother. This is exactly what the complainant did not want. He was certain that prayer was the most effective way of saving his wife. His duties to the children do not extend so far . . . that he would have had to abandon what he thought was a more promising aid in favor of medical treatment which he believed would be ineffectual without God's help. Admittedly, society's moral standards would dictate that the complainant follow both paths simultaneously. However, because his religious convictions would not permit him [to use both ways to save his wife], imposing criminal sanctions against him was not justified.[38]

Muslims in Germany have faced some limitations on the free exercise of their faith, but due to the expansive understanding Germany has of the free exercise of religion they have not faced as many limitations as they have in some other countries. Probably the most contentious issue has been the freedom of Muslim women who are teachers in government-run schools or other civil servants to wear the traditional Muslim headscarf or *hijab*.[39] In regard to students, there are no specific rules or court decisions regarding their wearing headscarves or other religious symbols to school, and they are generally permitted. The controversy has centered on the right of Muslim teachers to wear headscarves while teaching. The Constitutional Court ruled in 2003 that for a local area to prohibit teachers from wearing headscarves there must be a specific law permitting local authorities to make this prohibition, and the Federal Administrative Court has ruled that "all laws prohibiting religious garments in public schools must be interpreted in a way that treats all religions equally while respecting the German cultural tradition."[40] Berlin has passed legislation banning civil servants, including public school teachers, from wearing any signs of faith, including Christian crosses, Muslim headscarves, and Jewish yarmulkes. Other states have interpreted the Administrative Court's decision as allowing them to ban teachers from wearing headscarves while still allowing them to wear Christian symbols, since Christianity is a part of Germany's cultural tradition. The issue remains to be fully resolved, although it would seem likely that the strong German commitment to free exercise rights and religious neutrality will eventually lead—and should lead—either to allowing all teachers to wear symbols of their faith or banning all teachers from wearing such symbols as Berlin has done.

Questions have occasionally also arisen over issues such as coeducational physical education classes in elementary schools in which young girls have sometimes been required to participate in clothing considered immodest. Girls in this situation have been excused from physical education classes with little controversy, and in the 1990s the Federal Administrative Court ruled that Muslim girls in elementary schools would be excused from having to participate in coeducational physical education classes.[41] Also, as just noted, Muslim students are free to wear headscarves.

The construction of mosques has also sometimes raised free exercise issues. The construction of a mosque in Stuttgart, for example, became highly controversial, and was finally rejected by the local authorities. But they suggested other possible sites, arguing they were not opposed to the construction of a mosque but only the location that had been chosen. There have also been recent controversies over the construction of mosques in Cologne and Berlin. On the other hand, a large, traditional-looking mosque was constructed in Mannheim with little controversy, when Muslims, Catholics, and the Evangelical Church worked together and approached the local authorities jointly.[42] Some Muslims have felt discriminated against, but most of the controversies regarding the construction of mosques seem to involve questions of timing and location, not attempts to block their construction completely.

Although not without some problems and setbacks, on the whole German government and society appear to be making the sorts of adjustments needed to assure that Germany's Muslim population is able freely to practice its faith. Germany's strong tradition of free exercise rights has helped in this.

State Support for Churches

The concept of a church-state partnership has done much to frame questions related to various forms of state cooperation with or support for religion. A booklet put out by the Evangelical Church clearly makes this point: "State and Church, which consider themselves to bear responsibility for the same people in one and the same society, are thus obliged to strive for intelligent cooperation."[43] Robbers has expressed a similar outlook: "It is part of the special position of the Churches that they have in a special way a public mandate."[44] In an interview he stated: "Once you accept that religion is something public, government should also have something to do with it, the community as such should have something to do with it."[45] Church and state—throne and altar—are seen as having different responsibilities, but they both have public responsibilities, they are both important for society as a whole and its welfare, and thus cooperation between the two works to the benefit of society as a whole.

The result is a system that is far from a total separation of church and state, but one that the Constitutional Court has described as a "limping" (hinkende) separation.[46] In fact, von Campenhausen has written, "Religious freedom and complete separation of church and state are in a certain sense mutually exclusive."[47] When asked to explain this statement more fully, von Campenhausen answered:

> This is true. If the citizen has the right of religious freedom, the state is not allowed to say, "I will place your children in compulsory school. All their life I will occupy with my state school. You have liberty, but I occupy the life of the children." It can't be. That's contradictory. . . . Separation and religious liberty cannot be combined if you have an entire separation. The State has a responsibility not to prevent its citizens from being religious.[48]

One is back to the concept of religious liberty as a positive as well as a negative freedom. This is not to say that the state should favor any one religious group over another, or should even favor the religious over the nonreligious. One German observer after another whom we interviewed made this point. But it does mean that the state should cooperate with the church and should seek to create space or room for it to fulfill its responsibilities.

This mind-set results in government supporting and helping the churches in a number of ways. One way it does this is by granting the three main, historical religious communities—Evangelical, Catholic, and Jewish—status as public corporations.[49] This status helps assure these religious bodies of their legal autonomy. It means ecclesiastical law has the status of public administrative law, allows the churches to make treaties with the government in which they come to agreement on matters of mutual concern, and grants them several other privileges. Probably its greatest significance is the mind-set that it reveals, one that sees the major religious bodies as having a public, or societal, significance. Religion is seen as being more than a purely private concern. Public corporation status is granted by the state governments, and thus the religious bodies with that status vary somewhat from one state to another. Many small religious bodies other than the Evangelical, Catholic, and Jewish groups are now recognized as public corporations in one or more states. Included among these are many of the free Protestant churches and, as of 2006 in Berlin, under order of the Constitutional Court, the Jehovah's Witnesses.[50] But no Muslim organizations have thus far achieved public corporation status. More on this shortly.

The best-known and most important of the privileges granted to churches that have qualified as public corporations is the church tax (*Kirchensteuer*).[51] Under the church tax all members of the Catholic and Evangelical churches and of Jewish congregations are assessed a fee set by the churches that amounts to about 8 or 9 percent of what is owed the federal government in income taxes. This money is added to one's income tax bill—in fact, it is deducted from one's paychecks by employers along with the income taxes that are owed—and is forwarded to the churches by the government, after the government deducts a small fee (about 4 percent of the money collected) for collection expenses. People who do not pay are subject to the same penalties and means of collection as are taxes that are owed.[52] The only way a member can escape the church tax is to resign his or her membership in the church, which, due to the public corporation nature of the churches, involves a formal, legal process and an appearance before the civil authorities.

In 2006 the church tax provided about 7.8 billion Euros (about US$12 billion) to the Catholic and Evangelical churches, which amounted to about 80 percent of their total income.[53] It clearly is their major source of income. But the churches have been experiencing some financial pressures in recent years, since the amount of money coming from the church tax has been declining. This is due in part to members officially leaving the churches, a trend that is still present but that has slowed down in recent years.[54] Also, since the church tax is tied to the income tax, it is affected by economic downturns and by recent shifts from income taxes to indirect forms of taxation. And retirees who are not subject to the income tax also do not pay the church tax. As the number of retirees goes up, church tax collections go down. The money is used to finance both core church activities and wide-ranging charitable and educational activities.

The legal basis for the church tax is found in Article 137(6) of the Weimar Constitution, which has been incorporated into the current Constitution. It reads: "Religious communities that are public corporations shall be entitled to levy taxes in accordance with Land [state] law on the basis of the civil taxation." In a series of decisions the Constitutional Court has upheld the legality of the church tax system, but has also insisted—contrary to practices sometimes followed in the past—that it may only be applied to actual members of the religious bodies. In one case the Court ruled that the wages of a man, who himself was not a church member, could not be subjected to the church tax because his wife was a member: "[A] law may not be viewed as part of the constitutional order if it obligates a person to pay financial benefits to a religious association of which he or she is not a member. . . . [O]ne partner's connection with a church does not obligate the other partner."[55]

The origins of the church tax system go back to the early nineteenth century, when the state confiscated church property in most areas of Germany, and as compensation, the civil governments agreed to make annual payments to the churches. In time these cash payments were transferred into the right of the churches to tax their members, with the civil authorities cooperating in collecting the taxes.

It is important to be clear on what the church tax is and is not. It is not simply a matter of general tax revenues being turned over to the churches. It is a cooperative venture by the churches and the civil authorities, in which the churches levy certain fees on their own members and the civil authorities collect those fees and are reimbursed for their expenses in doing so. Thus one can argue that the church tax does not violate the norm of governmental neutrality—funds are collected only from the church's own members with the amount set by the church, the government is reimbursed for its expenses, and one can avoid their payment by simply leaving the church. Jewish as well as Christian congregations are beneficiaries of it. On the other hand, one can argue that the principle of neutrality is being violated since the coercive power of the state is being put at the disposal of the churches, a service that is not available to most other organizations and religious groups who have not qualified for public corporation status. Most noteworthy is the fact that to date no mosques or other Muslim associations—since they lack public corporation status—participate in the church tax system.

To the non-German observer the wide acceptance of the church tax system is surprising, especially given the apparent lack of religious zeal on the part of most church members. Most German church members are sporadic in their church involvements, yet they pay the church tax with little complaint. The Greens and the Left Party have come out against the church tax system, but neither of the two largest parties—the CDU/CSU and SPD—have opposed it, and the Free Democratic Party, after coming out against it in the 1970s, has tacitly abandoned its opposition to it. The church tax and its general acceptance, more than anything else, helps demonstrate that the concept of church-state partnership in German society is a concept that has permeated German society and is not merely a theoretical or elite principle. None of the persons we interviewed made an explicit comparison between the church tax and the United Way charitable contribution system in the United States, but we made that connection several times after listening to Germans explain the church tax and its acceptance. The churches are generally seen as socially important institutions; they strengthen German society and ably provide many charitable and educational services. The church tax is one means by which one can relatively painlessly—because of the wage deductions—fulfill one's financial obligation to these all-important cultural, charitable, and educational institutions. One study showed that roughly two-thirds of the Germans interviewed did not even know how much they were paying in the church tax.[56]

When asked about his perception of the fairness of the church tax system, a pastor in the Protestant Old Reformed Church in Lower Saxony—which is a free Protestant church and not a part of the church tax system—replied that he did not see it as a problem. In fact, he was happy not to be a part of the church tax system, since he felt his church obtained more contributions by a voluntary system than the Evangelical and Catholic churches do by church taxes. He went on to explain that most members of the EKD and the Catholic churches, once they have paid the church tax, feel that their financial obligation to the church is fulfilled, whereas the members of his church are used to giving more than they would under the church tax system.[57]

This is not to say that the church tax is without criticism or controversy. A Catholic journalist whom we interviewed and who has had his differences with the church hierarchy complained strongly that the church tax greatly strengthens the power of the central church hierarchy, since the money goes to the regional church offices and is distributed downward from there. Others have felt that the church tax has made the churches overly complacent. One person we interviewed compared the situation to one that is frequently alleged to occur when a developed nation gives too much money too freely to an underdeveloped nation: complacency, a strengthening of forces defending the status quo, and a sapping of initiative and creativity.

In addition to the church tax, there are some other forms of direct governmental support for the churches, usually at the state or local level. Some state or local governments help subsidize the salaries of certain church officials or help fund the construction or upkeep of church buildings. Such supports are largely holdovers from an earlier age when there were many such financial supports for the churches, and today are usually justified on the basis that nonreligious organizations often receive such help. As Robbers has expressed it: "Further, many churches receive allocations from the State for activities in the same way as other publicly funded events; it is a part of the idea of State neutrality that Church activities are not to be put in a worse position than that of State funded local athletic clubs."[58]

The financial arrangements between the church and the state demonstrate that although there is no legally, formally established church, the Evangelical, Catholic, and Jewish faiths have certain advantages that other religious bodies and competing secular ideologies do not fully share.

The sizable Muslim population in Germany does not share in the public corporation status and church tax systems. And as we will see shortly there are other areas where a way has not yet been found to integrate Muslims fully into the German system of church-state partnership. Doing so is proving more troublesome than the free exercise issues discussed earlier. There are about 3.2 million Muslims in Germany, constituting 4 percent of the population. This makes them the third-largest religious community in Germany. Three factors have posed roadblocks to the integration of the Muslim mosques and associations into the existing church-state system. The first and no doubt most important factor that has raised challenges to integrating Muslims into the existing church-state cooperative system is the Muslims' lack of a centralized organizational structure. Both the Catholic and Evangelical churches are hierarchical in nature and thus they have centralized councils and leaders who can deal with centralized governmental bureaucratic bodies and leaders. However, two scholars have noted that German "Muslims are divided less by that [federal] structure than by their differing ideologies and lack of a centralizing hierarchy." They go on to note the many ethnic divisions such as Turkish, Kurdish, and Arab, as well as other divisions that

are themselves partly based on conflicting interpretations of Islam, something the structure of the religion allows for. These very different conceptions of their place in European society in general, and in Germany in particular, provide a formidable barrier to the cohesion of Islamic groups, preventing them from presenting a united front to the German state in their efforts to obtain the goals which they seek.[59]

Robbers has written: "Muslim theology seems to prohibit or at least be alien to organizing Muslims in religious communities with their specific structures, hierarchies, religious offices and binding teaching authority."[60] He added in an interview that if there is to be church-state cooperation, there must be someone with whom to cooperate, for there to be a partnership there must be a partner.[61] But—with the Muslims broken up into thousands of individual mosques (which do not have a formal membership) and a host of decentralized ethnic, political, and theological subgroups—in most instances there are no unified Muslim groups with whom the authorities can work.

This has led to an impasse, with German authorities for the most part saying the Muslims need to organize themselves in such a way that they can qualify for public corporation status and other forms of cooperation with the government. Meanwhile, many Muslims are saying the Germans need to make allowance for their organizational structures. The deputy chairman of the Central Council of Muslims in Germany has described the situation this way: "It is not easy to qualify as a public corporation and Muslim efforts to qualify have thus far been unsuccessful. And the German authorities have not been too keen to do so. They say there is no central organization. . . . But to be fair, the failure to obtain public corporation status is as much the fault of Muslims themselves as of the German authorities."[62]

A second factor leading to problems in integrating Muslims into existing church-state partnerships is the lack of a German tradition of immigration and of integrating new ethnic or religious groups into German society. Most present-day Muslims or their forebearers originally arrived from Turkey in the 1960s and 1970s as guest workers. It was initially thought they would stay for a period of time and then go back to Turkey, and were not seen as immigrants who had come to make Germany their home. Obtaining German citizenship was an arduous process, a process that was made somewhat less cumbersome by 1999 changes in the law. But there still is a lingering mind-set among some Germans, and among some Muslims themselves, that considers Muslims more as foreigners temporarily living in Germany than as persons who have come to Germany to become Germans and share in the economic and cultural life of Germany.

A third factor making efforts to fit Muslims into existing church-state partnerships more difficult is the advent of 9/11 and the subsequent Madrid and London terrorist bombings, as well as the existence of a small, but real, militant, intolerant Islamist movement. When asked if these factors have changed relationships with Muslims, Cornelia Coenen-Marx, an official in the Evangelical Church's central office, replied:

> Yes, I think so. Before 9/11 we had an atmosphere in Germany to go together between Christians and mosques. At the time we had the feeling of belonging together with different religions. . . . Now people are very skeptical. I think the very good relationships between the leaders of our church who are responsible for Christian-Islamic relationships—people [in favor of good relationships with Islam] who had been the majority in the church are now the minority. The majority of Christian people and congregations are much more critical of Islam.[63]

One study found, "Since 11 September 2001 one can measure a rise [in the German news media] in the explicit blaming of Muslims for all kinds of crimes, including terror, forced marriages and honour killings, as well as the oppression of women."[64]

As a result of these three factors most forms of cooperation between church and state, such as public corporation status, the church tax, and other forms of cooperation considered later in the chapter have not yet been fully extended to Muslims.

Church, State, and Education

The distinguishing mark of Germany regarding religion and education was, until recently, the domination of public education by confessional schools (that is, schools that were public in the sense of being financed, owned, and controlled by government, and confessional in the sense of being marked by either Catholic or Evangelical religious exercises and teachings). At the time of the writing of the Weimar Constitution there was a strong movement to develop secular schools that would be committed to teaching loyalty to the new liberal political order, but the Catholic Center Party, with the help of conservative Protestants, was strong enough to force a compromise that made room for the continued existence of confessional schools.[65] As a result, confessional schools dominated public education in the interwar period. Of the 53,000 public schools, 55 percent were confessional Evangelical schools, 28 percent were confessional Catholic schools, 15 percent were interdenominational (that is, of a broadly Christian, nonsectarian nature), and a handful were either confessional Jewish schools (97) or secular (295).[66]

There was a strong effort during the Nazi era to undermine the diversity of the school system in favor of schools uniformly supportive of the regime. As one Nazi leader bragged, "The curriculum of all categories in our schools has already been so far reformed in an anti-Christian and anti-Jewish spirit that the generation which is growing up will be protected from the black [that is, clerical] swindle."[67]

Following World War II the occupying powers generally favored doing away with confessional schools in favor of unified, secular schools.[68] Again, this was resisted by church authorities, especially by the Catholic Church. In the western zone, therefore, the occupying authorities allowed local areas to decide whether they wished interdenominational schools or confessional schools. The 1949 Basic Law placed the responsibility for education with the state governments, not the national government. Initially, most Catholic areas opted for confessional schools and most Protestant areas for interdenominational schools. As recently as 1967, 40 percent of all schools in Germany were public Catholic schools, 17 percent were public Evangelical schools, 40 percent were interdenominational (or nonconfessional, sometimes referred to as "Christian") public schools, and 3 percent were private schools.[69] But things have changed. Protestants had for some time not seen the need for separate confessional schools, and starting in the 1960s the often inferior quality of the public Catholic schools—many of which were very small— drew public attention.[70] As a result many Catholic areas opted for interdenominational Christian schools. (The terminology here is confusing for Americans, since even the interdenominational or "Christian" schools are public schools.) In 1968, for example, Bavaria—a heavily Catholic area— voted by referendum to do away with Catholic schools in favor of interdenominational Christian schools. The religious nature of interdenominational schools is largely confined to prayers, separate voluntary classes in the religion of one's choice, and a general emphasis on the historical or cultural role of religion in Germany society.

Today four types of schools are found in Germany. The most common type is the interdenominational Christian public school, followed by the confessional public school (usually Catholic in nature, but sometimes Evangelical). There are also secular (or nondenominational) public schools—most often found in northern cities such as Bremen and Berlin—and private confessional schools.

The legal, constitutional basis for public schools that have confessional or religious exercises and instruction as an integral part of them—practices that would be clearly unconstitutional in the United States under current

Supreme Court interpretations—is found in subsections 2 through 4 of Article 7 of the Basic Law:

2. Parents and guardians have the right to decide whether children receive religious instruction.
3. Religious instruction shall form part of the curriculum in state schools except non-denominational schools. Without prejudice to the state's right of supervision, religious instruction shall be given in accordance with the doctrine of the religious community concerned. Teachers may not be obligated to give religious instruction against their will.
4. The right to establish private schools shall be guaranteed. Private schools as alternatives to state schools shall require the approval of the state and be subject to Land [state] legislation.

A 1975 case decided by the Constitutional Court dealt directly with the issue of religious instruction in public schools. The state of Baden-Württemberg had decided in 1967 to establish interdenominational Christian schools. Some nonreligious parents objected to the religious education their children were receiving. The Court ruled in favor of the interdenominational school. Its reasoning in doing so reveals much about the German approach to this issue and how it differs from the American one. The Court first noted that "the complainants' request to keep the education of their children free from all religious influences . . . must inevitably conflict with the desire of other citizens to afford their children a religious education. . . ."[71] It then went on to make a crucial observation that the U.S. Supreme Court has never accepted: "The elimination of all ideological and religious references would not neutralize the existing ideological tensions and conflicts, but would disadvantage parents who desire a Christian education for their children and would result in compelling them to send their children to a lay school that would roughly correspond with the complainants' wishes."[72] The key point made by the Court—and one that is hard to deny—is that a school stripped of all religious elements does not lie in a zone of neutrality between the religious and the secular, but is implicitly secular in nature. In such a school the children of the nonreligious parents would receive the exact sort of education their parents desire; the children of religious parents would not. Given this fact and the resulting necessity for compromise, the Court ruled that the state should be given the latitude to make the policy decision that it had. "As a result, the state legislature is not absolutely prohibited from incorporating Christian references when it establishes a state elementary school, even though a minority of parents have no choice but to send their children."[73] It then went on to state that the school may not proselytize, that no one may be forced to attend religion classes, and that Christianity in secular disciplines should be limited to references to it as a formative cultural force in western civilization.

Article 7(3) requires the government to assure the presence of religious instruction in state-run schools: "Religious instruction shall form part of the curriculum in state schools. . . ." The operative word here is "shall," not "may." Also important is the fact that religious instruction is to be a part of the standard curriculum, not an extracurricular or ancillary course of study. It is, however, to be voluntary. For children up to the age of fourteen, parents may choose the nature of the religious instruction they are to receive or decide they are to receive no religious instruction at all. At the age of fourteen, the decision rests with the students, not their parents. Thus the religious instruction made available in most German schools is similar to the in-school released time programs the U.S. Supreme Court rejected as violating the First Amendment in a 1948 decision.[74]

It is also important to note that the religious bodies themselves, not the public school authorities, control the content of the religious courses of study. Article 7(3) ("[R]eligious instruction shall be given in accordance with the doctrine of the religious community concerned.") has been interpreted to mean that the religious authorities, not the schools determine what is taught. One sees here the concept of church autonomy entering in. One Evangelical Church official explained to us that this helps assure the religious neutrality of the state.[75] He made clear it is the parents'—not the state's—responsibility to teach religion, values, and worldviews. This they accomplish by choosing what religious instruction their children are to receive and, through their religious community, determining the content of that instruction. The state neither assigns children to the religious instruction classes nor controls their content. In practice these classes are for two or three hours a week, and are taught by clergy specially appointed to this role or by regular public school teachers (although under Article 7(3) of the Constitution no teacher can be forced to teach a class in religion against his or her will).

This system poses a problem for small Christian religious groups, Jews, and Muslims. Given the overwhelming number of Germans that belong to either the Catholic or Evangelical church, it is difficult for this system to accommodate small religious communities. Almost all the classes now are in the Catholic or Evangelical religious traditions. Normally six to eight students are required to justify a special class for them, and given the role of the religious communities themselves in developing the actual courses of study to be followed, the religious communities need to be large enough and sufficiently organized to come together in agreement on a course of study the public schools can then implement. With only 100,000 Jews out of a population of eighty-two million, they almost invariably do not have enough students in any given school to qualify for a separate class. The same is true of small Christian groups. With about 700,000 students, the Muslims often have enough numbers, but as is the case with public corporation status, difficulties have arisen because the current German system was developed to accommodate the more structured, bureaucratized Catholic and Evangelical churches and does not accommodate the prevailing situation among the Muslims. As noted earlier, they consist of many different ethnic and theological groups and lack a centralized, hierarchical organization. Interviews with Muslim leaders indicated that this situation is viewed among Muslims as a more serious problem than either certain free exercise problems or difficulties in obtaining public corporation status. One scholar has noted that in "Germany the introduction of Islamic religious education is one of the most pressing problems in the relationship between Church and State."[76]

M. A. H. Hobohm, deputy chairman of the Central Council of Muslims in Germany and managing director of the King Fahd Academy in Bonn, when asked in 1996 if he thought this situation would be resolved in the next four or five years, gave evidence of both the hope and the frustration of Muslims on this issue:

> We hope it will happen earlier, of course we are aware this cannot be done overnight. One cannot overnight start religious instruction classes at all German public schools where there are Muslim children. But we have to start with three or four schools in one or two of the states, and then gradually, year by year, increase the schools where such instruction takes place. . . . It is a rather cumbersome and difficult process. The German authorities are not in principle against it. But they are also not very understanding, and not very helpful. And very often we have to face a situation where the German authorities tell us, "We do not know with whom to talk in such matters because there are so many Islamic communities and even Islamic faith organizations." They either do not really understand that in Islam there is no hierarchical order, no organization with a center, or they don't want to understand it. Sometimes I have the feeling we have stated this to them so often that if they really don't understand it, it is because they lack the will to understand it.[77]

Twelve years later this Muslim's hope that Muslim instruction in one or two states would be started and then gradually spread to other areas has been partly, but only partly, realized. The different German states have taken different approaches. North Rhine-Westphalia, for example, offers objective, factual instruction in Islam, although two scholars who have examined the instructional material being used report that it appears to have strong confessional elements in it.[78] To the extent that this instruction is indeed confessional, it raises constitutional questions, since the curriculum has been written by the school authorities, not by a Muslim association, and thus could be seen a violation of Article 7(3) of the Constitution. In Berlin the Islamic Federation of Berlin has worked with the Berlin school authorities to develop instructional material of a confessional nature and, as of 2003, 1,000 Muslim students in sixteen public schools were receiving instruction under this program.[79] Nevertheless, in most areas—even those with sizable Muslim populations—there is no religious instruction for Muslims comparable to what Catholic and Evangelical students have access to. In that sense, the 1996 comments of Hobohm appear to be overly optimistic.

In regard to religious exercises in the public schools, most confessional and interdenominational schools have prayers at the beginning of the school day and sometimes at the end. As Kommers has written, "The predominant German view is that such practices constitute an important aspect of religious liberty so long as freedom of choice prevails."[80] As seen earlier, in 1979 the Constitutional Court considered the question of the constitutionality of such prayers and ruled in favor of their constitutionality based on the positive right of religious parents to have their children pray in school, as long as the voluntary nature of the prayers is maintained.

One of the church-state issues that stirred up the most controversy in Germany in recent years concerned a Bavarian law that required a crucifix to be displayed in every public school classroom. In 1995 the Constitutional Court ruled that if any student objected to having a crucifix in the classroom, it would have to be removed. At the heart of its decision was the Court's conclusion that "freedom of faith as guaranteed by Article 4(1) of the Basic Law requires the state to remain neutral in matters of faith and religion."[81] The Court then went on to weigh the positive freedom of religious parents to have a religious symbol such as a cross present in their children's classrooms against the negative freedom of nonreligious or non-Christian parents to have their children's classrooms free of a Christian religious symbol. It concluded: "Parents and pupils who adhere to the Christian faith cannot justify the display of the cross by invoking their positive freedom of religious liberty. All parents and pupils are equally entitled to the positive freedom of faith, not just Christian parents and pupils."[82] It then pointed out that the key distinction it saw between the display of the crucifix in the classrooms and prayer and other Christian religious aspects in the public schools was the element of voluntarism.

In as much as schools heed the Constitution, leaving room for religious instruction, school prayer, and other religious events, all of these activities must be conducted on a voluntary basis and the school must ensure that students who do not wish to participate in these activities are excused from them and suffer no discrimination because of their decision not to participate. The situation is different with respect to the display of the cross. Students who do not share the same faith are unable to remove themselves from its presence and message.[83]

The dissenting justices argued that "the negative freedom of religion must not be allowed to negate the positive right to manifest one's religious freedom in the event the two conflict."[84] In taking this stand they stressed that the cross did not have a proselytizing purpose and did not require any overt acts of recognition or acceptance from the non-Christian students.

This decision unleashed a storm of criticism throughout Germany. The then chancellor, Helmut Kohl, condemned it. Newspapers and radio call-in shows debated it, with the clear preponderance of opinion indicating opposition to it. In fact, the criticism grew so intense and the calls for ignoring the Court's decision so frequent that there were fears for the constitutional order and the legitimacy of the Court. Justice Dieter Grimm, one of the Constitutional Court justices who had been in the majority, felt compelled to write a major statement in which he argued for the rule of law and called for obedience to the Court's decision, even by those who strongly disagreed with it.[85] The furor began to die down only when the Court made it clear that it had not ruled that all crucifixes in Bavarian classrooms must come down, but only that they must come down if students in a particular classroom register a complaint. The vast majority have stayed on the classroom walls.

This decision and the reactions to it illustrate several key points. First, to an American observer—coming from a political system where even the posting of the Ten Commandments in classrooms and the presence of a cross in a city's seal have been held unconstitutional[86]—it is surprising that the question of crucifixes in public school classrooms is even being debated. That this issue is at the cutting edge of church-state debate in Germany today illustrates the extent to which church and state are in a cooperative relationship. The uproar the decision created in the nation reveals the strong support that still exists for this relationship. Second, this case illustrates the broad acceptance of the concepts of neutrality and positive religious freedom. The reasoning of both the majority and dissenting justices revolved around these concepts. They were accepted by both sides in this case; they differed only on how they were to be applied in this instance. Both sides agreed the state should be neutral on matters of religion, neither favoring nor discriminating against any religious or ideological perspective, and in interpreting this neutrality, both agreed that a genuine neutrality sometimes requires the state to take certain positive steps in order to create the possibility or the space people of faith need to live their faith.

There are—compared to the other countries studied in this book—few private schools in Germany, either religiously or secularly based. Only about 4 percent of students attend private schools, a lower percentage than in Australia, Britain, the Netherlands, and the United States.[87] This no doubt reflects the German tradition of incorporating religious elements into the public schools. Of the students in private schools about 80 percent attend church-related schools, and of these about three-fourths attend Catholic schools and one-fourth Evangelical schools.[88] Private schools receive most of their current expenses—but not their capital expenses—from public funds, although the exact amount they receive can vary from 75 to 90 percent of their costs.[89]

The Constitution assures in Article 7(4) the right to establish private schools, but they must be approved by the state government and obtaining that approval can be a difficult, time-consuming process. The basic requirement for approval is a school's ability to demonstrate that it is equivalent to the public schools in terms of educational quality and that it does not discriminate in its acceptance of pupils on the basis of the economic means of their parents. But once such standards have been met, the Constitutional Court ruled in 1987, private schools must receive public funding. The Court did so largely on the basis that educational freedom requires that parents be able to choose for their children the school with the religious or ideological worldview with which they are in agreement. Without state subsidies this freedom would be only available to parents with wealth. "Only when [private schooling] is fundamentally available to all citizens without regard to the personal financial situation can the [constitutionally] protected educational freedom actually be realized and claimed on an equal basis by all parents and students. . . . This constitutional norm must thus be considered as a mandate to lawmakers to protect and promote private schools."[90]

There are two private Muslim schools, in Berlin and Munich, that follow the normal German curriculum in additional to providing Islamic instruction.[91] They have qualified for government funding, on the same basis as have other private confessional schools in the Catholic and Evangelical Christian traditions. Other Muslim schools that do not follow the German curriculum, but place a heavy emphasis on distinctive Muslim lessons and practices, do not receive government funds, since they have been unable to demonstrate that they offer an education equivalent to that of the public schools.

Once religiously based private schools receive official state recognition, they find few, if any, restrictions placed on their ability to integrate religious elements into their programs. They are free, for example, to appoint teachers on the basis of their church membership.[92] The key requirements are that they must meet the state-established curriculum standards and their students must be able to do well in the comprehensive exams that are an integral part of the German educational system.

One final note on private church-related education involves the widespread church-sponsored kindergartens. German children typically start school at the age of six and the regular school system does not contain kindergartens as in the United States. A majority of families send their children from three to five years of age to kindergartens, which are sponsored by churches or independent societies created for that purpose. The expenses are covered by state and municipal funds, parental payments, and church or society funds.[93] There are no state-imposed limits on prayers, Bible stories, or other religious elements in the kindergarten programs.

In summary, based on the constitutionally enshrined concept of parental control over the religious upbringing of one's children, the norm of governmental neutrality in matters of religion, and the concept of positive religious freedom, Germany allows various forms of religion into its public schools as long as the principle of voluntary participation is respected. It also permits widespread public financial support for religious schools without interference with their religious missions, as long as the educational quality of the schools—as determined by the state governments—is assured. The sizable Muslim minority in Germany has been included in the system of public funding of private religious schools, but has experienced only partial success in breaking into the system of religious instruction in the public schools. Creating new forms and procedures to allow greater accommodation of its Muslim population in the public schools remains the biggest challenge in the area of religious freedom and education.

Church, State, and Nonprofit Service Organizations

Helmut Anheier of Johns Hopkins University has noted that "in Germany a highly developed nonprofit sector *and* a highly developed welfare state coexist. As the welfare state developed, the nonprofit sector in Germany expanded."[94] This is the case because the German government relies extensively on private nonprofit organizations to deliver most of the social services that are the hallmark of the German welfare state. The Catholic-inspired principle of subsidiarity plays a crucial role here.

> The doctrine of subsidiarity essentially holds that the responsibility for caring for individuals' needs should always be vested in the units of social life closest to the individual—the family, the parish, the community, the voluntary association—and that larger, or higher level, units should be enlisted only when a problem clearly exceeds the capabilities of these primary units. . . . What is more, the doctrine holds that the higher units have an obligation not only to avoid usurping the position of the lower units, but to help the lower units perform their role.[95]

Anheier and Wolfgang Seibel report: "The principle of subsidiarity of public welfare became the most influential ideological counterweight to state-centered ideas of welfare provision."[96] It has been explicitly incorporated into several laws that require the government not to take over and provide social services directly if there are private social service agencies able and willing to provide them. Section 4 of the Social Assistance Act states that "if assistance in individual cases is ensured by free welfare associations, the [public] social assistance bodies shall refrain from implementing their own measures."[97] The Youth Welfare Act contains the provision: "In so far as suitable establishments and arrangements provided by the free youth assistance associations are available or can be extended or provided, the [public] Youth Welfare Office shall not offer such establishments and arrangements on its own."[98] The theory of subsidiarity has resulted, in the words of Anheier, in "no less than a protected, state-financed system of private service and assistance delivery."[99]

The practice of relying extensively on nonprofit private associations for the provision of social services has a historical as well as theoretical basis. A host of associations emerged in Germany in the nineteenth century and "became the elementary form of political opposition against the state; after the failed revolution of 1848, they also became a surrogate for the democracy that had not been achieved within the state order itself."[100] As a result, associations playing an intermediate role between the individual and the government gained a certain legitimacy. Germany's experience under the Nazis worked to reinforce this legitimacy, with private associations coming to be seen as a way to avoid a dangerous, overcentralized, dominant government.

There are six main associations of social service and health care organizations that are referred to as the free welfare associations. They carry out most of these privately delivered services. These associations are Diakonisches

Werk (the Evangelical Church's federation of social service and health agencies), Caritas (the Catholic counterpart to Diakonisches Werk), the Central Welfare Association for Jews in Germany (Zentralwohlfahrsstelle der Juden in Deutschland), the Workers' Welfare Association (Arbeiterwohlfahrt—an association of secular social agencies with ties to the Social Democratic Party), the German Equity Welfare Association (Deutscher Paritätischer Wohlfahrtsverband—an association of secular agencies not aligned with any political party), and the Red Cross (Deutsches Rotes Kreuz). The first three of these free welfare associations are all religious in nature and two of them, Caritas and Diakonisches Werk, are by far the largest among the free welfare associations.

These free welfare associations "provide 70 percent of all family services, 60 percent of all services for the elderly, 40 percent of all hospital beds, and 90 percent of all employment for the handicapped."[101] The nonprofit workforce in just the health and social services areas is 1.2 million persons.[102] It is estimated that over seven million persons volunteer for nonprofit organizations.[103] The nonprofit sector is heavily financed by government. Some 94 percent of the funds spent by private agencies in the health care area comes from the government, as does 66 percent of private social services spending.[104] Overall, 64 percent of the funds spent by the German nonprofit sector comes from the government, with most of the remaining funds coming from fees charged for services.[105] The religious associations share fully in the receipt of public funds. According to one estimate, 25 to 40 percent of Caritas's funds comes from public subsidies as does 25 to 30 percent of Diakonisches Werk's funds.[106] Through the Central Welfare Association for Jews in Germany the small Jewish community shares in the receipt of public funds, especially for the resettlement of Jewish immigrants from eastern European countries.

The difference between the American and German mind-sets on the issue of government funding of faith-based social service organizations is revealed in Robbers' statement that "it is generally acknowledged that, given a comprehensive support by the State of social activities, the religious communities may not be excluded from such support and so discriminated against."[107] As seen in chapter 2, in the United States President George W. Bush's faith-based initiative—which aimed to make government funds available to religiously based service organizations on the same basis as secular ones—was met by a storm of criticism on the basis that it would violate church-state separation. In Germany not to fund faith-based organizations while funding their secular counterparts is viewed as discriminating against the religious organizations.

There are some, but not many, nonprofit Muslim service organizations at the present time. Most Muslims look to their local mosque and informal mosque-based services when in need. Some Muslim social service organizations have received funding from individual state and local governments, but they are generally not included in the cooperative funding schemes of the federal government. As one report made clear: "Thus far, Islamic organizations have not gained such public status or revenues. The government has been slow . . . to subsidize mosque-centered Islamic social services for the Muslim community."[108] In theory they are eligible for such funding, but their small numbers and the lack of an organized, centralized push for such funds have thus far prevented them from sharing in national funding schemes as do the two large Christian communities and the Jewish community. We are again back to the dilemma posed by the organizational structure of the Muslim community—or, rather, the lack of a centralized organizational structure—combined with the German inability or unwillingness to develop ways to integrate splintered Muslim communities into its existing church-state practices.

Anheier and Seibel have made the additional important point that the nonprofit-government relationship goes beyond financial support by the government. "[A]s a result of both the principle of subsidiarity and the principle of self-governance, nonprofit organizations tend to be relatively well-integrated into the policy making function of government. In many areas of legislation, public authorities are required to consult nonprofit organizations in matters of economic, social and cultural policy."[109] There indeed is a nonprofit-government partnership in providing important social and health services, a partnership that includes the major religiously based organizations as full partners.

The concept of church autonomy is important for understanding the degree of freedom religious nonprofit service organizations have in pursuing their religious missions, even when working as partners with the government in providing services. The concept of church autonomy includes religious service organizations. Robbers has made this point clearly:

A church's right of self-determination is not restricted to a narrowly-drawn field of specifically "ecclesiastical" activities. The idea of freedom of religious practice extends to preserve the right of self-determination in other areas that are also based or founded upon religious objectives, such as the running of hospitals, kindergartens, retirement homes, private schools and universities.[110]

In an interview Robbers reemphasized this point. "Caritas, Diakonisches Werk, private schools, and kindergartens are a part of the church. They are ministries for the performance of persons' faith, for following Christ's example. They are the church being the church as much as saying prayers or lighting candles in a church. Therefore, the principle of self-determination applies to these ministries as fully as it does to the churches themselves."[111]

Article 137(3) of the Weimar Constitution, which was incorporated into Germany's current Constitution, reads in part: "Every religious community shall regulate and administer its affairs independently within the limits of the law valid for all." This provision—when combined with the previously made point that religiously based service organizations are considered an integral part of the church—has resulted in general agreement on the right of nonprofit service organizations to make hiring decision on the basis of religion, an issue that we saw in chapter 2 is under sharp debate in the United States. Germany for the most part allows faith-based organizations to take religion and moral behavior into account when hiring and firing employees. In the 1983 *Catholic Hospital Abortion Case* a Catholic hospital had dismissed a doctor after he had publicly stated he opposed the church's teaching on abortion. The Constitutional Court held that the hospital was an "affair" of the church and thus under church regulation.

> By laying down such duties of loyalty in a contract of employment, the ecclesiastical employer not only relies on the general freedom of contract, but he simultaneously makes use of his constitutional right to self-determination, [thus] permitting churches to shape [their social activity], even when regulated by contracts of employment according to a particular vision of Christian community service shared by their members.[112]

The Court went on to hold that, given the fact that Catholic canon law views abortion as the killing of innocent human life, to require the church to retain on staff a doctor who rejects this teaching would undermine the church's religious mission as it has defined it. Both the concept that a Catholic hospital is an integral part of the church and that under the Constitution the church has a right to self-determination entered into this decision. In an interview Gerhard Robbers more fully explained the current practice:

> The basic approach is that churches, religious communities running faith-based institutions with their own ethos, can decide on grounds of religion whom they employ and whom they do not employ. And so a Catholic church school would not be forced to have, say, an atheist director. And in case that a teacher in a Catholic school would openly and publicly act against Catholic doctrine by living together with a second or third wife or openly stating his

homosexuality, they could give notice. However, the situation is a little bit more complicated than this basic approach. . . . The nearer an employee or officerholder is to the general ethos, doctrine, teaching of that denomination, the more intensively he or she has to follow that doctrine, also in his or her behavior. It would not be the normal case and probably not allowed to give notice to a dishwasher in the kitchen of a hospital when he or she changes his or her religion. So Catholic, Protestant hospitals employ very many employees who do not adhere to their religious [teachings]. But in the case you have the leading medical doctor, then you would have to act not contrary to the teaching of the church. The nearer you are to the core issues the more they can expect from you.[113]

This issue has not been a highly controversial one, as it is in the United States.

There are still frequent struggles between the various religiously based service organizations and government regulators. But as seen in the Netherlands in chapter 3, most of the struggles revolve around the issue of the cutback of government funds in a time of retrenchment and issues related to professional performance standards, not issues of religion being integrated into the programs financed by the government. An official in the central office of Diakonisches Werk in Stuttgart told us: "We usually as a welfare organization really fight with different government departments in Bonn when they openly or covertly try to influence our autonomy. One is spiritual autonomy and the other is professional autonomy. In the case of spiritual standards they really do not interfere that much. But when it comes down to professional standards they try all the time."[114] This was a theme related to us by almost every person involved in religiously based service agencies that were receiving government funds. But we frequently were assured that when it comes to such questions as requiring agency employees to be members of the sponsoring church and to meet expected behavior standards, having devotional exercises as a part of their programs, and having salaried chaplains or pastors conducting religious services, they ran into no problems with government officials. One official in the central office of the Evangelical Church told us the big problem was not government interference, but finding enough young people with a deep religious life who wished to work for church social agencies.

In short, Germany has an extensive system of public funding of a wide variety of religiously based social service and health care associations. The strong German commitment to providing basic services, not through centralized bureaucracies but through private nonprofit associations, and its commitment to religious pluralism implied by the principles of neutrality and positive religious freedom, come together to support this system. The Evangelical and Catholic churches, with their large, well-established social and health ministries, share fully in this partnership, as does the Jewish community. But the few existing Muslim nonprofit service organizations have largely not been incorporated into this funding scheme.

Concluding Observations

At the beginning of this chapter we suggested that the German system of church-state partnership and church autonomy has some important parallels with both the principled pluralism of the Netherlands and the partial establishment of England. We return to that observation.

Germany clearly does not have a formally established church as does England. Nevertheless, the underlying mind-set that supports the concept of a church-state partnership has some similarities to the English mind-set that supports its partial establishment, resulting in Germany's church-state relationship possessing some elements of the informal, multiple establishment model mentioned in chapter 1. Leopold Turowski, a Catholic Church representative, has written that "religious and secular responsibilities are essentially aspects of a single common good, meant to fulfill the needs of one and the same human person in unified societal existence."[115] In so doing he has given expression to a concept at the heart of the German mind-set as it addresses issues of church and state. Church and state—throne and altar—are seen as twin pillars on which rests a strong, prosperous German society. Throne and altar are in a partnership. This means that most Germans see religion as having an important public role to play as a unifying, inspiring, educating, critiquing force in society. As one American scholar has noted: "The deeply rooted German tendency to think of church and state as joint bearers of the public order has been an enduring feature of German *Staatskirchenrecht* [church-state law]. . . . [T]he notion that religion is an integral element of the public realm remains."[116]

As a result Germany supports a number of practices in which the state cooperates with, assists, and makes room for religion, such as the church tax and certain religious elements in public schools. The formal ties between church and state such as those found in England are not present in Germany, but there are various informal means of church-state cooperation and support for consensual religious beliefs and practices, as there are in England. To the extent this constitutes an informal establishment, it is a multiple establishment, in that the cooperation and support extend to Protestants and Catholics alike and to smaller religious groups to some extent.

But this is not the full story. German church-state practice also has some important parallels with the principled pluralism of the Netherlands and its embrace of the pluralist church-state model. Germany places a strong emphasis on church autonomy and explicitly articulates principles such as state neutrality on matters of religion and freedom of religion as a positive right. These principles are similar to the principles of pluralism espoused by the Dutch and modify and qualify the German commitment to a church-state partnership. Germans see the partnership concept and the neutrality, autonomy, and positive religious freedom principles as complementing each other in such a way as to lead to greater religious freedom for all. Kommers has written that "the accommodationist stance of German constitutional law is often defended as a means of maintaining pluralism and diversity in the face of powerful secularizing trends toward social uniformity and moral rootlessness."[117] What many American observers would see as leftover elements of religious establishment that are subversive of religious pluralism and diversity, most Germans would insist are essential to religious pluralism and diversity.

The key to understanding these divergent perspectives is that the typical German observer has a concept of religious freedom as possessing both positive and negative aspects, while Americans tend to see religious freedom largely as a negative freedom. Rudolf Weth, the director of a federation of Evangelical social agencies in Neukirchen, referred, in an interview with us, to "positive religious neutrality."[118] This "positive religious neutrality" conceives of the state as not advancing any religious or philosophical viewpoint—it must be neutral. There was enough of that, he indicated, in the Nazi era and in the GDR. In that sense there is a separation of church and state. But, he argued, the state must also have a holistic view of human beings. People are religious, ideological beings. The state should not favor any one religion or ideology, but it must make room for the religious, ideological nature of humankind.

Under this perspective the state will be truly neutral only if it sometimes takes certain positive steps in order to make room for or to accommodate those who wish to live a religious life. Recall the Constitutional Court decision in the *Interdenominational School Case* that made the telling argument that "elimination of all ideological and religious references would not neutralize the existing ideological tensions and conflicts, but would disadvantage parents who desire a Christian education for their children. . . ."[119] A school that is made religiously "neutral" by removing all references to religion is neutral among contending religious traditions, but it is not neutral between religious and secular perspectives. Rather, it implicitly promotes a general secular "uniformity and moral rootlessness." German law—in contrast to American law—has recognized and sought to accommodate this perspective in its church-state stances.

There is a logic and an appeal to the German mind-set on church and state and especially to the principles of neutrality and positive religious freedom that underlie them. Germany is clearly and appropriately committed to religious freedom and pluralism. It has largely been successful in giving due recognition to the importance of religion in the life of the nation and in the lives of many of its citizens, and at the same time has assured the freedom of those without religious faith. It has an expansive concept of the free exercise of religion. Its efforts to integrate both religion and secular ideologies into the public schools and to fund both religiously and secularly based social service agencies and private schools are fully in keeping with religious pluralism and state religious neutrality. One can always question whether in specific instances—such as consensual prayers and crucifixes in the public schools—the German Constitutional Court has reached the conclusion most in keeping with religious neutrality and freedom for all. But the German emphasis on an expansive concept of the free exercise of religion, the commitment to governmental neutrality on matters of religion, and the concept of positive religious rights have led the German courts—at the very least—to frame issues such as these appropriately and to ask the right questions.

All this is not to say that the German approach to church-state questions is without problems. The German system evolved in a setting where there were essentially two religious bodies—the Catholic and Evangelical—and both of these thoroughly institutionalized, with regional and central administrative bodies. Thus the German church-state system depends on there being religious bodies that the government can recognize, accommodate, and negotiate with. As we have seen at several points throughout this chapter this system is not working well in relationship to the 3.2 million Muslims in Germany. They are anything but a unified, centralized religious community, but are divided along ethnic, theological, and political lines. As related earlier, the foremost German scholar of church-relations said to us in an interview while describing the challenges in forging a cooperative relationship between the government and the Muslims that for there to be a partnership there must be a partner. Even those German authorities who sincerely desire to integrate more fully the Muslim minority into the present church-state scheme of things often feel frustrated as they do not even know with whom to talk in order to develop a cooperative working relationship. And some German authorities are not all that eager to work at integrating Muslims into German society—or into the German church-state system. There are frustrations on both sides: many Muslims feel the civil authorities are not making a real effort to understand their noncentralized structure and adapt to it; many Germans feel the Muslim minority is not making a real effort to develop structures that can be accommodated by the German system.

All this has been made more difficult—and more urgent—by the events of 9/11 and other Islamist terrorist attacks and threats, which have aroused fears and suspicions on both sides. Compromise and flexibility on the part of the civil authorities as well as the Muslim population and its leaders are needed. This remains the major challenge to the German church-state system that seeks a church-state partnership while maintaining the autonomy of the religious bodies.

But the challenge of integrating the Muslim minority into the present church-state system ought not to deflect from the fact that Germany—building on the basic principles of neutrality, church autonomy, and positive religious rights and a strong emphasis on free exercise rights—has largely dealt successfully with issues of religious pluralism. It has done so while also paying deference to the traditional German sense of religion as a public force in society. It does not relegate religion to the private sphere as Enlightenment liberalism would do, but has created a public role, a public space for religion, and at the same time it allows for a plurality of religious and secular belief systems. This is what the liberal Enlightenment tradition in the United States has said cannot be done, which makes the fact that Germany has been largely successful in doing so all the more impressive.

Notes

1. On the autonomy or self-determination of German churches, see Axel Freiherr von Campenhausen, "Church Autonomy in Germany," in Gerhard Robbers, ed., *Church Autonomy: A Comparative Study* (Frankfurt am Main: Peter Lang, 2001), 77–85; and Gerhard Robbers, "State and Church in Germany," in Gerhard Robbers, ed., *State and Church in the European Union*, 2nd ed. (Baden-Baden: Nomos Verlagsgesellschaft, 2005), 77–94.

2. Robbers, "State and Church in Germany," 80.

3. Donald P. Kommers, *The Constitutional Jurisprudence of the Federal Republic of Germany*, 2nd ed. (Durham, N.C.: Duke University Press, 1997), 461.

4. Robbers, "State and Church in Germany," 77.

5. The terminology used to refer to the Protestant Church in Germany can be confusing to Americans. The *Evangelische Kirche in Deutschland* (EKD) is usually translated the Evangelical Church, and we follow this customary practice in this book. But this term ought not to be confused with the way in which "evangelical" is

often used in American and British contexts to refer to the more theologically conservative, biblically oriented wing of Protestantism.

6. Frederic Spotts, *The Churches and Politics in Germany* (Middletown, Conn.: Wesleyan University Press, 1973), 352.

7. Ronald Inglehart, et al. *World Values Surveys and European Values Surveys, 1981–1984, 1990–1993, and 1995–1997* [Computer file]. ICPSR version. (Ann Arbor, Mich.: Institute for Social Research [producer], 2000); and Bertelsmann Stiftung, "Religion and Society," at www.bertelsmann-stiftung.de/cps/rde/xchg/SID-0A000F14-8D3F5B99/bst_engl/hs.xsl/36787.htm.

8. Bertelsmann Stiftung, "Religion and Society."

9. Gerhard Robbers, "Religious Freedom in Europe," paper available at www.gobernacion.gob.mx/archnov/ponencia8.pdf, 4.

10. On the Constitutional Court, see Kommers, *The Constitutional Jurisprudence of the Federal Republic of Germany*, 3–29; and Donald P. Kommers, *The Federal Constitutional Court* (Washington, D.C.: Institute for Contemporary German Studies, 1994).

11. For good overviews of this period, see Stathis N. Kalyvas, *The Rise of Christian Democracy in Europe* (Ithaca, N.Y.: Cornell University Press, 1996); and Andrew C. Gould, *Origins of Liberal Dominance: State, Church, and Party in Nineteenth-Century Europe* (Ann Arbor: University of Michigan Press, 1999).

12. John S. Conway, "The Political Role of German Protestantism, 1870–1990," *Journal of Church and State* 34 (1992), 820. Also see Daniel R. Borg, "German National Protestantism as a Civil Religion," in Menachem Mor, ed., *International Perspectives on Church and State* (Omaha, Neb.: Creighton University Press, 1993), 255–67.

13. Paul Banwell Means, *Things That Are Caesar's: The Genesis of the German Church Conflict* (New York: Round Table Press, 1935), 84.

14. Article 136. The outlawing of a state church was found in Article 137.

15. Spotts, *The Churches and Politics in Germany*, 9.

16. Spotts, *The Churches and Politics in Germany*, 9.

17. Quoted in Spotts, *The Churches and Politics in Germany*, 11. On this declaration also see Conway, "The Political Role of German Protestantism," 830–33.

18. Spotts, *The Churches and Politics in Germany*, 291.

19. The then-West German authorities insisted on calling the Constitution a "Basic Law" (*Grundgesetz*), since it was seen as being of a provisional nature because of the Soviet zone (soon to become the German Democratic Republic, or East Germany) not being included in the government that was being created. In this book we will use Basic Law and Constitution interchangeably, since the Basic Law functions exactly as a Constitution.

20. All quotations from the Basic Law are taken from the English translation published by the Press and Information Office of the Federal Republic of Germany (1994).

21. On the church in East Germany see Karl Cordell, "The Role of the Evangelical Church in the GDR," *Government and Opposition* 25 (1990), 48–59; and John P.

Burgess, "Church-State Relations in East Germany: The Church as a 'Religious' and 'Political' Force," *Journal of Church and State* 32 (1990), 17–35.

22. Cordell, "The Role of the Evangelical Church in the GDR," 55.

23. Cordell, "The Role of the Evangelical Church in the GDR," 55.

24. See Bertelsmann Stiftung, "Religion in Society," 94–97; and Ronald Inglehart, et al., *World Values Surveys and European Values Surveys*.

25. Interview with Axel von Campenhausen (February 13, 1996).

26. *Religious Oath Case* (1972), 33 BVerfGE 23. Reprinted and translated in Kommers, *The Constitutional Jurisprudence of the Federal Republic of Germany*, 454.

27. *School Prayer Case* (1979), 52 BVerfGE 223. Reprinted and translated in Kommers, *The Constitutional Jurisprudence of the Federal Republic of Germany*, 464–65.

28. The Constitutional Court explicitly made this ruling in the *Rumpelkammer Case* (1968), 24 BVerfGE 236. Reprinted and translated in Kommers, *The Constitutional Jurisprudence of the Federal Republic of Germany*, 446–47.

29. *Rumpelkammer Case* (1968), 24 BVerfGE 236. Reprinted and translated in Kommers, *The Constitutional Jurisprudence of the Federal Republic of Germany*, 446.

30. *Religious Oath Case* (1972), 33 BVerfGE 23. Reprinted and translated in Kommers, *The Constitutional Jurisprudence of the Federal Republic of Germany*, 454.

31. *Religious Oath Case* (1972), 33 BVerfGE 23. Reprinted and translated in Kommers, *The Constitutional Jurisprudence of the Federal Republic of Germany*, 454–55.

32. Interview with Gerhard Robbers (February 23, 1996).

33. Quoted in Kommers, *The Constitutional Jurisprudence of the Federal Republic of Germany*, 494–95. The quotation is from the *Catholic Hospital Abortion Case* (1983), 70 BVerfGE 138.

34. Interview with Axel von Campenhausen (February 13, 1996).

35. Interview with Axel von Campenhausen (February 13, 1996).

36. *Blood Transfusion Case* (1971), 32 BVerfGE 98. Reprinted and translated in Kommers, *The Constitutional Jurisprudence of the Federal Republic of Germany*, 450.

37. *Blood Transfusion Case* (1971), 32 BVerfGE 98. Reprinted and translated in Kommers, *The Constitutional Jurisprudence of the Federal Republic of Germany*, 451.

38. *Blood Transfusion Case* (1971), 32 BVerfGE 98. Reprinted and translated in Kommers, *The Constitutional Jurisprudence of the Federal Republic of Germany*, 452.

39. Good summaries of this controversy in Germany can be found in Jytte Klausen, *The Islamic Challenge: Politics and Religion in Western Europe* (New York: Oxford University Press, 2005), 177–79; and Gerhard Robbers, "The Permissible Scope of Legal Limitations on Religious Freedom," *Emory International Law Review* 19 (Summer 2005), 865–68 and 881–82.

40. Robbers, "The Permissible Scope of Legal Limitations on Religious Freedom," 867.

41. See Robbers, "The Permissible Scope of Legal Limitations on Religious Freedom," 881; and Joseph Listl, "The Development of Civil Ecclesiastic Law in Germany 1994–1995," *European Journal for Church and State Research* 2 (1995), 15–16.

42. On both of these events see Joel S. Fetzer and J. Christopher Soper, *Muslims and the State in Britain, France, and Germany* (Cambridge, UK: Cambridge University Press, 2005), 118–19.

43. *The Evangelical Church in Germany: An Introduction* (Hannover, Germany: Church Office of the Evangelical Church in Germany, 1987), para. 6.1.

44. Robbers, "State and Church in Germany," 86.

45. Interview with Gerhard Robbers (February 23, 1996).

46. See David P. Currie, *The Constitution of the Federal Republic of Germany* (Chicago: University of Chicago Press, 1994), 268.

47. Quoted by Currie, *The Constitution of the Federal Republic of Germany*, 268.

48. Interview with Axel von Campenhausen (February 13, 1996).

49. On the public corporation status of religious communities and its significance see Robbers, "State and Church in Germany," 81–82.

50. For a complete listing of the religious organizations with public corporation status, see the website of the Institute for European Constitutional Law of the University of Trier (www.uni-trier.de/~ievr).

51. On the church tax see Robbers, "State and Church in Germany," 89–90; and Kommers, *The Constitutional Jurisprudence of the Federal Republic of Germany*, 484–89.

52. The churches have, however, opted out of the possibility of a taxpayer being imprisoned for nonpayment of the church tax.

53. Robbers, "State and Church in Germany," 89; Gerhard Robbers, e-mail message to the authors (December 19, 2007); and Nancy Isenson, "Quelling the Flight from the Church (Tax)," Deutsche Welle—World (April 13, 2004). Available at www.dw-world.de/dw/article/0,,1168497,00.html.

54. Interview with Gerhard Robbers (August 21, 2006).

55. *Mixed-Marriage Church Tax Case 1* (1965), 19 BVerfGE 226. Reprinted and translated in Kommers, *The Constitutional Jurisprudence of the Federal Republic of Germany*, 487.

56. See Kate Hairsine, "Economic Boom, Not Pope, Helps Catholic Church in Germany," Deutsche Welle—World (April 16, 2007). Available at www.dw-world.de/dw/article/0,2144,2441758,00.html.

57. Interview with Gerrit Jan Beuker (August 18, 2006).

58. Robbers, "State and Church in Germany," 90.

59. Carolyn M. Warner and Manfred W. Wenner, "Religion and the Political Organization of Muslims in Europe," *Perspectives on Politics* 4 (2006), 465.

60. Robbers, "The Permissible Scope of Legal Limitations on Religious Freedom," 856.

61. Interview with Gerhard Robbers (August 21, 2006).

62. Interview with M. A. H. Hobohm (November 20, 1996).

63. Interview with Cornelia Coenen-Marx, head of the Overseas Department, Ecumenical Relations, and Ministries Abroad for the EKD (August 16, 2006). Also see Open Society Institute, "Muslims in the EU: Cities Report, Germany" (2007), 53. Available at www.eumap.org/topics/minority/reports/eumuslims.

64. See "Muslims in the EU: Cities Report, Germany," 55.

65. See Charles L. Glenn, *Choice of Schools in Six Nations* (Washington, D.C.: U.S. Department of Education, 1989), 193–95.

66. Glenn, *Choice of Schools in Six Nations*, 195.

67. The writer was Alfred Rosenberg, quoted in J. S. Conway, *The Nazi Persecution of the Churches, 1933–1945* (New York: Basic Books, 1968), 182.

68. See Glenn, *Choice of Schools in Six Nations*, 197–201; and Spotts, *The Churches and Politics in Germany*, 212–19.

69. Spotts, *The Churches and Politics in Germany*, 219.

70. See Spotts, *The Churches and Politics in Germany*, 219–28.

71. *Interdenominational School Case* (1975), 41 BVerfGE 29. Reprinted and translated in Kommers, *The Constitutional Jurisprudence of the Federal Republic of Germany*, 469.

72. *Interdenominational School Case* (1975), 41 BVerfGE 29. Reprinted and translated in Kommers, *The Constitutional Jurisprudence of the Federal Republic of Germany*, 469.

73. *Interdenominational School Case* (1975), 41 BVerfGE 29. Reprinted and translated in Kommers, *The Constitutional Jurisprudence of the Federal Republic of Germany*, 470.

74. The decision was *McCollum v. Board of Education*, 333 U.S. 203 (1948).

75. Interview with Rüdiger Schloz (February 13, 1996).

76. Richard Puza, "The Rights of Moslems and Islam in Germany," *European Journal for Church and State Research* 8 (2001), 82.

77. Interview with M. A. H. Hobohm (November 20, 1996).

78. Fetzer and Soper, *Muslims and the State*, 113–14.

79. Fetzer and Soper, *Muslims and the State*, 114–15. Also see Puza, "The Rights of Moslems and Islam in Germany," 81–82.

80. Kommers, *The Constitutional Jurisprudence of the Federal Republic of Germany*, 472.

81. *Classroom Crucifix II Case* (1995),93 BVerfGE 1. Reprinted and translated in Kommers, *The Constitutional Jurisprudence of the Federal Republic of Germany*, 474.

82. *Classroom Crucifix II Case* (1995), 93 BVerfGE 1. Reprinted and translated in Kommers, *The Constitutional Jurisprudence of the Federal Republic of Germany*, 478.

83. *Classroom Crucifix II Case* (1995), 93 BVerfGE 1. Reprinted and translated in Kommers, *The Constitutional Jurisprudence of the Federal Republic of Germany*, 478.

84. *Classroom Crucifix II Case* (1995),93 BVerfGE 1. Reprinted and translated in Kommers, *The Constitutional Jurisprudence of the Federal Republic of Germany*, 481.

85. This statement, which appeared in the Frankfurter *Allgemeine Zeitung*, has been translated and reproduced in Kommers, *The Constitutional Jurisprudence of the Federal Republic of Germany*, 483–84.

86. On the Ten Commandments, see *Stone v. Graham*, 449 U.S. 39 (1980), and on the cross, see the 1996 Supreme Court denial of certiorari in a case in which the lower courts had ruled unconstitutional the incorporation of a cross in the seal of Ed-

mond, Oklahoma. See "Supreme Court Refuses Review of Oklahoma City Seal Cross Case," *Church and State* 49 (1996), 134.

87. Fetzer and Soper, *Muslims and the State*, 116. Also see Glenn, *Choice of Schools in Six Nations*, 203; and Manfred Weiss, "Financing Private Schools: The West German Case," in William Lowe Boyd and James G. Cibulka, eds., *Private Schools and Public Policy: International Perspectives* (London: Falmer Press, 1989), 193.

88. Weiss, "Financing Private Schools," 194.

89. Weiss, "Financing Private Schools," 199. Also see John E. Coons, "Educational Choice and the Courts: U.S. and Germany," *American Journal of Contemporary Law* 34 (1986), 5–7.

90. Quoted in Glenn, *Choice of Schools in Six Nations*, 204–5.

91. Interview with M. A. H. Hobohm (November 20, 1996).

92. Interview with Friedhelm Solms of Forschungsställe der Evangelischen Studiengemeinschaft (FEST) (February 22, 1996).

93. Heinz-Dieter Meyer, "Welfare between Charity and Bureaucracy: German Public and Church-Affiliated Pre-Schooling Compared" (unpublished paper, 1997), 6–7.

94 Helmut K. Anheier, "An Elaborate Network: Profiling the Third Sector in Germany," in Benjamin Gidron, Ralph M. Kramer, and Lester M. Salamon, eds., *Government and the Third Sector* (San Francisco: Jossey-Bass, 1992), 31. Anheier's emphasis.

95. "The Third Route: Subsidiarity, Third Party Government and the Provision of Social Services in the United States and Germany," in Organization for Economic Cooperation and Development, *Private Sector Involvement in the Delivery of Social Welfare Services: Mixed Models from OECD Countries* (Paris: OECD, 1994), 26.

96. Helmut K. Anheier and Wolfgang Seibel, "Defining the Nonprofit Sector: Germany," *Working Papers of the Johns Hopkins Comparative Nonprofit Sector Project*, no. 6 (Baltimore, Md.: Johns Hopkins Institute for Policy Studies, 1993), 7. Also see Lester M. Salamon, S. Wojciech Sokolowski, and Regina List, *Global Civil Society: An Overview* (Baltimore, Md.: Johns Hopkins University Institute for Policy Studies, 2003), 39–43.

97. Quoted in Anheier, "An Elaborate Network," 38.

98. Quoted in Anheier, "An Elaborate Network," 38.

99. Anheier, "An Elaborate Network," 38–39.

100. Wolfgang Seibel, "Government-Nonprofit Relationships in a Comparative Perspective: The Cases of France and Germany," in Kathleen D. McCarthy, Virginia A. Hodgkinson, and Russy D. Sumariwalla, eds., *The Nonprofit Sector in the Global Community* (San Francisco: Jossey-Bass, 1992), 213. Anheier and Seibel have also written, "The early development of the modern German non-profit sector happened in antithesis to an autocratic state." (Anheier and Seibel, "Defining the Nonprofit Sector: Germany," 29.)

101. Anheier, "An Elaborate Network," 41.

102. Lester M. Salamon, S. Wojciech Sokolowski, et al., *Global Civil Society: Dimensions of the Nonprofit Sector*, vol. 2 (Bloomfield, Conn.: Kumarian Press, 2004), 298.

103. Salamon, Sokolowski, et al., *Global Civil Society*, 297.

104. Salamon, Sokolowski, et al., *Global Civil Society*, 301.

105. Salamon, Sokolowski, and List, *Global Civil Society: An Overview*, 32.

106. Anheier, "An Elaborate Network," 44.

107. Robbers, "Religious Freedom in Europe," 3.

108. Congressional Research Service, "Muslims in Europe: Integration Policies in Selected Countries" (November 18, 2005), 34. Available at www.fas.org/sgp/crs/row/RL33166.pdf.

109. Anheier and Seibel, "Defining the Nonprofit Sector: Germany," 30.

110. Robbers, "State and Church in Germany," 83.

111. Interview with Gerhard Robbers (February 23, 1996).

112. Quoted in Kommers, *The Constitutional Jurisprudence of the Federal Republic of Germany*, 494. The quotation is from the *Catholic Hospital Abortion Case* (1983), 70 BVerfGE 138.

113. Interview with Gerhard Robbers (August 21, 2006).

114. Interview with Karl Dietrich Pfisterer (February 20, 1996).

115. Leopold A. W. Turowski, "The Church and the European Community: Developments and Prospects," *European Vision* 10 (1990), 15.

116. W. Cole Durham Jr., "Religion and the Public Schools: Constitutional Analysis in Germany and the United States" (paper given at the Western Association for German Studies, October 1977), 35.

117. Donald P. Kommers, "West German Constitutionalism and Church-State Relations," *German Politics and Society* 19 (Spring 1990), 11.

118. Interview with Rudolf Weth (February 14, 1996).

119. *Interdenominational School Case* (1975), 41 BVerfGE 29. Reprinted and translated in Kommers, *The Constitutional Jurisprudence of the Federal Republic of Germany*, 469.

CHAPTER SEVEN

~

Church and State in Pluralistic Democracies

In the first chapter we said our goal in this study was to give new guidance to democracies, and to the United States in particular, in their attempts to relate church and state to each other in a manner that is supportive of their citizens' religious freedoms and the role religion plays in these countries. After having described the church-state principles and practices followed by the democracies chosen for this study, we now seek to summarize the salient conclusions of the previous chapters and to consider what lessons and observations the experiences of these countries provide.

First, we summarize how each of the five countries has responded to the three questions we posed in our introduction.

- How far can a democratic polity go in permitting religiously motivated behavior that is contrary to societal welfare or norms?
- Should the state encourage and promote consensual religious beliefs and traditions in an attempt to support the common values and beliefs that bind a society together and make possible limited, democratic government?
- When religious groups and the state are both active in the same fields of endeavor, how can one ensure that the state does not advantage or disadvantage any one religious group or either religion or nonreligion over the other?

Second, we make five basic observations concerning what we believe can be gleaned from the experiences of the five countries whose church-state practices we have explored. Third, we respond to three objections that have sometimes been raised to religion playing a more fulsome role in the public life of nations.

A caveat is, however, in order. The material in our five country case studies shows that contemporary church-state practice has much to do with a nation's unique history and cultural assumptions. Practices that are largely unquestioned in one country, such as England's established church or Germany's church tax, are unimaginable in other countries, such as the United States or Australia. On the other hand, America's church-state separation is completely foreign to the Dutch or British experience. Having said that, we believe that countries can learn from each other and that the distinct church-state policy of these five countries is fertile and largely untapped soil for resolving what have historically been and what promise in the future to be persistent tensions between religious and political institutions.[1] These five states face common challenges, particularly in light of the immigration and settlement of large numbers of Muslims and other religious minorities in recent decades, as they negotiate the boundaries between religion and politics.

Summary Conclusions

Free Exercise Rights

The religious free exercise rights of the five countries vary a good deal in theory, but not as much as one might expect in practice. The pattern that emerges from our review of these democracies is that each basically protects religious liberty (which is no small achievement), but struggles with how to interpret that right in specific instances.

There are three principal mechanisms by which these countries secure religious freedom: constitutional provision, legislation, and cultural attitudes and assumptions. With the exception of England, a basic right to the free exercise of one's religion is enshrined in the constitutions of each of the countries in our study. Our review of the practices of the remaining four countries has shown, however, that in many instances the courts do not consistently defend those rights. Cases from the United States and Australia have established the precedent that constitutions do not always protect individuals and groups when their religious practice violates otherwise valid regulatory laws, irrespective of how important and deeply held the religious beliefs that underlie their practice. The U.S. Supreme Court abandoned the compelling state interest test in its 1990 decision *Employment Division v. Smith*, while the Australian High Court has never applied that standard in religious free exercise cases. The German Constitutional Court, by contrast, has been more aggressive in protecting religious liberty. While the Court does balance the religious rights of individuals and groups against the state's interest in public safety and health, it has been more likely than its judicial counterparts in Australia and the United States to overturn laws that conflict with religious belief and action.

Australia and the United States have gone the farthest with legislation to protect people against religious discrimination. Most of the Australian states have established antidiscrimination boards that defend people against religious discrimination; the United States also has a variety of laws against religious discrimination. In England, there are fewer laws that specifically protect religious groups against discrimination, although the recently passed Human Rights Act (HRA), which incorporated the European Convention on Human Rights (ECHR) into British law, has moved Britain closer to the other countries in our study in having legal protection for religious free exercise rights.

Constitutional and legal rights are significant, to be sure, but public opinion and the cultural assumptions underlying them seem just as important a safeguard for religious liberty. England does not have a constitutional protection for religious liberty but the nation's practice is not far different from that of the United States, which does. The British protect religious liberty not so much because of the law, at least until recently, but because the British public values that right. Public attitudes in England have liberalized over the past century, and public policy has become more accommodating to the rights of religious minorities. The Netherlands also demonstrates the importance of cultural assumptions about religious freedom. The Dutch Constitution provides for religious liberty, but the judiciary does not have the power of judicial review over acts passed by the States-General. In theory, the States-General could pass laws that violate a person's or group's right of religious free exercise, but in practice this rarely has happened because there is widespread public support for religious liberty and the Dutch may do a better job at securing religious rights than almost any other country in the world.

This is not to suggest that constitutional protections are meaningless. They provide the opportunity for religious groups to litigate when they believe that the state has violated their rights, as many have done in the United States, and in some cases the Supreme Court has used that litigation to extend religious free exercise rights. Much the same is true in Australia, where the High Court has at times been more assertive in protecting constitutional rights against state action. Ideally, the courts would interpret a constitutional protection of religious rights as a mandate to defend minority religious groups whose views are unpopular and for whom the political process is not consistently a sufficient safeguard. Constitutional cases can provide the springboard for expanding free exercise rights, but a culture supportive of religious liberty has been as significant a force for extending religious rights in most of these countries.

The protection of free exercise rights, in whatever form it assumes, is an important expression of governmental neutrality on matters of religion. It sends a strong message that the government will not advantage or disadvantage people's religious choices by seeking to favor or burden any particular religion, but will instead ensure that there are no disabilities or advantages associated with adherence to any specific religion or secular belief system. This is particularly important for minority faiths whose religious free exercise rights the state might not otherwise secure.

There is one other significant pattern that emerges in these countries as it relates to free exercise rights. Germany and the Netherlands have a far more expansive and, we contend, appropriate understanding of religious liberty than England, the United States, or Australia. German practice recognizes that religious belief presupposes action based upon that belief; consequently the right to believe includes the right to act on one's beliefs. The German Constitutional Court explicitly acknowledged this point when it stated that religious freedom encompasses "the individual's right to align his behavior with the precepts of his faith and to act in accordance with his internal convictions."[2] In Australia and the United States, by contrast, the courts have adopted an Enlightenment liberal understanding of religion that views faith primarily as a private matter of individual conscience. Seen in this light, to secure religious liberty the state needs simply to protect an individual's right to believe what he or she will. The weakness of this idea is apparent in the failure of the U.S. Supreme Court to preserve the right of an Orthodox Jewish air force officer to wear a yarmulke as required by his faith, and the Australian High Court case that allowed the government to ban the Jehovah's Witnesses during World War II without any discussion of whether the church's teachings or practices threatened the state. Having abandoned or having never advocated a compelling state interest test, American and Australian courts lack a mechanism for discerning when people can legally act on the basis of their beliefs, which restricts religious free exercise rights for those people whose faith clashes with otherwise valid regulations.

The Dutch contribution to a more complete understanding of religious liberty is found in Article 6 of its Constitution, which protects religious belief whether one exercises it as an individual or "in community with others." This communitarian emphasis contrasts with the Enlightenment liberal idea that protecting individuals' right to religious worship guarantees their religious liberty. In liberal theory, the state protects religious rights indirectly, by guaranteeing freedom of worship without fear of state discrimination. Theorists as diverse as Michael Sandel, Alisdair MacIntyre, Will Kymlicka, and Bhikhu Parekh have noted, however, that the modern individual is a creation of community.[3] Individuals do not choose or live a religion in isolation from others, so the liberal attempt to elucidate the right of religious liberty apart from the community is insufficient. As we have demonstrated in the country chapters, religion has a strong public facet to it and religious groups are actively involved in a wide variety of service activities. A more robust form of religious freedom requires the state to take positive measures aimed at protecting and promoting the religious expression of *groups* or *communities*, since people live out their religious lives within faith communities and associations.

This is precisely what the Dutch model of pillarization historically recognized, with policies geared toward the main Catholic, Reformed, and secular groups in society. As we have noted, pillarization in the Netherlands has changed radically in recent decades, but in their public policy the Dutch have retained the idea that it is appropriate for the state to accommodate both secular and religious organizations because people naturally want to express their principles, secular or religious, within and through groups. The Dutch view the issues of public support for religious schools and organizations as matters of the right of religious free exercise, and not an establishment of religion, as would be the case in the United States. The result is a cooperative arrangement between church and state, but the Netherlands still maintains the idea of governmental neutrality. It does so not by equating neutrality with the government withdrawing all support for religion, but by equally accommodating and supporting all communities' desires for education and social services within their religious or secular traditions. The state is thereby neutral among all religions and between religious and secular systems of belief.

In theory and in practice, each of the five countries recognizes that there are some values that are so fundamental to human existence and democratic society that religious freedom cannot be the basis for their violation. Chief among them are the public health, safety, and social welfare of citizens. On these grounds, none of the countries would tolerate human sacrifice, child sexual abuse, or violence even if it was part of a group's religious beliefs. These easy cases belie how difficult it is to draw a precise boundary between free exercise rights and the state's various interests, particularly in those cases when a religious group's teaching or practice violates social values but endangers no one. It does, however, establish the appropriate precedent that there are times when the government legitimately may regulate and even outlaw religious practices because they undermine the social norms that are the basis for social unity and democratic governance. The debate about the need for a democratic society to invest its citizens with certain key values leads us directly to the second question in our discussion.

Consensual Values

There is a strong impulse in each of the countries studied in this book to promote consensual values, even religious values, as a way of assimilating individuals and groups into democratic society. The norms often cited as being crucial for a democratic polity are tolerance, respect for the rule of law, public spiritedness, commitment to the democratic process, and recognizing the importance of diversity. The key places in which these issues are raised are citizenship and educational policies. In terms of citizenship norms, some of the countries in our study have refined their tests for immigrants seeking citizenship in the past several years. The impetus in each case was the enormous inflow of foreigners, particularly Muslims, and the fear that these newer immigrants were not successfully integrating into the values of the host country. Citizenship tests are administered in the language of the country where the immigrants are seeking citizenship, sending a strong message about the link between competence in their new country's tongue and full membership in the political community. Immigrants are expected to learn the basic facts about the country's history, political institutions, and cultural values. Some countries, however, seem to have designed portions of their tests to alienate potential citizens, particularly those with certain religious sensibilities. In the Netherlands, for example, before they are even admitted to the country, potential immigrants are shown images of topless female bathers and gay men kissing as a way to expose them to Dutch cultural practices, and presumably to Dutch ideas on tolerance. The German state of Baden-Württemberg includes on its test questions about potential citizens' views on forced marriages, homosexuality, and women's rights, all presumably designed with an eye toward the growing Muslim population.[4]

The issue is not whether the state should promote particular values. We believe that a democratic state must advance those norms that will help to sustain the polity, and support for the nation's political institutions and familiarity with its cultural practices are consonant with that purpose. The question is how those values should be promoted. While it may be reasonable for the Dutch to show potential citizens a picture of topless female bathers in order to give them an example of Dutch liberalism at work, the purpose of this practice ought not to be to deny citizenship to persons who might be offended by that practice. The same is true for the German citizenship test that asks respondents about their views on homosexuality and women's rights. It is understandable that the state would want to alert potential citizens to the fact that German law recognizes same-sex partnerships and thereby affirms the legal equality of gay persons. The promotion of consensual values goes too far, on the other hand, if the intent of this education is to deny citizenship to persons who might be opposed to gay unions.

The institution that has historically had the key role as the incubator of national values is the school. The common public schools in the United States were designed to be institutions of assimilation for the waves of newly arriving immigrants at the end of the nineteenth century. More recently, many of the countries in our study have refined their curricula for public schools to become much more explicit about defining and teaching national values. In Australia, the National Framework for Values Education in Australian Schools identifies nine key values, including freedom, integrity, respect, understanding, tolerance, and inclusion in order to promote the Australian way of life to all schoolchildren.[5] Since 2002, secondary schools in England must meet statutory requirements in the area of citizenship, which include knowledge and understanding to become informed citizens, developing skills of enquiry and communication, and developing skills of participation and responsible action.[6] The goal of this citizenship education is cultural assimilation.

The five countries in our study differ, however, in the extent to which this goal of integration is the province of the public schools, as opposed to public and private schools, particularly religious ones. The United States is alone in providing virtually no aid to private religious schools, partly because of a belief that the common public schools should be the basic means by which children of all classes and religions are taught social and political values. There is a perception that private religious schools undermine this model because they segregate children on the basis of religion and allegedly on the basis of social class and race, and fail somehow to inculcate children with important democratic norms. There are two problems with this picture. First, it idealizes common schools as institutions that are inherently diverse. Due to the multiplicity of school districts in metropolitan areas, public schools in the United States are in fact segregated by race and social class. Second, the argument that separate religious schools do not promote key democratic values is an empirical claim, for which there is no supportive evidence of which we are aware.

There will be some cases of religious or secular groups that do not support basic democratic norms and they should properly be excluded from programs of public aid and participation in cooperative church-school released time programs. A private religious school that preaches hatred and violence toward others or does not provide an adequate education for children to function in the modern world has not signed on to the core consensual values of a democratic society and should not receive public support. If religious schools become nurseries of fundamentalism—which seems to be the implicit fear of them in many quarters—and they fail to reach their objectives in citizenship education they should not receive state funding. The same is true for a religious counseling center that, for example, advises the female victims of violent domestic disputes to submit to the wishes of their abusive husbands.

As a general rule, however, religious schools and agencies do not undermine democratic values, but support them. Despite the concerns of liberals who stress the importance of the cultural assimilation of minority groups, there is very little evidence that religious schools or social service agencies fail to socialize citizens with the values necessary for life in a liberal democratic polity. There has been virtually no resistance among Muslims, for example, to laws in each of these countries that ban polygamy, female circumcision, and arranged marriages if they are entered into under duress. The states that have gone the farthest to recognize group differences in their public policy—the Netherlands and Australia—seem not to have compromised their commitment to cultural assimilation or suffered any serious negative cultural effects because of their policies.[7] There is no necessary tension between the need for society to reach some consensus on key social values with a public policy that accommodates group identities. Bhikhu Parekh notes that "a multicultural society cannot be stable and last long without developing a common sense of belonging among its citizens . . . [but] commitment or belonging is reciprocal in nature. Citizens cannot be committed to their political community unless it is also committed to them, and they cannot belong to it unless it accepts them as belonging to it."[8] The problem with some of the states considered here is not so much that their public policies accommodate group differences, but that they fail to do so equitably. This is true in Germany, which has not met the religious instruction needs of Muslim students to the same degree it has for Protestant and Catholic students; and in the United States, which restricts tax-supported educational options to the state sector.

There is clearly a market for Christian, Jewish, and Islamic schools in each of these five countries. With or without state aid these schools will attract students. The question then becomes what policy is most likely to ensure that those students will receive the kind of education necessary to instill in them key social and political values. We believe that bringing those schools into the state system with the promise of state aid is a better guarantee that they will promote consensual democratic values than consigning them to a status where they have virtually no contact with state educational officials and are less beholden to state regulations. It is a compromise position in which the state supports separate schools, but with some common curriculum, particularly as it relates to the promotion of common values.

Having said that, we do not believe that the public schools can or should be the place for the inculcation of shared *religious* values. The experience of countries that include state-sponsored religious instruction and worship in public schools—as do England, Australia, and to a lesser degree, Germany—suggests that the pursuit of consensual religious beliefs in public institutions is doomed to failure. Each of these societies is religiously pluralistic and it is no longer possible, if it ever was, to discern consensual religious values that significant minorities of the population would not question. This is a myth fostered by nineteenth-century Enlightenment liberal educational reformers who mistakenly believed that one could suppress particularistic religious beliefs, but retain key values shared by all religious traditions. It is possible for a country to come up with guidelines for religious instruction and worship that satisfy the majority, of course, but this denies the rights of religious and secular minorities. The German Constitutional Court correctly recognized this fact in its 1995 decision that overturned a Bavarian law that required the display of a crucifix in every public school classroom, even when some students objected. Religious pluralism is a reality in each of the countries in our study, which makes it unfair for the state to promote a single religious worldview, and unlikely that it will succeed if it tries. A far better approach is for the state to allow separate, in-school religious education classes as the basic means for religious instruction, as both Germany and Australia do—and the United States Supreme Court has found unconstitutional.

The debate in England, where the law not only permits but actually requires Christian religious instruction and worship, demonstrates the problems that come when public schools attempt to promote a single religious vision. The religious education curriculum in England focuses as much as possible on consensual religious values and on the country's religious pluralism, but the results have dissatisfied non-Christians, nonbelievers, and many Christians as well. Non-Christians and nonbelievers fear that the schools will indoctrinate their children in the Christian religion, while many Christian groups contend that a focus on common religious values distorts and trivializes their faith. Not surprisingly, a majority of the schools have failed to meet the requirements of the Education Reform Act of 1988. The controversy illustrates that even when a majority of the people want religious instruction in the public schools, there is little agreement about what forms of religious worship and instruction the state should promote. The same is true for Australia's chaplaincy program, which rather naively assumes that a chaplain from a specific faith tradition can provide generic religious and pastoral advice to persons from diverse religious backgrounds. The program is not necessary for the promotion of shared values, and the fact that it is voluntary does not ensure that it can work in a way that is faithful to diverse religious beliefs or equitably between religious and nonreligious worldviews.

Public Aid to Religious Schools and Nonprofit Organizations

Religious organizations in each of the five countries in our study provide a wide variety of educational and social services to the public similar to those the five governments provide. Each state is committed to governmental neutrality on matters of religion, but they differ on what that means in terms of public financial support when religious groups and the state are active in the same field of endeavor. The issue that crystallized the tension between state and church authorities was state provision of education in the nineteenth century. Religious communities traditionally provided education for group members, but the distribution of that service was so uneven that the state gradually began to provide education for all its citizens. Educational reformers believed that the state should not provide aid to religious schools because they encouraged sectarian disputes and worked against the assimilationist goal of the public schools. Enlightenment liberal reformers in each nation saw particularistic religious beliefs as inherently dangerous, but they included in the public school curriculum what they considered to be "rational," consensual religious beliefs. This position engendered conflict from many church leaders, particularly Roman Catholics in each of the countries and conservative Protestants in the Netherlands, who argued that this state action threatened the power and autonomy of religious communities. This was not an unfounded fear. Political theorist Michael Walzer has written: "State welfare undercuts private philanthropy, much of which was organized within ethnic communities; it makes it harder to sustain private and parochial schools; it erodes the strength of cultural institutions."[9]

The reformist ideal never took hold in Germany, where the government-sponsored schools originally were confessional in nature and most have gradually become schools that are broadly Christian in a nondenominational, nonsectarian sense and where provision is made for in-school religious instruction for the children of the major faith traditions. In the Netherlands and England church leaders secured state funding for denominational schools on an equal basis with state-supported schools. Church schools received little or no state aid in the United States and Australia, largely because the dominant Protestant groups joined forces with liberal reformers to stop money going to Roman Catholic schools. In the early 1960s, Australia dramatically changed its policy and began offering substantial support to church schools, while at the same time the U.S. Supreme Court was articulating a policy of strict church-state separation that ruled government could not provide funding to religious schools.

Neutrality in the United States has come to mean that the state withdraws its financial support for religious schools because of a concern that this aid would demonstrate a preference for a religious over against a nonreligious perspective. In the remaining four countries, by contrast, the justification for government support is that the state can only be truly neutral between secular and religious perspectives if it does not dominate the provision of so key a service as education, and makes it possible for people to exercise their right of religious expression within the context of public funding.

Religious schools have thrived in those countries where state aid is available; a higher percentage of citizens attend religious schools in England, the Netherlands, and Australia than are members of a church, mosque, or synagogue combined. The tension in those countries has come over the issue of which religious groups to include within the system. Australia and the Netherlands have gone the farthest and for the longest time to ensure that all religious groups are eligible for state aid, and there is a great diversity of religious as well as secular private schools in both countries. Because of its tradition of incorporating religious elements into public schools, Germany has relatively few religiously based private schools, but has provided state funding for those that exist and meet state standards. Recently, England has begun to support schools that exist outside the long-established system of aid to Christian and Jewish schools.

There was less conflict between church and state when each of these governments began to expand its social welfare role in the twentieth century. The fact that Enlightenment liberal thinking did not place as great an importance on the services these agencies offered as it did on public education, which involved issues of national unity and the inculcation of democratic values, no doubt made it easier to adopt public policies that included religious associations. As a result, each of the five countries relies extensively on religious agencies to provide social welfare services. All five countries fund religious agencies and generally give them the autonomy to run their organizations as they see fit. This is not unexpected, since four of the five countries in our study also finance religiously based schools. What is somewhat surprising is that the United States funds religious agencies even though it does not fund religious schools. Because of the strict separation principles that led to the rejection of funding for religious schools, however, the religious autonomy of U.S. religious social service agencies is in more doubt in the United States than in the other countries. This can be seen in the controversy engendered by President George W. Bush's faith-based initiative, with many on the political left insisting that a nonprofit, religiously based social service organization that receives public funds loses its right to take religion into account in its hiring decisions.

Observations

We wish to make five observations that we believe are supported by the experiences of the democracies reviewed in this book. The basic norm of governmental neutrality on matters of religion we originally set out in the introductory chapter has been our guide in making these evaluative observations. This neutrality is substantive or positive in the sense of sometimes supporting positive governmental actions and sometimes governmental inaction. The basic, directing goal is that the state should neither favor nor disfavor any particular religion or religious belief structures as a whole or secularly based belief structures as a whole. Only in this way can the state ensure that people are neither advantaged nor disadvantaged by their adherence to their secular or faith-based tradition.

Government Neutrality and the Free Exercise of Religion

We are convinced that governmental neutrality is gained, first, when free exercise rights are limited only because of compelling societal interests. When government imposes certain burdens on religious practices—even when it does so in pursuit of what in most circumstances are valid regulatory purposes—governmental policy disadvantages those religions whose practices are being burdened. In the nineteenth century, U.S. laws against polygamy constricted the Mormons' free exercise of their religious beliefs. In England, the Netherlands, and Germany, problems have arisen over such issues as the right of Muslims to insist that their young girls not be required to wear what they consider immodest clothing in coeducational gym classes. Australia effectively banned Jehovah's Witnesses at the time of World War II, and Germany has struggled with allowing Muslim women teachers and government officials to wear distinctive Muslim clothing.

We are not saying that neutrality demands that the claim of the religious group must always trump the broader society's need for order or other societal interests. What we do insist is that if governmental religious neutrality is to be maintained, the state must only restrict the practices of communities of religious or secular belief when there is a compelling, significant societal purpose in doing so. We believe it is more important that this be the standard that is fairly and honestly applied than any particular outcome in specific instances. Given the grave danger from foreign invasion the Australians were facing in World War II and given the clear antigovernment beliefs of the Jehovah's Witnesses at that time, the government justifiably sought to protect itself against organizations that actively sought to overthrow the state. A compelling state interest of the highest order—survival of the state itself—was at stake. Our problem with the action taken by the Australian High Court related in chapter 4 lies in its failure to justify its decision on the basis of whether or not the Jehovah's Witnesses did, in fact, threaten a vital state interest. Similarly, our concern with the U.S. Supreme Court's decision in regard to Mormon polygamy in the nineteenth century lies less in the outcome of the decision than in its basis (that the free exercise protection encompass only religious beliefs, not religiously inspired actions). If Germany or the Netherlands would continue or strengthen limits on the wearing of Muslim headscarves or other distinctive Muslim attire, they should only do so on the basis of protecting key society-wide interests, not out of fear or prejudice.

Our purpose is not to say how other countries—whose specific conditions and circumstances we can only know in general terms—should decide these sensitive, often difficult issues. We do, however, insist that they should not be decided on the basis of conventional, majoritarian practice or the political and social power of long-dominant religious groups. They should be decided in a fair, honest attempt to allow the maximum amount of religious freedom congruent with societal order, health, and safety. Anything less would put the adherents of those religions at a disadvantage without there being a compensating societal advantage. In doing this, government's religious neutrality would be violated.

Government Neutrality and the Promotion
of Consensual Religious Beliefs

Our second observation is that it is extremely difficult for states to promote consensual religious values and still maintain their religious neutrality. England and Germany have sought to do the most along these lines, and in the case of Germany it has self-consciously sought to do so in a manner respectful of differing religious traditions. Yet in reviewing their practices we came away convinced that their success in doing so, while maintaining governmental religious neutrality, is less than complete. Most efforts to inculcate consensual religious values have been directed at public elementary and secondary schoolchildren. (We are thinking here of religious or worship experiences that are made a part of the school day or—as is the case in some German schools—the presence of religious symbols in public school classrooms, not released time programs where schoolchildren receive religious instruction in the faith or secular beliefs of their families.) The fact that many British schools do not follow the clear legal mandate to include prayers and worship experiences of a "broadly Christian character" reveals the difficulty many school officials feel they have in doing so in a manner fair to all students in a society that is increasingly religiously pluralistic. The provisions that the German Constitutional Court has insisted upon for the right of children to be excused from public prayers in the schools or to insist that a crucifix be removed from their classroom have put a large burden on these children and their parents. Such children must choose between living in an atmosphere that goes against their religious beliefs and distinguishing themselves as being different from other students. The problem inherent in all such efforts is that religion and secular belief structures are particular and concrete in nature, not general or vague. It is simply not possible to find religious common ground that has enough content to be at all meaningful. Those who dissent from whatever religious common ground the state seeks to identify and then promote find themselves being put at a state-created disadvantage.

Government Neutrality and Church-State Separation

Our third observation is that efforts at the strict separation of church and state—in which the United States engaged for a time and that still exert a strong influence today—also violate state religious neutrality. The state violates religious neutrality when under the auspices of strict separation public schools ban released time programs, schools sponsored by religious groups are denied funds, and religious social and health service agencies must downplay or put at risk their religious character in order to receive public funds all other agencies are receiving. Government is no longer treating religious and nonreligious viewpoints and groups in an evenhanded manner. It collects taxes from citizens who are adherents of a wide range of religious and secular viewpoints and from members of a wide range of religious communities (and, for some, secularly based communities of belief), and then distributes those tax funds in support of only some of them. Strict separation policies advantage those whose implicit or explicit beliefs lead them to be comfortable with public schools stripped of religion or with social service agencies whose religious character is left in question. But those who desire their children to receive religious instruction in keeping with their particularistic beliefs or wish to support or receive services from religiously based service agencies are put at a competitive disadvantage.

Strict separation was born in the context of eighteenth-century debates over the appropriateness of public funding for churches and their clergy. In that situation strict separation properly says the state should strictly separate itself from the church, not funding any or all churches. Even funding all religions equally would still discriminate against or disadvantage those citizens who are adherents of no religious faith. In addition, when the issue is direct government funding of churches and clergy, for the government not to do so does not disadvantage religion generally, since the state would not be funding competing secular belief structures. The state is being neutral. That, however, is not the issue today. None of the five democracies included in this study directly funds churches or clergy to any significant extent. It is no longer even an issue.

Instead the issue has shifted to the arena of schools and social and health service organizations. Here the state, religiously based organizations, and secularly based organizations—all three—are providing the same services. Under strict separation the state may, of course, fund its own secularized services and presumably could fund and otherwise cooperate with private secularly based organizations, but could not fund or cooperate too closely with religiously based organizations (or at least could not fund them if they integrate their religious aspects into the services they render). But this is not neutrality. The state is favoring schools and organizations of a nonreligious nature over those of a religious nature. All of the democracies considered in this book except the United States have recognized this. Time and again in our interviews, and especially in the Netherlands, Australia, and Germany, people made reference to the fact that funding religiously based schools or social service agencies or making provision for released time religious classes in public schools constitutes an attempt at fairness or neutrality. In a statement quoted earlier, Sophie van Bijsterveld of the Netherlands made a key point that is widely recognized outside the United States—but often not recognized within it:

> There have also been court decisions [ruling] that government doesn't have to subsidize social work, charitable work, or youth work, but when it subsidizes this type of work it should make no discrimination on the basis of religion or belief. So if a "neutral" organization applies for this work it may receive it, but

if a church or religious organization wants to carry out this work, it should not be excluded because that would not be equal treatment.[10]

Government Neutrality and Released Time Programs

A fourth observation relates closely to the point with which we closed our third observation. We would argue that public policies that provide for released time instruction in public schools or that provide equally for public funding of private religiously and secularly based schools and social service organizations are fully in keeping with state religious neutrality, and may sometimes be required by the neutrality norm. This is a counterpart to the point we made in our first observation, dealing with free exercise protections. We argued there that if, in the absence of a compelling societal interest, the government were to limit the rights or practices of certain religious groups, it would be putting them at a disadvantage in a way that other religious or nonreligious groups were not. Similarly, if government were to fund a variety of schools (either public or private), but not fund religious schools, it would be putting the religious schools at a state-created disadvantage. Or, if government were to fund its own social and health services and private secular social and health services, but not fund religious social and health services, it would be putting those religious service organizations at a state-created disadvantage.

Not quite as clearly, if the public schools provide all sorts of secular instruction in a wide variety of fields, but make no allowance for the various religious groups to instruct the children of their members in their faith, one can argue that religion is being disadvantaged. Here there is, however, an easy counterargument in that the various religions could instruct their adherents' children during nonschool hours. That point can be countered, however, by the fact that the schools normally monopolize the prime morning and early afternoon hours outside of summer and holiday periods, leaving the religions with the leftover, less prime times. We do not need to take a stand on whether the lack of a released time program in government-sponsored schools violates state neutrality. What we do argue is that public policies that provide for released time programs for in-school religious instruction do not violate the norm of state religious neutrality. As long as schools provide classes for all or most of the religious groups represented among the students and alternative classes in secular values systems or other topics, government is being evenhanded. It is not favoring any particular religious or secular belief system. The Australian and German approaches to religious instruction are a good example of this. They are marked by representatives of virtually all of the religious traditions in Australia and Germany developing their own religious instruction programs, which are then offered to the children from their own traditions in separate classes. Children of nonbelievers attend classes in secularly based ethical issues.

Government Neutrality and Funding for Religious
Schools and Service Organizations

Our fifth observation is that government funding of religious schools and organizations is not only in keeping with the norm of state religious neutrality, but that it also actively promotes three key values often associated with liberal democracy: choice, social pluralism, and participatory democracy. We want to elaborate at some length on how state aid promotes these social norms.

Public funding makes religious education more affordable for low- and middle-income parents who choose to exercise that option. Parents who want a religious education for their children have more choice in Australia, the Netherlands, England, and Germany than in the United States. Similarly, without public finance of religious social service organizations there would be less diversity in those services. Citizens in each nation have access to services that have a specific philosophical basis in such key areas as mental health, drug and alcohol rehabilitation, residential aged care, and marriage services. The current policies being followed by all five countries—with the exception of schools in the United States—encourage greater citizen choice and are neutral among religions and between a religious and a nonreligious perspective. To the extent that choice is a value (and we do not suggest that it is the only value in a liberal democracy), public funding of religious schools and agencies is preferable.

Genuine choice is only possible, however, if the state grants nongovernment schools and welfare organizations a significant degree of autonomy. We believe that nongovernment organizations should be accountable to the government for the funds they receive and that they must meet standards in the services they offer, but nongovernment organizations must also have freedom in how they operate, within limits. The state should not allow religious or secular associations to engage in or advocate illegal actions that would undermine public order, health, and safety. Nor should they be allowed to foment hatred and the violation of norms of civility and respect for the rights of others. The government should not, however, seek to impose a standardized model into which Muslim, Catholic, Jewish, and secular child care or marital counseling services would be forced. The imposition of common rules and standardized services onto such agencies would threaten the diversity that is a virtue of contemporary policy. To the extent that there are groups of citizens who want services tailored to a specific value system, schools and agencies must be free to retain their specific character with policies on hiring, admissions, and service delivery.

State funding for religious schools and service agencies also promotes social pluralism and cultural identity. Religious schools enable groups to maintain and instill the tenets of their faith and relate them to the contemporary world. This is particularly true for immigrants who do not necessarily support assimilation if this implies that they must absorb all of the values, ethos, and practices of that society. Since government schools and agencies typically support consensual religious or secularized perspectives, people who belong to religious communities with distinctive, nonmajoritarian religious beliefs will tend to find themselves put under significant disadvantages. Pluralism asserts that the state should tolerate competing educational and social service ideas because the diverse religious and secular communities that make up a nation have a right to exist in the context of freedom to live out their beliefs uncoerced by the state. Pluralism challenges the idea that the intent of public education or social services is to unify a diverse polity by supplanting particularistic identities through cultural assimilation.

As each of these societies becomes more pluralistic, the demand for particularistic services grows and the issue becomes whether or not each state will accommodate group differences through public finance of religious schools and social service organizations. So long as there is a clear demand for services to be organized through ethnic and religious communities, we believe that it makes sense for the state to finance those organizations. Public aid reinforces group identities, which gives greater recognition to the fact that religious and ethnic life is lived out through community organizations like the school. While we recognize that the state has an interest in assuring that these organizations meet certain minimal levels of service by establishing uniform standards, centralized service provision is economically inefficient and potentially dangerous, particularly for those groups that want to retain a distinctive perspective. We argue that genuine pluralism is preferable because it demonstrates public recognition and support of the religious group differences that are a part of each of these societies. There is also evidence that services provided through faith-based groups are as efficient, cost-effective, and successful as those provided by the government.[11]

Public aid to religious schools and welfare organizations also strengthens participatory democracy and localized decision making. Public aid to religious schools and agencies empowers groups at local levels to participate in the decisions that are most important to them. It reinforces what Paul Hirst describes as "associative democracy."[12] Associationalism claims that "individual liberty and human welfare are both best served when as many of the affairs of society as possible are managed by voluntary and democratically self-governing associations."[13] In an associational democracy, the state provides the finance for public goods, such as education or social welfare, but allows local associations to administer them. These groups are accountable to the government for use of the funds, but are more responsive to those for whom the service is provided.

Hirst and other communitarian theorists have made a case for the notion of group rights. The idea is that the state encourages groups to organize themselves by assigning to them rights and political power. The Dutch corporatist arrangement is the clearest indication of this policy in practice. We do not suggest that corporatism is the appropriate model for any one of these states, but we do believe that there are legitimate ways for the state to step in to structure and encourage religious group life. With the exception of the United States, the countries in our study have taken positive and, we believe, legitimate steps to ensure that religious groups can live out their faith in what is probably the most important public institution, the school. Each of the states has allowed group life to flourish in social welfare services, although the autonomy and status of those organizations are in some question in some of the countries. Germany has followed a restricted form of pluralism by its failure to incorporate religious instruction for Muslim children into the public school system. We believe that governmental neutrality demands public finance for all religious groups, as long as they support basic democratic norms. We also contend that state aid promotes the socially beneficial goals of choice, social pluralism, and participatory democracy.

Two Objections

In this book we have made clear the extent to which the U.S. church-state practices—especially as they relate to establishment of religion issues such as state funding of religious schools and social and health service organizations—differ from those followed in the other democracies considered here. We have also argued that this strict separationist approach of the United States to these establishment issues—which, although weakening, still exerts a continuing influence—has led it to violate the norm of state neutrality toward religion. Clearly, we believe the other democracies considered here—especially the Netherlands and Australia—have done a better job of meeting the norm of state religious neutrality and thereby of assuring the full religious freedom of all than has the United States.

It is appropriate for us to close this book by briefly considering two objections often raised in the United States to the practices and principles followed by other democracies and advocated by us. One key point that opponents of public funds going to religious schools and service organizations often make is that doing so leads to invidious distinctions in society along religious lines and undermines key goals of a liberal polity, including societal unity, tolerance, and respect for women.[14] According to this argument it is a mistake to recognize and accommodate group differences, and especially religious group differences, because doing so leads to dangerous divisions in society and encourages the kinds of social demarcations that are unhealthy for democracy. A successful democracy assumes a minimum of consensus that a truly pluralistic society cannot achieve. A policy of public funding for the educational and social service efforts of separate religious groups is unacceptable because doing so reinforces the tendency of people to separate along ethnic, class, gender, and religious lines. Sectarian conflict such as what Northern Ireland and the former Yugoslavia experienced, and what Kosovo and Iraq are experiencing today illustrate the dangers one courts when religion and politics are allowed to mix. What is preferable is a model of strict church-state separation, in which religion is privatized, and of liberal individualism, which evaluates people on the basis of their individual achievements, and not according to their membership in groups. A commitment to these liberal values provides the common bond for the nation's citizens and overcomes the problems inherent in a more pluralistic system.

This is a powerful and, in some cases, persuasive argument. Northern Ireland, the former Yugoslavia, and Iraq are indeed terrifying examples of what can happen when a polity makes invidious distinctions between people based solely upon their group membership. Liberal individualism rightly calls attention to the horrors that can result when the notion of group identity gets out of hand. We recognize the grave dangers in a rigid, extreme form of separatism that elevates group loyalty—whether based on religion, ethnicity, language, or other considerations—to a position of preeminence over all other loyalties. Loyalty to one's religious or other group then becomes all-consuming and is not balanced by loyalties to the nation-state, community, and other forces present in a pluralistic society. Separatism of such a nature is not the democratic ideal, either for society as a whole or for the minority groups in question.

Two facts need to be recognized, however. One is that religion does not pose a unique danger of being the source of an extreme separatism that threatens societal unity. One has only to think of the American Civil War, the tragic fighting that Kenya experienced in recent years, the breakup of the

Soviet Union, and the ongoing, sometimes violent struggle of the Kurds in Iraq and Turkey for a separate nation-state to realize that many forces other than religion can lie behind societal disunity and actual or threatened civil war. Religion does not pose a uniquely dangerous source of societal division.

A second fact in need of recognition is that historically religion has become a dangerous, divisive force in society when one or more religious groups asserted monopolistic claims. It is when religion asserts the right to monopolize state or societal power and force its will on the rest of society or to claim prerogatives or advantages denied other religious groups that tensions and possibly violent conflict arise. This was true in the case of Europe's religious wars in the seventeenth century and the civil war in Bosnia-Herzegovina in the 1990s. Similarly erring are those people and groups in the United States who today advocate a constitutional amendment that would declare the United States a Christian nation or who seek to reinstate organized prayer in the public schools. The problem in these cases lies with the idea that the government should promote or endorse a particular faith over other religious and secular worldviews. This naturally leads to bitter social and political disputes among people who are not of the preferred faith.

Thus the key question becomes whether a likely effect of aid to religious schools and social service agencies, and perhaps other positive actions to recognize or accommodate the whole range of religious and secular belief structures, is to intensify cultural differences in unhealthy ways that breed an extreme separatism that will place loyalty to one's religious groups above all other loyalties and will lead to attempts to assert monopolistic claims. We believe that the answer to this question is clearly no. We can think of no instance when a genuine pluralism accompanied by mutual respect and freedom for all religious groups led to dangerous societal divisions.

The countries in our study with the most pluralistic system of state aid to religious schools and organizations—the Netherlands and Australia—have witnessed less conflict among religious groups and fewer problems of social divisiveness than countries with less extensive systems of support, notably England and the United States. What is remarkable from the Dutch and Australian experience is the extent to which a political coalition among the various faiths—Catholic, Protestant, Jewish, Islamic—has formed to protect their shared status. In a curious twist of fate, British Muslims have arguably become the most vocal advocates for retaining the Established Church of England. The pluralistic policy of aid to all religious schools and organizations gives them a common stake in the political system, which has helped to domesticate religious disputes in these countries. This is no small accomplishment. By contrast, the United States is experiencing many religiously based disputes and conflicts because many religious groups contend, with some justification, that the state disadvantages them due to the influence of strict church-state separation thinking.

We argue, further, that state aid to religious and ethnic organizations' educational or social efforts can promote the state's goal of integrating immigrant groups into society while at the same time encouraging social pluralism.[15] Surveys of Jewish and Muslim communities in Australia, for example, indicate that involvement with ethnic or religious organizations has helped, not restricted, the assimilation process for immigrant groups. According to one report, involvement with Jewish organizations provides new immigrants "with important avenues for acculturation that eventually allow them to broaden the areas of social interaction with the host society."[16]

We are well aware of the potential dangers to democratic stability of the politicization of religious disputes, but we conclude that those problems inhere in countries that provide aid in a discriminatory manner, either to one or a small number of religious groups or only to secular perspectives. A pluralistic policy of funding for religious schools and social agencies has not intensified social divisiveness in those countries that have adopted this policy, and there is no reason to believe that it would engender greater conflict among religious groups if the United States followed this example.

A second basic concern often expressed by American strict separationists is that a strict separation, no-aid-to-religion approach is necessary to safeguard the welfare of religion. The argument is that state support for religion—even its educational and social service activities—inevitably leads to a weakening of religion as government imposes regulations along with its support and religion becomes fat and complacent. In fact, American strict separationists often point to the experience of European countries such as England, Germany, and the Netherlands to make their case. The argument is that in these countries religion receives much public aid of one type or another and the churches are moribund; in the United States religion does not receive public aid and the churches are alive and active. If churches and their respective schools and service agencies are receiving ample government funds, what purpose is served in people committing their own time and money to the work of those religious organizations?

Works by Roger Finke, Rodney Stark, and Anthony Gill that have applied a supply-side economic theory to religious activism make a similar point.[17] It is difficult to overstate the influence of this rational choice perspective in the sociology of religion. What makes religious groups strong, according to this theory, and what accounts for variations in religious participation rates among nations is the degree of state regulation of religion. They argue that an unregulated religious economy increases the overall levels of religious commitment and participation as churches appeal to specific segments of the religious market in order to survive. A highly regulated economy, by contrast, creates an unnatural religious monopoly that depresses competition among the churches and decreases religious activism and vitality. That public support for religion is bad is suggested by the secularization of Europe, where the state provides aid to religious organizations, and the absence of as powerful a secularization movement in the United States, where aid is not as available to religious organizations.

We would make two responses to these suggestions. One is that the key to church vitality in the United States according to a rational choice theory has been competition among the churches, and not the American model of church-state separation per se. This model has historically allowed for the formation of a genuine religious pluralism in America. It is undoubtedly the case that competition among religious groups in eighteenth- and nineteenth-century America encouraged higher rates of religious participation than did the state monopoly of religion in England at the same time. However, church-state separation is not a necessary institutional condition for the type of competition that makes religious groups strong. We believe that the state can provide funds to religious schools and social agencies without inhibiting competition among the churches. Our policy of state neutrality among the churches and between religious and secular perspectives would arguably enhance religious competition: a closer look at church activism in these countries will show that the issue is not so much the presence or absence of a strict church-state separation, as some suggest, as public policies that inhibit competition among religious groups.

American religion acquired a uniquely entrepreneurial tone or spirit because of the extreme religious diversity found in the United States and the unsettled, changing social conditions of a new, rapidly expanding nation. That the state did not generally restrict religious competition provided a better atmosphere for new, upstart religious movements that formed to appeal to the common people, responded to their needs and desires, and lured members away from the more "respectable" established churches ("established" in a social not political sense). In the early United States the Presbyterians, Baptists, and Methodists challenged the more established Anglicans and Congregationalists. Now they are the respected mainline churches and have been losing members to the newer Assemblies of God, evangelical "megachurches," charismatics and Pentecostals, and new religious movements. All this means churches in the United States have to be entrepreneurial—they must compete for new members and hold their present members by responding to the needs of their members and potential members. If they do not, there will always be other churches who will be willing to do so. The absence of a state-imposed religious monopoly gave new religious movements the freedom to form and made American churches populist and sensitive to the desires of their adherents and potential adherents, thereby increasing church attendance and other measures of religious commitment. This compares dramatically with England and Germany, where the state historically regulated the religious economy in such a way as to inhibit the development of religious pluralism and vitality. Church-state policies of both countries restricted access to the religious market for new churches and gave the established church or churches built-in advantages. Church activism suffered as the established churches did not have to be sensitive to religious market demands in order to survive. The fact that even today the German church tax continues to be collected by the state may mean that clerics still feel less pressure to recruit a congregation or tailor their "product" to meet specialized religious market demands (in the terms of Finke, Stark, and Gill).

The important difference between the United States and Europe according to this account is the presence or absence of a pluralistic and highly competitive religious scene. While we are not prepared to say that this is the *only* reason for the different levels of religious commitment in the countries considered here, and there has been much debate about the utility of a rational choice theory,[18] it is certainly *a* reason. A church-state policy that restricts competition among the churches, such as a religious establishment, is unhealthy for religion. From a rational choice perspective, however, the European "problem" is not that states artificially restrict competition (none of the countries in our study do that in any meaningful way) but that Europe has not witnessed the kind of religious pluralism that has inspired competition and vigorous religiosity in the United States. That could, however, be changing. The immigration and settlement of Muslims in Western Europe, Caribbean and African Christians in England, and a diversity of religious groups in Australia are leading to levels of religious competition that many of these countries have never before experienced. As we noted in the country chapters, this religious diversity has already spawned political controversy; it might be that the next stage is a revitalization of religion as a whole. It would be wonderfully ironic, or possibly the work of a benign deity with a supremely active sense of humor, if the introduction of religious competition into Europe proved to be the catalyst that reinvigorated the old, and apparently dying, religious traditions.[19]

We see no reason to conclude, however, that a policy of strict church-state separation is the only one that would facilitate competition among the churches. Our proposal would not inhibit competition or make America more like its European counterparts in terms of religious vitality. Our policy calls for the elimination of any state-imposed monopoly—religious or secular—that is discriminatory among ideological perspectives and leads to the kinds of market failures highlighted by Finke and Stark. The key point that American discussions of church-state issues often miss is that church-state separation is not neutral among ideological perspectives, but advantages secular ones. Government assistance that is genuinely neutral can increase the pluralism that seems a natural state of a religious economy and is so important for religious vitality. Government aid to religious schools and agencies in the Netherlands and Australia did not restrict competition but enhanced it as new religious organizations formed to represent their distinctive perspectives. We believe that much the same thing would occur if the United States allowed public money to go to religious schools.

Our second response to the argument that a neutral governmental policy of aiding religious and secular schools and social agencies weakens religion is that there is almost no evidence linking the secularization—or diminishing church activism—of the British, Australian, Dutch, and German societies with state aid to religious schools and organizations. In the Netherlands, for example, there was a clear secularization trend that swept through Dutch society in the 1960s and 1970s.[20] If government funding of religious schools and social service organizations caused this trend, however, it was a long time coming, since there had been significant public funding of such organizations since the end of the nineteenth century. In addition, the Dutch secularization trend started not so much in the schools and religious social service agencies, but in the churches themselves. And the churches receive no governmental support or aid. If government support and recognition of religion is a causative factor in the secularization of Dutch society, one would expect it to be most advanced where the most aid is found—the schools and social service organizations—and the least advanced in the churches themselves who do not receive aid. This relationship does not, however, hold up. Similar points can be made in regard to all four of the countries studied where the state has made public provision of funds available to religious schools and social service agencies. In all four of these countries, for example, we interviewed people from religious schools and social service organizations whose religious commitments were strong, vigorous, and upfront. Yet they all also received public funding. At the very least this demonstrates that there is not a necessary causative link between public funds and the atrophy of distinc-tive religious commitments. The same point can be made by noting that, al-though not included in this study, France has largely followed a strict church-state separation model. If in fact strict separation, no-aid-to-religion policies lead to large, active religious congregations, the churches of France should be overflowing with worshippers. This, however, is hardly the case. A causative link between an absence of significant governmental support for religiously based schools and social service agencies and vigorous religion simply does not exist.

At the close of this book we return to the theme of religious freedom for all—the freedom to believe and follow the eternal truths one's conscience dictates without the involvement of government either to favor or to hinder. This becomes an ever more elusive goal in an era marked by increasing lev-els of religious pluralism, and with the growth of the modern welfare state that involves the government in almost all aspects of society. There is much that liberal democracies can learn from each other. We are convinced there is especially much to be learned from those practices rooted in an acceptance and even celebration of religious diversity. Those practices seek to attain re-ligious neutrality, not by a blanket, no-aid-to-religion standard nor by seek-ing and supporting consensual religious beliefs, but by treating all faiths and secular systems of belief in a manner that accepts them for what they are, protects them to the extent vital societal interests allow, and in programs of governmental support and cooperation, treats them in an evenhanded man-ner. There is much wisdom in such a course.

Notes

1. This was a point rather ironically raised by Justice Scalia in his dissenting opin-ion in the case of *Roper v. Simmons*, 543 U.S. 551 (2005). In that case, the Court held that it is unconstitutional to impose capital punishment for crimes committed by per-sons under the age of 18. The Court's opinion relied in part on international law and the practices of other western democracies to support the holding. The United States, Justice Kennedy noted, stood alone in allowing juveniles to be executed. In his dissenting opinion, Justice Scalia, citing our book as a source, noted that the Court is oblivious to international norms when it comes to religious establishment is-sues such as public funding for religious schools. He argued that the Court should similarly reject international norms when it came to directing American practices re-garding executions. In our view, a more consistent and reasonable standard would be for democratic states to learn from each other on issues as diverse as funding for reli-gious schools and executions for juveniles.

2. *Religious Oath Case* (1972), 33 BVergGE 23. Reprinted and translated in Donald P. Kommers, *The Constitutional Jurisprudence of the Federal Republic of Germany*, 2nd ed. (Durham, N.C.: Duke University Press, 1997), 454.

3. See, for example, Michael Sandel, *Liberalism and the Limits of Justice* (Cambridge, U.K.: Cambridge University Press, 1982); Alisdair MacIntyre, *After Virtue: A Study of Moral Theory* (Notre Dame, Ind.: University of Notre Dame Press, 1984); Will Kymlicka, *Liberalism, Community, and Culture* (Oxford: Clarendon Press, 1989); and Bhikhu Parekh, *Rethinking Multiculturalism: Cultural Diversity and Political Theory* (London: Macmillan, 2000).

4. Deanne Corbette, "Testing the Limits of Tolerance," *Deutsche Welle* (March 3, 2006). Available at: http://www.dw-world.de/dw/article/0,2144,1935900,00.html.

5. "National Framework for Values Education in Australian Schools" (Canberra: Australian Government Department of Education, Science and Training, 2005).

6. "Inspecting Citizenship 11–16 with Guidance on Self-Evaluation" (London: Crown Copyright, 2002).

7. See Arend Lijpart, "Self-Determination versus Pre-Determination of Ethnic Minorities in Power Sharing Systems," in Will Kymlicka, ed., *The Rights of Minority Cultures* (Oxford: Oxford University Press, 1995), 275–87.

8. Parekh, *Rethinking Multiculturalism*, 341–42.

9. Michael Walzer, "Pluralism: A Political Perspective," in Kymlicka, ed., *The Rights of Minority Cultures*, 153.

10. Interview with Sophie C. van Bijsterveld (February 9, 1996).

11. See Stephen V. Monsma and J. Christopher Soper, *Faith, Hope, and Jobs: Welfare to Work in Los Angeles* (Washington, D.C.: Georgetown University Press, 2006).

12. Paul Hirst, *Associative Democracy: New Forms of Economic and Social Governance* (Amherst: University of Massachusetts Press, 1994).

13. Hirst, *Associative Democracy*, 19.

14. See, for example, Amy Gutman, *Democratic Education* (Princeton, N.J.: Princeton University Press, 1987); and Susan Moller Okin, *Is Multiculturalism Bad for Women?* (Princeton, N.J.: Princeton University Press, 1999).

15. For a good analysis of this position, see Iris Marion Young, "Together in Difference: Transforming the Logic of Group Political Conflict," in Kymlicka, ed., *The Rights of Minority Cultures*, 155–78.

16. John Goldlust, *The Melbourne Jewish Community: A Needs Assessment* (Canberra: Australian Government Publishing Service, 1993), 85.

17. Rodney Stark and Laurence R. Iannaccone, "A Supply-Side Reinterpretation of the 'Secularization' of Europe," *Journal for the Social Scientific Study of Religion* 33 (1994), 230–52; Rodney Stark, *The Rise of Christianity: A Sociologist Reconsiders History* (Princeton, N.J.: Princeton University Press, 1996); Roger Finke and Rodney Stark, *The Churching of America: Winners and Losers in Our Religious Economy* (New Brunswick, N.J.: Rutgers University Press, 2005); and Anthony Gill, *The Political Origins of Religious Liberty* (Cambridge, U.K.: Cambridge University Press, 2008).

18. Steve Bruce, *Choice and Religion: A Critique of Rational Choice* (New York: Oxford University Press, 1999).

19. For a similar argument, see Jytte Klausen, *The Challenge of Islam: Politics and Religion in Western Europe* (Oxford: Oxford University Press, 2005).

20. One historian who has carefully studied the Dutch secularization trend of the 1960s sees the chief causative factor lying not in the Dutch pluralistic system of recognition of and aid to religious and secular schools and social agencies, but in the religious, political, and social elites' response to the cultural changes moving through western societies in the 1960s. That response emphasized accommodating and accepting rather than resisting these changes. See James C. Kennedy, *Building New Babylon: Cultural Change in the Netherlands During the 1960s* (Ph.D. dissertation, University of Iowa, 1995).

~

Selected Bibliography

Alley, Robert S., ed. *The Supreme Court on Church and State*. New York: Oxford University Press, 1988.

Andeweg, Rudy B., and Galen A. Irwin. *Dutch Government and Politics*. New York: St. Martin's Press, 1993.

Bader, Veit. *Secularism or Democracy? Associational Governance of Religious Diversity*. Amsterdam: University of Amsterdam Press, 2007.

Bakvis, Herman. *Catholic Power in the Netherlands*. Kingston, Ontario: McGill-Queen's University Press, 1981.

Bax, Erik H. *Modernization and Cleavage in Dutch Society*. Aldershot, U.K.: Avebury, 1990.

Bebbington, D. W. *Evangelicalism in Modern Britain*. London: Unwin Hyman, 1989.

Beckford, James A., and Sophie Gilliat. *Religion in Prison: Equal Rites in a Multi-Faith Society*. Cambridge: Cambridge University Press, 1998.

Bellah, Robert, Richard Madsen, William M. Sullivan, Ann Swindler, and Steven M. Tipton. *Habits of the Heart*. New York: Harper & Row, Perennial Library, 1986.

Bijsterveld, Sophie C. van. *The Empty Throne: Democracy and the Rule of Law in Transition*. West Lafayette, Ind.: Purdue University Press, 2002.

Black, Amy E., Douglas L. Koopman, and David K. Ryden. *Of Little Faith: The Politics of George W. Bush's Faith-Based Initiative*. Washington, D.C.: Georgetown University Press, 2004.

Bolt, John. *A Free Church, a Holy Nation: Abraham Kuyper's American Public Theology*. Grand Rapids, Mich.: Eerdmans, 2001.

Bouma, Gary D. *Mosques and Muslim Settlements in Australia*. Canberra: Australian Government Publishing Service, 1994.

Boyd, William Lowe, and James G. Cibulka, eds. *Private Schools and Public Policy: International Perspectives.* London: Falmer Press, 1989.

Breward, Ian. *A History of the Australian Churches.* Sydney: Allen and Unwin, 1993.

Campbell, Tom, Jeffrey Goldsworthy, and Adrienne Stone, eds. *Protecting Rights Without a Bill of Rights: Institutional Performance and Reform in Australia.* Aldershot, U.K.: Ashgate, 2006.

Carlson-Thies, Stanley. *Democracy in the Netherlands: Consociational or Pluriform?* Ph.D. dissertation, University of Toronto, 1993.

Community Cohesion: A Report of the Independent Review Team Chaired by Ted Cantle. London: Home Office, 2001.

Currie, David P. *The Constitution of the Federal Republic of Germany.* Chicago: University of Chicago Press, 1994.

Daalder, Hans, and Galen Irwin, eds. *Politics in the Netherlands: How Much Change?* Totowa, N.J.: Cass, 1989.

Davie, Grace. *Religion in Modern Europe: A Memory Mutates.* Oxford: Oxford University Press, 2000.

DiIulio, John, Jr. *Godly Republic: A Centrist Blueprint for America's Faith-Based Future.* Berkeley: University of California Press, 2007.

Dreisbach, Daniel L. *Real Threat and Mere Shadow: Religious Liberty and the First Amendment.* Westchester, Ill.: Crossway, 1987.

Edge, Peter W., and Graham Harvey, eds. *Law and Religion in Contemporary Society: Communities, Individualism, and the State.* Aldershot, U.K.: Ashgate, 2000.

Fetzer, Joel S., and J. Christopher Soper. *Muslims and the State in Britain, France, and Germany.* Cambridge: Cambridge University Press, 2005.

Finke, Roger, and Rodney Stark. *The Churching of America: Winners and Losers in Our Religious Economy.* New Brunswick, N.J.: Rutgers University Press, 2005.

Gay, Peter. *The Enlightenment: An Interpretation.* New York: Knopf, 1966.

Gill, Anthony. *The Political Origins of Religious Liberty.* Cambridge: Cambridge University Press, 2008.

Glenn, Charles Leslie, Jr. *The Myth of the Common School.* Amherst: University of Massachusetts Press, 1987.

———. *Choice of Schools in Six Nations.* Washington, D.C.: U.S. Department of Education, 1989.

Gutman, Amy. *Democratic Education.* Princeton, N. J.: Princeton University Press, 1987.

Hamburger, Philip. *Separation of Church and State.* Cambridge, Mass.: Harvard University Press, 2002.

Handy, Robert. *A Christian American: Protestant Hopes and Historical Realities.* New York: Oxford University Press, 1984.

Hatch, Nathan. *The Democratization of American Christianity.* New Haven, Conn.: Yale University Press, 1989.

Hogan, Michael. *The Sectarian Strand.* New York: Penguin Books, 1987.

Jupp, James, ed. *The Australian People: An Encyclopedia of the Australian Nation, Its People and Their Origins* (Cambridge: Cambridge University Press, 2002).

Kaye, Richard, ed. *Anglicanism in Australia: A History.* Melbourne: Melbourne University Press, 2002.

Kennedy, James Carleton. *Building the New Babylon: Cultural Change in the Netherlands During the 1960s.* Ph.D. dissertation, University of Iowa, 1995.

Klausen, Jytte. *The Islamic Challenge: Politics and Religion in Western Europe.* New York: Oxford University Press, 2005.

Kommers, Donald P. *The Federal Constitutional Court* (Washington, D.C.: Institute for Contemporary German Studies, 1994).

———. *The Constitutional Jurisprudence of the Federal Republic of Germany*, 2nd ed. Durham, N.C.: Duke University Press, 1997.

Kuyper, Abraham. *Calvinism: Six Stone Foundation Lectures.* Grand Rapids, Mich.: Eerdmans, 1931.

Kymlicka, Will. *Liberalism, Community, and Culture.* Oxford: Clarendon Press, 1989.

Kymlicka, Will, and Wayne Norman, eds. *Citizenship in Diverse Societies.* Oxford: Oxford University Press, 2000.

Levy, Leonard W. *The Establishment Clause: Religion and the First Amendment*, 2nd ed. Chapel Hill: University of North Carolina Press, 1994.

Lewis, Philip. *Islamic Britain: Religion, Politics and Identity Among British Muslims.* London: I. B. Tauris, 1994.

Lugo, Luis, ed. *Religion, Public Life, and the American Polity.* Knoxville: University of Tennessee Press, 1994.

Lyons, Mark. *Third Sector: The Contribution of Nonprofit and Cooperative Enterprise in Australia.* Sydney: Allen and Unwin, 2001.

MacIntyre, Alisdair. *After Virtue: A Study of Moral Theory.* Notre Dame, Ind.: University of Notre Dame Press, 1984.

Marsden, George M., and Bradley J. Longfield, eds. *The Secularization of the Academy.* New York: Oxford University Press, 1992.

May, Henry A. *The Enlightenment in America.* New York: Oxford University Press, 1976.

Mead, Sidney E. *The Lively Experiment.* New York: Harper & Row, 1963.

Means, Paul Banwell. *Things That Are Caesar's: The Genesis of the German Church Conflict.* New York: Round Table Press, 1935.

Moller Okin, Susan. *Is Multiculturalism Bad for Women?* Princeton, N.J.: Princeton University Press, 1999.

Monsma, Stephen V. *Positive Neutrality.* Westport, Conn.: Greenwood, 1993.

———. *When Sacred and Secular Mix: Religious Nonprofit Organizations and Public Money.* Lanham, Md.: Rowman & Littlefield, 1996.

———. *Putting Faith in Partnerships: Welfare-to-Work in Four Cities.* Ann Arbor: University of Michigan Press, 2004.

Monsma, Stephen V., and J. Christopher Soper. *Faith, Hope, and Jobs: Welfare to Work in Los Angeles.* Washington, D.C.: Georgetown University Press, 2006.

Moon, Jeremy, and Campbell Sharman, eds. *Australian Politics and Government: The Commonwealth, the States, and the Territories.* New York: Cambridge University Press, 2003.

Nielsen, Jørgen. *Muslims in Western Europe*, 2nd ed. Edinburgh, UK: Edinburgh University Press, 1995.

Norton, Philip. *The British Polity*, 4th ed. New York: Longman, 2001.

Organization for Economic Cooperation and Development. *Private Sector Involvement in the Delivery of Social Welfare Services: Mixed Models from OECD Countries.* Paris: OECD, 1994.

———. *School: A Matter of Choice.* Paris: OECD, 1994.

Parekh, Bhikhu. *Rethinking Multiculturalism: Cultural Diversity and Political Theory.* London: Macmillan, 2000.

Ploeg, Tymen J. van der, and John W. Sap, eds. *Rethinking the Balance: Government and Non-Governmental Organizations in the Netherlands.* Amsterdam: VU University Press, 1995.

Post, Harry. *Pillarization: An Analysis of Dutch and Belgian Society.* Aldershot, U.K.: Avebury, 1989.

Ramadan, Tariq. *To Be a European Muslim.* Leicester, U.K.: The Islamic Foundation, 1999.

Reichley, A. James. *Religion in American Public Life.* Washington, D.C.: Brookings Institution, 1985.

Robbers, Gerhard, ed. *Church Autonomy: A Comparative Survey.* Frankfurt am Main, Germany: Peter Lang, 2001.

———. *State and Church in the European Union*, 2nd ed. Baden-Baden, Germany: Nomos Verlagsgesellschaft, 2005.

Rossiter, Clinton. *Seedbed of the Republic.* New York: Harcourt, Brace & World, 1953.

Sachs, W. L. *The Transformation of Anglicanism from State Church to Global Communion.* Cambridge: Cambridge University Press, 1993.

Saeed, Abdullah, and Shahram Akbarzadeh, eds. *Muslim Communities in Australia.* Sydney: UNSW Press, 2001.

Salamon, Lester M., and Helmut K. Anheier, eds. *Working Paper of the Johns Hopkins Comparative Nonprofit Sector Project, no. 35.* Baltimore, Md.: The Johns Hopkins Institute for Policy Studies, 1999.

Salamon, Lester M., S. Wojciech Sokolowski, et al. *Global Civil Society: Dimensions of the Nonprofit Sector, vol. 2.* Bloomfield, Conn.: Kumarian Press, 2004.

Sandel, Michael. *Liberalism and the Limits of Justice.* Cambridge: Cambridge University Press, 1982.

Sniderman, Paul M., and Louk Hagendoorn. *When Ways of Life Collide: Multiculturalism and Its Discontents in the Netherlands.* Princeton, N.J.: Princeton University Press, 2007.

Spotts, Frederic. *The Churches and Politics in Germany.* Middletown, Conn.: Wesleyan University Press, 1973.

Stark, Rodney. *The Rise of Christianity: A Sociologist Reconsiders History*. Princeton, N.J.: Princeton University Press, 1996.

Tash, Robert C. *Dutch Pluralism*. New York: Lang, 1991.

Wald, Kenneth D. *Religion and Politics in the United States*, 2nd ed. Washington, D.C.: Congressional Quarterly, 1992.

Wilson, James Q. *The Moral Sense*. New York: Free Press, 1993.

Index

~

About the Authors

Stephen V. Monsma is a research fellow at the Henry Institute for the Study of Christianity and Politics, Calvin College (Grand Rapids, MI) and a professor emeritus of political science at Pepperdine University (Malibu, CA). He has published widely in the fields of church-state relations and faith-based nonprofit organizations. In addition to the first edition of *The Challenge of Pluralism: Church and State in Five Democracies*, his best-known works are: *Faith, Hope and Jobs: Welfare-to-Work in Los Angeles* (2006, with J. Christopher Soper), *Putting Faith in Partnerships: Welfare-to-Work in Four Cities* (2004), *When Sacred and Secular Mix: Religious Nonprofit Organizations and Public Money* (1996), and *Positive Neutrality* (1993).

Chris Soper is the Frank R. Seaver Professor of Political Science at Pepperdine University in Malibu, California. He is coauthor of *Faith, Hope, and Jobs: Welfare to Work in Los Angeles* (2006), *Muslims and the State in Britain, France, and Germany* (2005), and *The Challenge of Pluralism: Church and State in Five Western Democracies* (first edition, 1997); coeditor of *Equal Treatment of Religion in a Pluralistic Society* (1998); and author of *Religious Beliefs and Political Choices: Evangelical Christianity in the United States and Great Britain* (1994), as well as numerous essays and articles in scholarly journals.